M000035213

Providence Tales
and the
Birth of American Literature

Providence Tales

and the

Birth of American Literature

James D. Hartman

THE JOHNS HOPKINS UNIVERSITY PRESS
Baltimore & London

© 1999 The Johns Hopkins University Press
All rights reserved. Published 1999
Printed in the United States of America on acid-free paper
2 4 6 8 9 7 5 3 1

The Johns Hopkins University Press
2715 North Charles Street
Baltimore, Maryland 21218-4363
www.press.jhu.edu

Library of Congress Cataloging-in-Publication Data will be found
at the end of this book.
A catalog record for this book is available from the British Library.

ISBN 0-8018-6027-x

To Evelyn

Contents

Preface

In the following pages I present an analysis of the providence tale in seventeenth-century England and New England, particularly of its adumbrations in its two main New England forms, the witchcraft tale, brought over from England, and the Indian captivity narrative, the first providence tale form to use uniquely American materials. My study, which began as an examination of the late-seventeenth-century New England Indian captivity narrative, follows the course of my recognition of those stories as providence tales, and then charts the transmission of the providence tale form from England to the colonies and how it then flourished there.

Seventeenth-century New England writers wrote thousands of prose narratives. Some of these, such as Indian captivity narratives, have received significant critical attention recently.[1] Another popular narrative form, the criminal narrative or biography, has recently been anthologized by Daniel Williams and analyzed by Daniel Cohen.[2] Narratives of witchcraft cases and of apparition tales have long been used as proof texts in assorted attacks on Puritan culture, particularly against its attitudes and practices toward women and other races and religions. In their popular narratives, the Puritans provided generous evidence their critics could use to fix Puritanism high up upon their critical scaffolds, well bound in their hermeneutical stocks. This study, however, attempts to convey the power, complexity, and literary and cultural importance of the above texts and of other related ones, all of which I look at as examples of providence tales.

Materials abound for the critic who wishes to examine seventeenth-century New England narratives. Captivity narratives have appeared in numerous editions, alone and anthologized. New England witchcraft discourse is prodigiously represented in current editions of S. G. Drake's meticulous nineteenth-century collection of witchcraft narratives, *Annals of Salem Witchcraft* (1866, reprinted 1970), in reprints of W. E. Woodward's *Records of Salem Witchcraft* (reprinted 1969 from the 1864 original), in Charles W. Upham's *Salem Witchcraft* (1867, re-issued 1966), in George Lincoln Burr's *Narratives of the Witchcraft Cases, 1648–1706* (1914, 1968), and in contemporary collections such as Paul Boyer and Stephen Nissenbaum's *Salem Witchcraft Papers: Verbatim Transcripts of the Legal Documents of the Salem Witchcraft Outbreak of 1692* (1977) and David Hall's *Witch Hunting in Seventeenth Century New England: A Documentary History, 1638–1692* (1977). Even the two most extensive New England providence tale collections remain in print, albeit in quite expensive editions: Increase Mather's *Essay for the Recording of Illustrious Providences* (1684, reprinted 1977) and Cotton Mather's *Magnalia Christi American* (1702, reprinted 1972). These last two works together comprise a vast depository of early American narrative art in general and of providence tales, the most popular form this art took, in particular.

This brief inventory of New England Puritan narratives in print reflects the continuing critical interest in them. In spite of this attention, however, the providence tale itself, as a distinct and significant genre, remains, critically speaking, virgin soil. Aside from some interesting introductory remarks in anthologies and in facsimile reprint editions by critics such as James Levernier, Kathryn Derounian-Stodola, Coleman Parsons, Richard Dorson, and John Demos, there exists no in-depth, formal analysis of the New England providence tale genre.[3] This study sets out to correct that deficiency, and in so doing, to trace some of the neglected roots, both indigenous and transatlantic, of American prose narrative discourse.

During the course of my studies, I began to feel that the basic providence tale model I kept finding in every tale I read, British or American, constituted a viable paradigm for the then just-emerging novel. I came to construe the unique combination in these tales of supernatural, gothic, and sensationalistic elements with the concrete, empirical spirit of the new science as a near-mathematical formula, through which a writer could present a supernatural or unseen, in other words *imaginary* world, using concrete evidence, resulting in a proto-typical novel, that is to say, a vivid, concrete, believable depiction of a fictional world. The key to this discourse lay in its adding the layer of scientific evidence to the supernatural, gothic world being invoked in its pages.

My extensive reading of English providence tales, and my ideas about the novelistic or fictional characteristics of these texts, led me eventually to Michael McKeon's classic *Origins of the English Novel*. After reading so many critics deriding and discounting the works I'd been studying, it came as a pleasant surprise to find McKeon studying many of the very same English texts and authors

I had been reading. He also focused on many of the same specific aspects of these texts as I had been noting. Moreover, whereas I was only suggesting the importance of these works in the development of American fiction, McKeon flatly stated they were the direct precursors of the English novel.

McKeon's work supports my providence tale model and my own suggestions about the impact of the providence tale on subsequent American prose narratives, an impact I touch on only briefly in the introduction, since a full treatment of this topic would require another book-length manuscript. I further introduce my study by briefly laying out a few key points from the first part of McKeon's book. First, though, I present a summary of the ideas of the American historian of religion and popular culture David D. Hall, in his study of New England Puritan religious belief in the seventeenth-century, *Worlds of Wonder, Days of Judgment*. Hall seeks to locate New England religiosity somewhere outside "what went on in the spare meeting houses of New England . . . , [beyond the] sermons and sacraments . . . the church covenant and the obligations of community it imposed" (17), and he finds it in what he calls "wonder" stories. Basically, these are the same stories I call providence tales, and Hall, like McKeon, identifies many of the same English sources for them as I do, points out many of the same characteristics and tropes in them, and suggests they played a similarly significant role in the development of future American writing.

In critically locating my own study alongside McKeon's and Hall's, I am emphasizing both the transatlantic and interdisciplinary perspectives in my work, two broad critical approaches which, in the hands of certain contemporary critics, have reconfigured many traditionally held views of early American culture. Many of the texts I study, especially the Indian captivity narratives, have already been used in other "reconceptualizing" critical works. These texts make up part of what Annette Kolodny, for example, has called "frontier literature." Kolodny cites these as a heretofore-neglected collection of discourse which, in fact, must be considered and appreciated in any attempt to reassess our notions of early American culture in light of the many previously neglected voices who, we now realize, played such important roles in it. For Kolodny and others, this frontier discourse has generally meant work by Native Americans, by women, and by Hispanic and French explorers in the New World. Adding providence tales, especially Indian captivity narratives and witchcraft relations, adds another substantial body of texts to this list of neglected voices.

Equally important, though, is the shift back across the Atlantic to England, and the shift to other disciplines such as history and religion, which my providence tale model suggests are also necessary and useful methodologies for studying early New England literature. Crossing the Atlantic created as wild and dangerous a barrier behind the colonists to the east as the barrier that lay to the west of them.[4] It seems as necessary to reconsider what influenced those colonists across that ocean boundary, and what changes they made on those influences, as it is and has been necessary to consider the same questions regarding the colonists's western influences. In addition, archival materials, such as the court records and probate wills analyzed by historians, are two types among a wide range of materials from other disciplines which, as discussed in the works of writers such as Hall and John Demos, provide essential insights into early American discourse and culture overall.

This book, then, looks at early New England culture as a transatlantic culture with two frontiers, and views this model with an interdisciplinary praxis. Finally, I am also attempting to reconsider traditional ideas about the relationship between science and religion, and about the role of religion in modern culture generally. I look at religion as an imaginative art form with many literary and scientific characteristics; that is to say I consider it as "true" as the mythic worlds created by Blake, Homer, Shelley, and Einstein. In so doing I am also consciously suggesting that religion and science have not developed so much as antithetical practices, but have rather evolved dialectically, each taking from and enriching the other to create some entirely novel branch of knowledge. The particular brand, in the case of this study, is the art of prose narrative, and the early manifestations of American fiction.

Introduction

Providence tales are stories that relate the activities of God on earth. Accounts of miracles, of answered prayers, and of judgments—often in the form of natural catastrophes executed upon the high and mighty[1]—can all be construed as providence tales. Stories of any remarkable, "unnatural" events not explainable by natural law can also be read as providence tales. Such wonders go back at least as far as Pliny the Elder's *Natural History* and the Bible—and as far forward, in some instances, as the *National Inquirer*; whenever God's agency is factored into a tale of the bizarre, a case study in natural history or philosophy, or a popular legend, it also becomes a providence tale.

Owing to several sweeping and converging cultural and historical changes, English providence tales from around the second half of the seventeenth century underwent a figurative, and a quite literal, sea change. Empiricism, skepticism, and atheism were all becoming increasingly vital cultural forces, fueled by the age of exploration, by the new science, and by a widespread turn against the religious enthusiasms responsible for the divisiveness of the Reformation generally and of the period of the English Civil War in particular. In response to these new challenges, religious leaders began to adapt providence tales toward the purpose of defending themselves. These religious writers appropriated the empirical methodology of the new science promulgated by the Royal Society of London by including "scientific" evidence in their providential relations. They also reinforced their own custom of recounting miraculous incidents by appropriating the tradition of writing about "wonders"—about prodigies and bizarre occurrences—which the new science had also adopted. Finally, they infused their tales with the violence, sentimentality, and melodrama that a variety of other popular forms in this new age of print, including pamphlets, broadsides, merriments, and ballads, had been exploiting in England and in New England with the aid of the new printing technology. Together, these appropriations forged a new hybrid providence tale, one neither strictly religious, solely scientific, nor merely entertaining. The new providence tale set out to entertain and moralize while proving—scientifically, legalistically, and beyond all reasonable doubt—that God and his supernatural hosts both existed and were still actively managing mankind's daily affairs on earth.

The New England providence tale, then, had two primary objectives. One was to counter skepticism, materialism, and atheism and to reassert God's dominion on earth. But rather than being simply a backward-looking form, the last literary gasp of a dying theocracy which critics have so often characterized them as, these tales more importantly attempted to synthesize the Puritan religious outlook of the late Reformation with the merging scientific spirit of the early Enlightenment.[2] In such a union, these tales heralded the future discourse of the new nation and served as a formative crucible in which that discourse and culture could develop.

David D. Hall, in *Worlds of Wonder, Days of Judgment*, calls relations of "wonders," among which he includes witchcraft tales, a dominant form of discourse in seventeenth-century New England. As Hall notes, this culture contained an unusually high percentage of readers and writers, thus making these "wonders" particularly influential. Besides witchcraft relations, Hall places in his category of "wonders" the very same types of tales that comprise various subcategories of providence tales in my model. These include sea deliverances and sea catastrophes, stories of pious children's last words such as those in the British writer James Janeway's *Tokens for Children*, and any other story that recognized "God's power to work 'special providences'" (59). Hall also adds to this genre of "wonders," stories of people speaking in tongues or foreign languages they had never learned, apparition tales, and stories of the awesome and strange powers of nature. In Hall's view, "wonders" made up one of the three main "story frameworks [New Englanders] invoked repeatedly" (Hall 69). His other two frameworks were execution stories and Indian captivity tales, simply other types of providence tales in my model.

Hall specifies many of the same British and Continental sources for these New England tales as I do. He cites Pliny, other natural historians, and the new science as some of the important sources. He traces these tales back to the Bible and the Romans, but as their most immediate precursors he spotlights John Foxe's *Acts and Monuments* and other British providence tale writers such as Stephen Batman, Thomas Beard, Samuel Clarke, and William Turner, all discussed in detail below. What these tales did, in his view, was to incorporate Puritan religiosity into a popular, sensationalistic form of discourse becoming

increasingly widespread and significant in this new print culture. He emphasizes how these tales straddled the line between the godly and the sensational,
and how they were a composite form which synthesized the godlier texts of
writers such as Richard Baxter and the Mathers with more common forms such
as street ballads, prose romances, histories, and merriments. For Hall, these
tales were "veins of proven popular appeal" (52). Forged, he says, in an alliance
between printers and ministers, "they mated terror and the evangelical inquiry
with genres that had proven sales appeal" (56). They "moved in and out of for-
mulas and genres that were clearly popular" (70), and in so doing, combined in
one story the reading public's interest in sensationalism, violence, strangeness,
truth, and God's power and providence on earth. Hall's comments about sensationalism and an overall gothic atmosphere echo essential providence tale
tropes.

For Hall, these tales of wonder constituted one of the primary vehicles
through which popular religious belief was transmitted and defined in seventeenth-century New England. He further points out that these narratives depicted everyday events; they were "histories in which people spoke of their
struggles against doubt and sin" (57). In these tales, he says, there was, "a common and consistently used metaphor of life as 'warfare,' as an unremitting battle against temptation, as a struggle to keep oneself in the straight and narrow
path that led to heaven [so that] ordinary people thus learned that, whatever
their worldly circumstances, they were actors in the greatest drama of them all"
(57). In short, Hall notes how these narratives contributed to the emergence of
the novel: "These writers dramatized the lives of ordinary men and women,
long before the novel emerged as a genre that encompassed everyday (that is,
not royal or chivalric) experience. Evangelical writers were turning to biography and autobiography" (57).

Hall's definition of "wonders" as any tale which included "strange and
wonderful" events which were meant to be construed as truthful, reflects the
combination of empiricism and strangeness which is the most essential textual
element of my providence tale model. On the other hand, he does not, as I do,
credit wonder tales with incorporating the age's scientific outlook in its skeptical entirety. Hall finds in writers such as Increase Mather an irreconcilable
conflict between science and sensationalism which resulted in their producing
totally different works for different audiences. So, in citing Mather's *Kometographia* (1683), he says Mather "tries there to be a 'man of learning'[;] though
admitting he lacked access to the latest books, he assumed the stance of a skeptic judiciously weighing the evidence" (106). Hall says that in this work and his
Angelographica: A Discourse Concerning the Nature and Power of the Holy Angels
(1696), Mather questioned the divine origin of many supposed preternatural

wonders, but when addressing a common audience with one of his wonder tales, he simply didn't open up this skeptical side (Hall 106/107).

Hall also doesn't fully recognize the aim in these tales to oppose atheism by detailing evidence of the supernatural. He still ascribes to them the same roles as have been traditionally ascribed to this discourse. They were, in his view, either jeremiads depicting judgments or impending doom, calls for improved morals, or reminders of the chosen mission of New England and Protestantism in general. However, he does show that wonder tales did provide "a recognition of God's power to work special providences," and he overall distinguishes and defines an important new core of texts that speaks significantly to the origins of American prose and American culture in general.

Whereas Hall's quarry is the religious soul of Puritan New England, Michael McKeon seeks the discourse responsible for the emergence of the eighteenth-century English novel. In locating this English discourse, McKeon, in *The Origins of the English Novel,* focuses on three of the main providence tale forms that figure prominently in my analysis: the apparition tale, the criminal biography, and the sea deliverance story. The importance and uniqueness of these narratives, for McKeon as for me, lies in the new and higher standards of empirical truth they embodied, even as they retained, and even augmented, a sensationalistic and gothic flavor that their own precursors had had for centuries.

In his analysis, this new narrative form evolved out of a cultural matrix that included Protestantism, the new science, and the seventeenth century's proliferation of printed material. The interplay of these forces led to what McKeon identifies as the overriding question in all these narratives: "What kind of authority or evidence is required to permit [a narrative] to signify truth to its reader?" (20). This question then led to the attempt, common throughout the Restoration, to separate "the factual from the [merely] historical" (267), to write what he calls more "historicized," that is, more factual, history. This attempt, among other factors, led to the eighteenth-century novel, in McKeon's view.

McKeon traces how the new science and printing worked together to place empirical knowledge and the evidence of one's senses in the forefront of what could be considered truth. The deluge of printed matter in the seventeenth century created "competing accounts of the same event" (43), which raised the burden of proof on writers and forced them to present more evidence, whatever their subject. Such evidence, in that time, had to be empirical rather than based on traditional authors. The new science heralded

> objective research, understanding through the systematic collection, comparison, categorization, collation, editing and indexing of documentary objects . . . , [and] the notion of scientific inquiry suffused [seventeenth century] historical research.

In the antiquarianism of the late part of the century it encouraged the archeological study of 'objects,' of non or quasi literary objects like charters, coin inscriptions, and statutes . . . but documents are also objects. Empirical attitudes in the study of history and the practice of law helped stimulate an unprecedented dedication to the collection of records, and validated both the first hand 'evidence of the senses'—eye and earwitness reports—and the 'objective' testimony of documentary objects. (43)

Not only did the new science, particularly as practiced by the Royal Society, emphasize firsthand, empirical knowledge over tradition and received authority; it also sought to examine and deduce new theories from unique, unusual phenomena rather than draw conclusions from universals, which had been the general method of Aristotelian scholasticism. In *Novum Organum* Francis Bacon makes clear this change from continually solidifying established traditions to discovering the unknown:

We have to make a collection or particular natural history of all prodigies and monstrous births of nature, of everything in short that is in nature new, rare, and unusual. This must be done, however, with the strictest scrutiny, that fidelity may be ensured. Now those things are to be chiefly suspected which depend in any way on religion, as the prodigies of Livy, and those not less which are found in writers on natural magic or alchemy, and men of that sort, who are a kind of suitors and lovers of fables. But whatever is admitted must be drawn from grave and credible history and trustworthy report. (178–79, lib. 11, Aph. 29)

Thus, hand in hand with a mania for factuality went an obsession with the unusual. Like Hall, McKeon points out that bizarre stories, or "unnatural natural history," had been a popular genre going back to Livy and Pliny, and he shows how they now became even more significant because of the age's conflation of the unusual with the scientific. Discussing news ballads, "sold throughout the [seventeenth] century by itinerant chapmen like Shakespeare's Autolycus [which] recall the [aforementioned] unnatural natural history tradition . . . in their naive dedication to the wonderful and the incredible," McKeon notes that now,

The claim to historicity has . . . become far more elaborate, exploiting especially the techniques of authentication by firsthand and documentary witness that have developed during the late medieval and early modern periods. As a result, the increasing validation of empirical modes of truth actualizes the latent tension between the claim to truth and the nature of the material whose truth is claimed. . . . [T]he old claim that a story is "strange, but true," subtly modulates into something more like the paradoxical formula, "strange, therefore true." The fact of "strangeness" or "newness" ceases, that is, to be a liability to empirical truth telling, and becomes instead an attestation in its support. As we will see, the printed ballad is only one of the contexts in which this unstable reversal can be seen in seventeenth-century discourse. At its most striking, the formula "strange, therefore true" amounts to the insistence that the very appearance of the incredible itself has the status of a claim to historicity. (47)

So science and printing helped create more bizarre and detailed narratives. McKeon then shows how these cultural forces joined with the skepticism and materialism of Protestantism, and with the age's growing sense of unbelief and atheism, to produce the most striking and widespread type of seventeenth-century narrative, the apparition tale.

The Reformation witnessed the publication of countless and conflicting religious interpretations of events and narratives. This multiplicity of views, coupled with Protestantism's emphasis on an individual's reading of Scripture, were sources of contention, skepticism, and doubt. For these and other reasons, McKeon concludes that

> Protestant belief became so intertwined with the evidence of the senses that in the end the truth of Scripture itself seemed to require vindication as the truth of "true history"....[Protestantism associates] knowing with the empirical act of seeing. [It is the] religion of the book, of the documentary object; its proverbial elevation of the printed Word over the graven image only made reformed religion more compatible with a visual epistemology that associated knowing with the empirical act of seeing.... The new revealed word of God now also becomes subjected to the skeptical scrutiny of empirical norms of revelation. Miracles have not ceased and their persistence may be objectively documented and verified.... People increasingly take vision—what is seen with one's own eyes—as the only sound basis of knowledge. (76)

In response to this need for material evidence and to the new Hobbes-, Descartes-, and Deist-influenced materialists and atheists, the new apparition tales arose, whose "explicit and overriding aim [was] ... to proclaim the reality of the spiritual world in a materialistic age that has come to doubt it. .... These narratives assert the truth in the terms that are now the most persuasive, and derive their techniques of authentication from the very stronghold of skepticism which it is their purpose to refute" (84). In other words, as McKeon says, "There were many ... apparition narratives whose most concrete political end was to rebut freethinkers and atheists by showing that divine revelation is still being manifested, quite literally, before our eyes" (84).

These apparition stories, or accounts of the acts of demons, devils, and witches were described by one of their most famous creators as "sensible manifestations of the certain existence of Spirits of themselves Invisible [and were] a means that might do much with such as are prone to judge by Sense" (Richard Baxter, cited in McKeon, 84). They were particularly necessary because "even of the mysteries of the Gospel, I must needs say with Mr. Richard Hooker, *Ecclesiastical Polity*, that whatsoever men may pretend, the subjective certainty cannot go beyond the objective evidence" (Baxter, cited in McKeon, 77).

These factors which McKeon cites as bringing about the seventeenth-century apparition tale in England are comparable to those I discovered in tracing the development of all the seventeenth-century New England providence tales. McKeon goes on to show that forms such as apparition tales had unstable boundaries; using material means to assert supernatural "facts," these tales' methods could as easily be allies of atheism and materialism as weapons against it. McKeon's point is that this instability led to the creation of an entirely new form, the novel. Moreover, that "complex pattern of circumstantial and authenticating details—name, place, date, events, eye and earwitnesses, attentiveness to stylistic sincerity, confirmation of good character, denials of special bias" which McKeon finds articulated and framed in his texts dovetails with my own findings among English and New England providence tales.

To further illustrate these elements, McKeon uses a form, the travel, exploration, or discovery narrative, which typically reflected all the providence tale's main characteristics except for its overriding interest in proving God's existence. At times, too, these tales could become providence tales by factoring God's agency into the plot, but in general, discovery narratives such as those found in Hakluyt were not providence tales.[3] They were, however, deeply influenced by the ideas of Robert Boyle promulgated by the Royal Society, ideas which directly influenced all providence tale writers. New England providence tale writers such as Increase and Cotton Mather refer repeatedly to, and were members of, the Royal Society, just like the English authors they learn and borrow from, such as Joseph Glanvill and Henry More. McKeon's discussion, then, of these discovery narratives is quite pertinent to a discussion of providence tales. Travel narratives are a literary bridge between the old and new providence tale, just as the technology invented to cross the oceans and conquer the new world, and the sights seen while doing so, augmented the change from a scholastic worldview to the ideas and views of the new science and the Reformation.

McKeon first points out the ancient lineage of the discovery tale genre, how it was fashioned by writers such as Pliny and Mandeville (he might have mentioned Homer and Virgil in verse). The genre, he asserts, had become associated with "tall tales," in that travelers were associated with liars (101). He then shows, however, how the new travel literature became a popular form for proponents and practitioners of the new science, as well as for the commercial interests who supported some of their scientific ventures. The new travel narrative, McKeon writes, became "preoccupied with the question of [its] own historicity and how it might be authenticated" (101). Given such concerns, the Royal Society published instructions "on how to keep the daily travel journals" on which the narratives were based. Robert Boyle, the preeminent Royal Society member as well as a man who led a society devoted to spreading the Gospel among the world's heathen, set forth the basic tenets of these narrative principles in an early issue of the Society's *Philosophical Transactions* (1665/66). These tenets were abstracted from his 1663 "Some Considerations of the Usefulness of Experimental Natural Philosophy," in which he included his "General Heads for the Natural History of A Country," the part included in the *Transactions*. Thus Boyle and the Royal Society added their scientific methodologies to the recipe for a new travel narrative, whose outline had earlier been suggested by writers such as Francis Bacon, in his essay "Of Travel" (1625) and in the earlier quoted section of *Novum Organum*, where he called for a collection of well-documented prodigies.

McKeon describes how Boyle gave "instructions on the composition of a good natural history," and adds that in the instructions the "principles of materialistic epistemology," rather than the authority of "overarching truth of a great Author" prevailed (105). In short, McKeon clearly distinguishes the importance of the Royal Society and of the new science in these travel narratives and in the new narratives in general. The same influences are clearly evident in the providence tales written in early New England and in their English precursors, as will be described in depth.

McKeon also highlights some other specific tropes essential to my providence tale model, such as the plain style of these narratives; "the fundamental trope," he says, "of the anti-rhetorical style [essential in providence tales] is the self-reflexive insistence on its own documentary candor, as well as on the historicity of the narrative it transparently mediates" (105). In locating the emergence of this style, McKeon cites another place in the Royal Society's *Philosophical Transactions* where the style is commended, in this instance in a prologue to John Fryar's "A New Account of East India and Persia" (*P.T.* 20 (1668)). He notes (109) that in travel narratives "plainness of style seems almost a precondition for the documentary authenticity—the truth—of a text." He then quotes the English providence tale writer so influential throughout New England, Richard

Baxter, praising another important English providence tale writer who greatly influenced New England writers, Samuel Clarke; Baxter calls Clarke "a man of great sincerity, a hater of lying, and [a] great lover of truth" (cited by McKeon, 94n, taken from the preface to Clarke's *Lives of Sundry Eminent Persons in this Late Age*). McKeon also cites Clarke when he quotes from one of the period's major travel narrative collections, edited by Awnsham and John Churchill, *A Collection of Voyages and Travels*, 1704. In an introduction to a narrative by Edward Pelham[4] about a fishing voyage to Greenland which Clarke included in *A Mirrour or Looking Glass for Saints and Sinners*, Thomas Sprat, author of *The History of the Royal Society*, applauds the insistence on plain style and an unbiased narrative voice: "The narrative has nothing of Art or language, being left by an ignorant Sailor, who, as he confesses, was in no better part than Gunnar's Mate, and that to a Greenland Fisher; and therefore the Reader can expect no more than bare matter of Fact, delivered in a homely Stile" (McKeon 109, quoting from Churchill).

Sea deliverances were another important genre in providence tale collections in New England and in their English precursors' collections, and McKeon finds in them, too, important sources for the English novel. James Janeway wrote many stories which were rewritten by New England writers. His most famous sea collection was called *James Janeway's Legacy to his Friends, Containing Twenty Seven Famous Instances of God's Providence in and about Sea Dangers and Deliverances, with the Names of several that were Eye Witnesses to Many of Them.* An opening epistle by John Ryther sets Janeway's tales firmly within the providence tale genre, and McKeon mentions another piece by Ryther, "A Plat for Mariners," which contains instructions on how to specifically "improve" sea voyages through "self documentation . . . [which] can closely resemble those [instructions] of the Royal Society on how to improve them scientifically" (McKeon, 115).

Finally, McKeon refers again to the Churchill collection and to some other discovery tale collections such as the "Prologue to the Readers" from William Lithgow's *History of 19 Years of Travel* (1682) for other evidence of the importance of documentation and plain style. McKeon summarizes them by noting: "It is a generally accepted principle that the credibility of a travel account is enhanced by the confirmation of other travelers, but a far more important principle is the superiority of eyewitnesses to hearsay testimony, however reputable the source." A writer's integrity, sincerity, and modesty are essential: "Nor . . . should they be thought capable of having any practical interest in, or emotional bias toward, the fabrication of untruths" (McKeon 108).

As I will show, all these concerns with truth and plainness are clearly echoed in providence tales written by Joseph Glanvill, Henry More, Increase and Cotton Mather, Mary Rowlandson, John Williams, and Quentin Stockwell. The travel narratives and apparition tales analyzed by McKeon feature the same essential elements as the providence tales under my purview. Although this certainly would suggest a role in the rise of the American novel for the New England providence tale similar to the role McKeon posits for his English tales in the development of the English novel, such a case must be left for further study, and I only ask the reader to keep such a possibility in mind. But in the following pages what I do try to show is how many of these English concerns mentioned by McKeon also affect New England writers and their narratives which constitute a substantial and compelling body of prose which, at the very least, must be dealt with far more fully than it has been to date. After examining this discourse closely, and seeing clearly what it contains, it becomes evident that a great deal of subsequent American discourse has been influenced by it. A quotation from Lord Shaftesbury from 1712, in which he parodies the travel and discovery narratives so in vogue then, is most evocative of the impact these tales had on future American novels:

> Yet so enchanted are we with the *Travelling Memoirs* of any Casual Adventurer; that be his Character, or Genius, what it will, we have no sooner turn'd over a Page or two, than we begin to interest our-selves highly in his Affairs. No sooner has he taken Shipping at the Mouth of the *Thames*, or sent his Baggage before him to *Gravesend*, or *Buoy in the Nore*, than strait our Attention is earnestly taken up. If in order to his more distant Travels, he takes some Part of EUROPE in his way; we can with patience hear of Inns and Ordinarys, Passage-Boats and Ferrys, foul and fair Weather; with all the Particulars of the Author's Diet, Habit of Body, his personal Dangers and Mischances, on Land, and Sea. And thus, full of desire and Hope, we accompany him, till he enters on his great Scene of Action, and begins by the Description of some *enormous Fish*, or *Beast*. From monstrous *Brutes* he proceeds to yet more *monstrous Men*. For in this race of Authors, *he* is ever the compleatest, and of the first Rank, who is able to speak of things the most *unnatural* and *monstrous*. (qtd. in McKeon, 117)

It does not take much imagination to notice in Shaftesbury's remarks quite a perfect outline for *Moby Dick*. Indeed, other critics have also pointed out connections between these early American narratives and our later literature. Recently Christopher Castiglia (*Bound and Determined*) has traced captivity narrative tropes as far forward as Patty Hearst's memoirs of her captivity with the Symbionese Liberation Army. Writers such as James Levernier and Richard VanDerBeets with Hennig Cohen have anthologized captivity narratives published well into the nineteenth century, and have discussed captivity motifs in authors such as Catharine Sedgwick, Lydia Marie Childe, Charles Brockden Brown, James Fenimore Cooper, William Gilmore Simms, and Robert Montgomery Bird. Coleman Parsons, who edited providence tale collections by Joseph Glanvill and George Sinclair, noted their connections to Edgar Allan Poe's interests in the mathematics of horror. Levernier and Parsons have both seen echoes of the providence tale's supernatural vision of the material world in the American Transcendentalists' spiritualized views of nature. None of these critics, however, have gone far in mapping the extent of the providence tale's effects throughout American cultural history.

Such a map would entail another book-length work. This work would show how frequently the essential providence tale markers appear in American literature, and how these markers combine to create an essential American myth in which the sublime, the transcendent, the supernatural—in other words, God—are invoked in a "scientific" way. The innocent narrator, Ishmael, those gothic prodigies Ahab, the *Pequod*'s crew, and Moby Dick himself, and Melville's precise rendering of the whaling business in all its mundane concreteness can all be taken as providence tale markers which, in Melville's masterful hands, invoke the presence of the sublime which generations of readers have felt. The providence tale was created to reassert God's existence, and thus, whenever its peculiar matrix of tropes is reassembled, God, or some sense of divinity, sublimity, or holiness, is also being invoked, in conjunction with post-Enlightenment beliefs in empirical proof. Early in the seventeenth century, Daniel Defoe set the fictional pattern for embedding providence tale markers in novels in his preface to *Robinson Crusoe*:

> If ever the story of any private man's adventures in the world were worth making public, and were acceptable when published, the editor of this account thinks this will be so.
>
> The wonders of this man's life exceed all that (he thinks) is to be found extant; the life of one man being scarce capable of a greater variety.
>
> The story is told with modesty, with seriousness, and with a religious application of events to the uses to which wise men always apply them (viz.) to the instruction of others by this example, and to justify and honour the wisdom of Providence in all the variety of our circumstances, let them happen how they will.
>
> The editor believes the thing to be a just history of fact; neither is there any appearance of fiction in it. And however thinks, because all such things are disputed, that the improvement of it, as well to the diversion, as to the instruction of the reader, will be the same; and as such, he thinks, without further compliment to the world, he does them a great service in the publication. (7)

The continued reappearance of providence tale motifs in American discourse suggests the importance of both science and religion in American mythology. Many classic American texts contain these markers. Hemingway's *Old Man and the Sea* is based on a confrontation, narrated in great detail, between innocence, in the form of the old, peasant fisherman, Santiago, and an immense and unyielding gothic universe, symbolized by the terrifying shark. King Kong and Fay Wray play out the paradigm on the silver screen, while the "innocents" Huck Finn and Jim revitalize the myth on a Mississippi River teeming with criminality, insanity, and murder. Pearl, and perhaps Hester Prynne and Dimmesdale, are the tarnished innocents facing a gothic wilderness and a gothic social order in *The Scarlet Letter*, while in *The Great Gatsby*, Nick Carraway looks up in reverential, naive awe at the crass evil of Meyer Wolfsheim and his "Swastika Holding Company," at the surreal "eyes of Dr. T. J. Eckleburg" set in their "valley of ashes" in the horrible gothic landscape of western Long Island, and at the much darker mysteries of Jay Gatsby and his twinkling, nearly supernatural green light. In the *Harper American Literature* anthology's introduction to its selections from Phyllis Wheatley, we read that "the circulation of a book of poems by a nineteen-year-old slave was regarded as so unusual that Wheatley's work [*Poems on Various Subjects, Religious and Moral*, 1773] . . . had to be prefaced by the testimony of eighteen prestigious Bostonians, including John Hancock and the Reverend Byles Mather, certifying the poems' authenticity" (McQuade 502). This obsession with truth in the face of the prodigious is again echoed near the end of Washington Irving's "Rip Van Winkle," where we read the following "Note":

> The foregoing Tale, one would suspect, had been suggested to Mr. Knickerbocker by a little German superstition about the Emperor Frederick *der Rothbart* and the Kypphauser mountain. The subjoined note, however, which he had appended to the tale, shows that it is an absolute fact, narrated with his usual fidelity:
>
> "The story of Rip Van Winkle may seem incredible to many, but nevertheless I give it my full belief, for I know the vicinity of our old Dutch settlements to have been very subject to marvelous events and appearances. Indeed, I have heard many stranger stories than this, in the villages along the Hudson, all of which were too well authenticated to admit of a doubt. I have even talked with Rip Van Winkle myself, who, when last I saw him, was a very venerable old man and so perfectly rational and consistent on every other point that I think no conscientious person could refuse to take this into the bargain; nay, I have seen a certificate on the subject taken before a country justice and signed with a cross, in the justice's own handwriting. The story, therefore, is beyond the possibility of doubt." (53–54)

I also offer a few excerpts from George Catlin's classic and generally unnoted nineteenth-century narrative *Letters and Notes on the Manners, Customs, and Conditions of the North American Indians: Written during Eight Years Travel (1832–1839) Amongst the Wildest Tribes in North America*. In his very first letter, after self-consciously confessing that he has actually written this "first" letter several years after the letter which now follows it in the text, Catlin goes on to humbly say, "Amidst the multiplicity of books which are, in this enlightened age, flooding the world, I feel it my duty as early as possible, to beg pardon for making a book at all; and in the next . . . to take some considerable credit for not having trespassed too long upon their time and patience" (1).

From Mary Rowlandson onward, humility has been a sign of innocence and credibility in providence tales. Catlin invokes other providence tale markers when he describes the gothic wilds he enters, emphasizes the care and attention to detail with which he (a painter) records his experiences of a race which, in his descriptions, is not only prodigious but also, like the supernatural world itself, vanishing and already nearly invisible:

> I started out in the year 1832, and penetrated the vast and pathetic wilds which are familiarly denominated the great "Far West" . . . , inspired . . . and devoted to the production of a literal and graphic delineation of the living, manners, customs and characters of an interesting race of people, who are rapidly passing away from the face of the earth—lending a hand to a dying nation, who have no historians or biographers of their own to portray with fidelity their native looks and history; thus snatching from an hasty oblivion what could be saved for the benefit of posterity, and perpetuating it, as a fair and just monument, to the memory of a truly lofty and noble race. (1–2)

Later he adds, "I have spent about eight years . . . immersed in Indian country . . . identifying myself with them as much as possible . . . to familiarize myself with their superstitions and mysteries which are the keys to Indian life and character" (3), while later still he further evokes the gothic element while reemphasizing his own credibility: "I will carry you a few degrees further into my stories of conjuration. . . . I [will] relate a scene of the tragic, and yet of the most grotesque character, which took place in the fort a few day since, and to all of which I was an eye witness. The scene I will relate as it transpired precisely, and call it the story of the 'doctor,' or the Blackfoot medicine man" (3).

Providence tale markers appear in texts from different disciplines and genres throughout American discourse. Tracing them through our culture helps us broaden our view of that culture and recognize previously neglected texts. This brief sketch of the overall impact of providence tales in American culture is mainly meant to remind the reader that the ensuing texts and reflections on them should not be viewed as quaint but now archaic vestiges of a dead era, but as the germinations of cultural motifs that have reverberated throughout American culture.

1

Remapping Colonial Discourse
from Providence Tale
to Indian Captivity Narrative

Critics have been examining early Indian captivity narratives since the 1940s. Generally they have viewed the pre-1700 narratives as variations of other forms of Puritan writing, such as spiritual autobiography and jeremiad, applying models canonized by Perry Miller and Sacvan Bercovitch. Although captivity narratives written after 1700 have received attention, critics have generally seen the form to have become by then a low and sensationalistic one, one which pandered to the violent and racist part of the American psyche.[1]

Recent scholarly work asserting the significance of Native American culture and history for an understanding of all periods of American literature has renewed interest in the captivity narratives. Annette Kolodny has shown the importance of what she calls frontier narratives, among which she includes captivities.[2] Lucy Maddox's *Removals* describes cultural myths about Native Americans which influenced the works of several major nineteenth-century writers. She traces some origins of these myths to seventeenth-century captivity narratives and other early American histories of Indian wars. The most striking recent study of the captivities has been John Demos's narrative history of Eunice Williams, *The Unredeemed Captive*. Demos portrays, in the relationship of John, Stephen, and Eunice Williams, an early American tragedy. He explains how Indian captivity affected every aspect of colonial life, from the family to international politics and trade. Demos's combination of novelistic sensitivity with the exhaustiveness of his historical research has produced the most compelling view to date of the relationship between the colonists and the Native Americans, surpassing the excellent work already done by Francis Jennings, James Axtell, Alden Vaughan and Daniel Richter, Maddox, and Kolodny.[3] Taking a different approach entirely, Leonard Tennenhouse and Nancy Armstrong have shown the influence of Mary Rowlandson's captivity narrative on the English epistolary novel.

All these studies have expanded the boundaries of colonial American literature. Demos's use of the John Williams family materials in itself enlarges the field of captivity studies by focusing on a relatively neglected but clearly essential set of texts. Even a brief look at the relations between Native Americans and English colonizers in seventeenth-century New England demonstrates the important historical and cultural role captivity played there and justifies the increasing attention devoted to stories about it.

According to Alden Vaughan and Daniel Richter, approximately seven hundred English settlers in New England were taken captive between 1675 and 1713.[4] This period included more than twenty years of declared war between the English colonists, the Native American tribes, and the French. Richard Slotkin estimates that at least twice as many New England settlers than the records indicate were actually seized (97). Such figures are not disproportionately high in relation to population estimates of approximately fifty to seventy-five thousand English in New England in 1675. However, these settlers did not become prisoners at a steady rate throughout the period Vaughan and Richter study. More became captives in certain years, such as 1675–77, 1688–97, and 1702–1714, than in others because these periods were those when war had been declared between France and England. Moreover, those captured came from sparsely populated frontier settlements. Using even the most conservative estimates, seven hundred people taken primarily in a few years from the midst of a small group of settlers struggling to establish themselves would surely have been a subject of intense interest.

Not surprisingly, captivity narratives were among the most popular literary forms in America from 1681, when Mary Rowlandson's narrative first appeared, until about 1720, six years after the end of Queen Anne's War. They remained widely read for well over a century and a half thereafter.[5] This interest is reflected in measures of best sellers during the seventeenth and early eighteenth centuries in New England. Mary Rowlandson's captivity narrative was one of only seven books that sold more than one thousand copies during any decade between 1660 and 1690. Jonathan Dickinson's *God's Protecting Providence Man's Surest Help . . . In Time of the Greatest Difficulties*, a Quaker captivity narrative set in Florida, was the only book that sold over two thousand copies in the 1690s. From 1700 to 1710 only three books sold three thousand copies. One was John Williams's *The Redeemed Captive Returning to Zion*, published in 1707.[6]

These narratives describe the capture of English settlers by war parties consisting largely of Indians, sometimes aided by the French. Many of the captives' family members, often small children, were killed, and the accounts of their deaths are usually detailed and brutal. The narratives then relate, in what is usually their longest section, the journey of the captives and the Indians through the woods to Canada. In this section the tales emphasize captives' suffering, the continual imminence of death for them, their various adaptations to Native American forest culture, and their religious interpretations of their struggles. In some narratives, this middle section also concerns the treatment of the captives by the French, to whom the Indians would sell them. The Indians sought either revenge, adoption of their captives, or some form of payment for them, while the French sought some combination of marriage, captives' conversion or taking of religious orders, or an exchange with the English for money or prisoners, French or Indian. The last section of the narratives generally deals briefly with the captives' redemption and return.

One striking fact about the captivity narratives is that they were generally published as parts of providence tale collections. Even when published separately, the captivities were saturated with providence tale ideology, and thus clearly belonged to the same genre. Through use of the providence tale as a model for the captivity narratives, many overlooked literary and cultural features of the captivities emerge, as do new perspectives on all seventeenth-century narrative prose literature in England and New England. The seventeenth-century providence tale, especially the apparition story, served as a laboratory in which Enlightenment empiricism and religious faith were joined to form a new cultural synthesis. The stories examine, and celebrate in that examination, the material world, even as they insist that God's presence fills that world. The stories prove God exists by presenting undeniable evidence of inexplicable occurrences. They are realistic tales of the supernatural which depict imaginary worlds concretely and convincingly.

Their claim became much more empirically valid in the setting of the American wilderness. Apparitions, the main prodigies in the English providence tales, could only be seen in their effects, while in New England, the Indians were flesh-and-blood "demons." Viewed as a providence tale, the captivity narrative clearly functions as a negotiation site where the sensibilities, ideas, and practices of the age of faith merged with the spirit of the new science to help usher in the American Enlightenment.

The providence tale background of the captivity narratives illustrates the strong connections between early American literature and English literary movements. The captivity narratives' inflections on the providence tale model help to explain the more gothic turn in the main line of subsequent American literature compared to the English epistolary novel and the realistic novel of social manners. Finally, this view of the captivity narrative afforded by the providence tale model lets us see how early American literature already distinguished itself in important ways from its European precursors more than one hundred and fifty years before critics usually say such literary distinction occurred in America.

Providence Tales in Seventeenth-Century England

The Bible, of course, is *the* providence tale, the story of God's activity on earth. Augustine, Boethius, Aquinas, and Calvin all wrote about the idea of providence, God's control or influence over earthly events.[7] Medieval exempla, "edifying tales of judgements upon sinners and mercies shown to the pious" (Thomas 93), are later variations of the form. Thomas mentions Lydgate's *Fall of Princes* (1430) and the Tudor *Mirror for Magistrates* (1559) as early Renaissance examples. In the sixteenth century, providence tales written by Protestants proliferated, for several reasons. In that Protestants sought ways to prove their faith's superiority to Catholicism, their providence tales demonstrate the power of prayer in influencing God over the so-called power of Romanist rituals. Works such as *A Golden Chain* (1592) by William Perkins, the English Puritan theologian so influential to William Ames and John Robinson particularly, were written in part to refute papist claims to supernatural power. Protestants also had to defend themselves against the challenge of the ever-increasing ranks of atheists and skeptics influenced by the rediscovery of classical writers and by the discoveries of Copernicus, Galileo, Kepler, and other scientists. Protestant writers responded with popular providence tale collections such as Henry Parker's *Dives and Paupers* (1493), Arthur Munday's *A View of Sundry Examples* (1580), and John Feilde's *A Godly Exhortation* (1583), which include stories about the downfalls of wicked kings, Sabbath breakers, drunkards, and other sinners. Pamphlets described disasters as providential judgments on "blasphemers, cursers, perjurers, murderers, adulteresses, and Sabbath breakers" (Thomas 93). Such stories "proved" that God's moral order existed, and that he would destroy anyone who upset it. The tales are generally short, with limited characterization, simple plots, and few concrete details. Stubbes's *Anatomie of Abuses* (1583), John Fox's third book of his martyrology, *Acts and Monuments* (1563), containing accounts of the fates of persecutors, and Stephen Batman's 1581 compendious *The*

Doome Warning All Men to the Judgement all tell tales of God's divine intervention on earth.[8] Believers eagerly read them and joined in discovering new examples of divine providence. Recording providential acts in diaries and autobiographies became a religious duty for Protestants.

By the seventeenth century, the new science, increasing atheism, and the expanding sectarianism helped produce a large skeptical readership which required empirical evidence in order to consider a divine origin for events. To meet these needs, writers of providence tales used descriptive, concrete prose and borrowed ideas of presenting evidence from science and the law. Paradoxically, they also made their accounts as sensational as possible; people who no longer believed in God, they thought, had lost their reason, so the writers could only persuade them convincingly through their emotions and senses.

Seventeenth-century providence tales were written by Protestant ministers who believed that religious faith could be fully justified on grounds compatible with reason. Many of these ministers themselves were interested in science, and some were members of the Royal Society. One of them, Henry More, belonged to a group which came to be known as the Cambridge Platonists. Based at Emmanuel College at Cambridge, they reacted against the rigorous Calvinism of that institution. Studying Plato and Plotinus, they determined that reason was God's highest gift to man, and accordingly they asserted their right to investigate any question in the light of reason, no matter how sacred to the Church. They wanted to create a scientific theology.[9]

At first, Cambridge Platonists such as More, Benjamin Whichcote, Ralph Cudworth, and John Smith wrote theological treatises disputing, with philosophical abstractions, the positions of Deists, materialists, and atheists, especially Descartes and Hobbes. Some of these "Sadducees" described the world as a machine operating automatically, which God had originally set in motion and then left alone. More's *True Notion of the Spirit* (a version of the last two chapters of his 1671 *Enchiridion Metaphysicum* which he added to the posthumous 1681 version he edited of Glanvill's *Saducismus Triumphatus: A Full and Plaine Evidence Concerning Witches and Apparitions*) was an attempt to refute those two philosophers and their respective schools, called the Nullibists and Holenmerians. In this work, More tried to imagine and describe in intricate detail how the supernatural, nonmaterial world could act upon the physical world. By the middle of the seventeenth century, however, Enlightenment materialism had already become dominant. The Cambridge Platonists and other ministers closely associated with them, such as Matthew Poole, Richard Baxter, and Joseph Glanvill, recognized that ideas alone could not affect godless men. To restore faith, they decided they would have to arouse readers' senses rather than their sleeping reason. Despite the Neoplatonists' aversion to popular art forms such as storytelling, some of them, as well as Nonconformists like Baxter, reluctantly determined to compile striking and sensational accounts of the workings of the invisible world on earth. Because of their scientific backgrounds, these writers rendered their sensational accounts according to empirical, Baconian methods, gathering well-documented, physical evidence before any hypotheses or theories were formulated.[10] These two conflicting intentions, to be both sensational and factual, produced a crucial transformation in the providence tales.

The new science further encouraged the choice of sensational subject matter in reaction to centuries of Aristotelian scholasticism which had searched out "norms" and deduced universal "laws" from them. Glanvill, More, Baxter, and others began to write accounts of bizarre occurrences which could not be explained by natural law, both to stimulate the senses and to discover new laws according to the principles of the new science. The Cambridge Platonists believed it was reasonable for God to act in ways that were beyond man's comprehension. Providence either imposed its own will on events at these times, or else so recombined natural occurrences that something inexplicable happened.[11] Their narratives had to prove, according to the standards of evidence set down by Francis Bacon in his essays and in works such as *Novum Organum*, that those providential acts had occurred. The centuries-old call, in the words of Cotton Mather's captivity narrative heroine Hannah Swarton quoting from Psalm 118, to "declare the works of the Lord," was taking an increasingly scientific, "enlightened," or empirical turn. Versed in Baconian rubrics, the Cambridge Platonists were well equipped to gather and then publicize evidence of the supernatural world that would be both convincing and shocking.

By the end of the century, their tales had developed into an increasingly complex dramatic form. Forced to be factual, providence tale compilers created believable characters, plots, motivations, and settings. Despite their religious intentions and sometimes dry empiricism, these authors inadvertently created new ways to tell exciting stories in prose. In the ensuing mammoth collections of apparition, ghost and witchcraft tales, shipwreck adventures and stories of hangings, horrible injuries, natural catastrophes, and wilderness adventures, they sought the suspension of their readers' disbelief. Ironically, their attempt to restore God to his heavenly throne brought him down to earth faster than the skeptics and atheists alone could have done.

Providence tales were as popular and influential in seventeenth-century New England as they were in England. Among the six books that sold at least one thousand copies in any decade before 1690 in New England were the *Essays* of Francis Bacon, a major influence on the new science, and Richard Baxter's *Call to the Unconverted*, while James Janeway's *Tokens for Children* was, according to Frank Luther Mott, among the period's "better sellers." Janeway's stories of dying children and their visions of Christ were a common type of providence tale, exemplifying "remarkable," or preternatural, faith, which could only have come from God.[12] Janeway also wrote a famous account of providential deliverances and judgments of shipwrecked people, *Mr. Janeway's Legacy to His Friends, Containing Twenty-Seven Famous Instances of God's Providence in and about Sea Danger and Deliverances, with the names of several that were Eyewitnesses* (1674). Baxter published his first providence tale collection in 1650, called *The Saints Everlasting Rest*, and he assembled a collection of all his providence tales in his last work, *The Certainty of the World of Spirits* (1691). Many of these tales, revised in varying degrees, were included in New England providence tale collections.

Increase Mather first used the English Neoplatonists' providence tale form in New England. A member of the Royal Society himself, and an illustrious minister fully involved in the Bay Colony's political affairs and deeply troubled by his church's declining power,[13] Mather found the form perfectly suited to his needs. In his preface to his first collection of providence tales, *An Essay for the Recording of Illustrious Providences* (1684), he recounts how he first became interested in a New England providence tale collection during a visit to England in 1658. There he read a manuscript of Matthew Poole's which outlined such an English collection. The project languished until 1670, when Mather found, while going through the papers of the recently deceased John Davenport, an anonymous text outlining the same plan. In a 1677 sermon, "A Discourse Concerning the Dangers of Apostasy," he discusses New England's long-standing desire for such a collection, citing a meeting of the Commissioners of the United Colonies as early as September 9, 1646, where plans for one were drawn up.[14] In this same sermon, he also mentions Thomas Shepard's interest in the idea, expressed in Shepard's 1672 sermon entitled "Eye Salve," where Shepard calls for a "Book of Records, and of God's dealings with his Church and people in Memorial of mercies, judgements, and great feats of the Lord" (71). Still, it wasn't until a meeting of the Ministers of the United Colonies in May 1681, that the plan was set in motion, resulting in the publication in 1684 of the *Essay*. At the 1681 meeting, as described in Mather's 1684 preface to his *Essay*, the ministers resolved to collect and publish "such divine judgements, tempests, floods, Earthquakes, Thunders as are unusual, Strange Apparitions, or what ever else shall happen that is Prodigious. Witchcrafts, Diabolical Possessions, Remarkable Judgements upon noted sinners: eminent Deliverances, and Answers of Prayers, are to be reckoned among illustrious providences" (Mather, *Essay*, A7).[15]

Mather expresses in this preface his desire to have included a lengthier, more complete collection, especially regarding stories about the Indian wars:

> I could have mentioned some very memorable Passages of Divine Providence Wherein the Countrey in general hath been concerned. Some Remarkables of that kind are to be seen in my former *Relation of the Trouble occasioned by the Indians in New England*. . . . I have often wished that the Natural History of New England might be written and published to the World, the Rules and method described by that learned and excellent person, Robert Boyle Esq., being duly observed therein. (A3)

Here Mather includes Indian tales in his list of potential providence tales. In praising Boyle's plan, he adds the ideas of another figure who combined scientific interests with religious passion in his thinking.[16]

The rest of the preface and the *Essay* itself contain an extensive collection of contemporary judgments, deliverances, and "magnalia dei." All of these share methodology of empirical analysis and a style employing gothic effects. Throughout the *Essay*, Mather refers to the inspiration he drew from many of the English providence tale writers, and rewrites some of their stories.

Mather closes the preface with several apparition tales. He opens the first chapter with deliverances at sea from storms and shipwrecks. To make them more convincing, he only uses stories with New England characters or which occur in New England waters. Chapter 2 offers a wider assortment of remarkable salvations. The fifth tale in chapter 2 is the Indian captivity narrative of Quentin Stockwell, presented merely as one of many providence tales.

Mary Rowlandson's *Sovereignty and Goodness of God* begins with a preface by "Per Amicum," who critics generally agree was Increase Mather.[17] This preface superimposes the providence tale model onto the ensuing narrative. "Per Amicum" calls Rowlandson's narrative a "memorandum of God's dealing with her, that she might never forget." She was persuaded to publish it because of the "many passages of working providence discovered therein . . . that God might have his due glory." In order to declare, the writer continues, what God has done for her soul, "this Narrative, particularizing the several passages of this providence, will not a little conduce thereunto." The whole narrative, he continues, shows the power, glory, and compassion of God. In other words, *A True History of the Captivity and Restoration of Mrs. Mary Rowlandson* (the title of the first English edition) is a providence tale.

Cotton Mather compiled a more complete providence tale collection than his father did. Published in 1702, the *Magnalia Christi Americana* includes, among hundreds of other narratives, a selection of short captivity narratives and several lengthier accounts of the Indian wars. Two of the captivities in the 1702 collection first appeared in a sermon, printed in 1697. That sermon's title demonstrates that the stories were conceived as providence tales: *Humiliations follow'd with deliverances. A Briefe Discourse On the Matter and Method Of that Humiliation which would be an Hopeful Symptom of our Deliverance from Calamity, Accompanied and Accommodated With A Narrative of the Notable Deliverance lately Received by some English Captives From the Hands of Cruel Indians. And some Improvement of that Narrative. Whereto is added a Narrative of Hannah Swarton, containing a great many wonderful passages, relating to her Captivity and Deliverance* (Mather, in Orians 87). The sermon refers primarily to Hannah Dustan, who had just returned from captivity with the scalps of the ten Indians she and two of her friends had killed to escape. Mather delivered the sermon to Dustan, who sat in the audience as he spoke. He pointed her out to his listeners to increase the drama of his remarks.

The Hannah Swarton story appears in book 6 of the *Magnalia*. This book is by itself an extensive providence tale collection called: *Thaumaturgus . . . Wherein very Many Illustrious Discoveries and Demonstrations of the Divine Providence in Remarkable Mercies and Judgements on Many Particular Persons among the People of New England are Observ'd, Collected and Related; Or, Remarkables of the Divine Providence Among the People of New England.*

Mather first recycled Dustan's story in *Decennium Luctuosum: A History of Remarkable Occurrences, in the Long War, Which New-England hath had with the Indian Salvages, From the Year 1688 to the Year 1698*. It appears as article 25, "A Notable Exploit; wherein Dux Faemina Facti." He published *Decennium Luctuosum* in 1699; subsequently it became the appendix to book 7 of the *Magnalia*. Book 7, another providence tale collection, is titled: *Ecclesiarum Praelia: Or, A Book of the Wars of the Lord . . . Relating the Afflictive Disturbances which the Churches of New=England have Suffered . . . and the Wonderful Methods and Mercies whereby the Churches have been Delivered out of their Difficulties.*

Like Increase in the *Essay*, Cotton Mather began book 6 with a preface relating the growth of the providence tale collection through his father's connection to Poole. He then described more contemporary proposals for a collection made to the ministers from the leaders of Harvard College, including his father. They proclaimed in March 1693/94 that "to observe and record the more illustrious discoveries of the divine providence, in the government of the world, is a design so holy, so useful, so justly approved, that the too general neglect of it in the Churches of God, is as justly to be lamented" (C. Mather, *Magnalia*, bk. 6, 1).

Cotton Mather then continued to pattern his own work after his father's by beginning with a chapter of "wonderful Sea Deliverances," followed by a second chapter of "Salvations experienced by others beside the Sea Faring," where, after a few "Remarkable Answers of Prayer" and recoveries from horrid injuries, appears "A Narrative of Hannah Swarton, containing Wonderful Passages relating to her Captivity and her Deliverance" (C. Mather, *Magnalia*, bk. 6, 10).

The *Magnalia* is more comprehensive than Increase's *Essay*; even the last two books, 6 and 7, exceed their precursor in length and scope. Cotton Mather's final two books contain a vast storehouse of narratives of corrupt ministers, converted Indians, penitent criminals on their way to being executed, murderous, insane, and lewd Quakers, witches and apparitions, separatists and zealots, dying God-fearing children, and a wide range of other stories. Some came from English sources but most were New England tales, selected to reveal God's providence. The Indian captivity narratives were presented as an integral part of the overall structure, just as they were in Increase Mather's *Essay*.

Cotton Mather also scattered references to other providence tale writers and collections throughout these books. He named one section of his work (book 6, chapter 6, section 3, appendix, 6) after Joseph Glanvill's *Saducismus Triumphatus* (Glanvill's subtitle: *Full and Plain Evidence Concerning Witches and Apparitions*). The fact that books 6 and 7 of the *Magnalia* are providence tale collections is not a mystery. The evidence seems equally "full and plain" that the Indian captivity narratives within these collections are providence tales as well.

John Williams's great narrative of 1707, *The Redeemed Captive Returning to Zion*, was also published separately, like Rowlandson's, but it too was set quite clearly in a providence tale framework. An introductory dedication to Governor Dudley and Williams's homecoming sermon appended to the end of the narrative demonstrate the narrative's generic identity. In the dedication, Williams says he "maintains the most lively and awful sense of divine rebukes which the most holy God has seen meet in spotless sincerity to dispense to me" (Clark and Vaughan 169); he also says

> God has given us plentiful occasion to sing of mercy as well as judgement. The wonders of divine mercy, which we have seen in the land of our captivity and deliverance therefrom, cannot be forgotten without incurring the guilt of blackest ingratitude.
>
> To preserve the memory of these, it has been thought advisable to publish a short account of some of those special appearances of divine power and goodness

for hoping it may serve to excite the praise, faith, and hope of all that love God . . . and to render the impressions of God's mighty works indelible on my heart, and on those that with me have seen the wonders of the Lord. (Clark and Vaughan 169–70)

In the final line of his sermon, "Reports of Divine Kindness; or Remarkable Mercies Should be Faithfully Published for the Praise of God the Giver," written under Cotton Mather's guidance, he proclaims that "God accounts the forgetting of mercies, a forgetting of himself" (Clark and Vaughan 168). Clearly then, the need to depict in vivid terms God's remarkable feats of mercy, judgment, and deliverance, to write, that is, ever more exciting and exacting providence tales, was among the most primary forces inspiring the creation of the Indian captivity narratives.

Common Characteristics of Providence Tales and Indian Captivity Narratives

Providence tales and captivity narratives share, most significantly, an overall concern with truth—scientific, empirical, Baconian truth. This concern appears on several levels. On the most abstract and theoretical level, authors and editors argue, in digressions, "cases of conscience," prefaces, introductions, "advertisements," dedications, and other places in the metanarratives, against skeptics who resist the very idea of the truth.[18] Thus we find Cotton Mather attacking Godefridas de Valle and his book *About the Art of Believing Nothing* (*Magnalia*, bk. 7, 61), in the introduction to *Decennium Luctuosum*. More concretely, but still on the margins of the narratives themselves, authors and editors continually assert their own claims to truthfulness and maintain the credibility of the authors they are editing or of the characters whose testimony they are reporting. Thus, at various points in Henry More's second posthumous edition of Joseph Glanvill's witchcraft collection, *Saducismus Triumphatus* (1683), More defends, in brief essays, letters, and other forms of testimony, the integrity of his co-author Glanvill and of Glanvill's most famous tale, "The Tedworth Demon."

More also uses Glanvill's reluctance to publish another edition of "Tedworth" with new supporting evidence as further proof of Glanvill's moral spotlessness, of his being above sordid considerations of revenge or material gain. Similarly, in Increase Mather's preface, he lauds Mary Rowlandson's innocence, and thus her credibility, shown by her reluctance to "thrust" her tale before the public.[19]

Major characters in these tales frequently provoke questions concerning what is real or true. In one dispossession story of the early 1600s, a melodramatic mystery and theological debate unfolds over the veracity of the claims of the exorcist John Darrell regarding the boy he "dispossessed," John Somers. The chief villain in "Tedworth" is a con artist, a drummer traveling and working with forged papers, but the reality of the curses he inflicts in retribution for being sent away and having his drum confiscated is adamantly maintained by Glanvill, More, and a host of witnesses. The presence and actions of such characters represent the slipperiness of truth which these tales dramatize.

The boundary between truth and deception becomes hotly-contested territory in these providence tales, and presenting the testimony of numerous witnesses becomes a popular providence tale technique. Writers imitate trial accounts such as Thomas Potts's narrative of the trial of the Lancashire witches (1613). Valentine Greatrakes, the "Irish stroker," adds an appendix to the end of his providential narrative, in which he defends his preternatural cures with eyewitness accounts from many of the leading scientists and theologians of his day.[20] In a famous apparition tale, both Increase Mather and Glanvill tell how the devil himself, through a witch named Julian Cox, creates illusions just as painters do (Glanvill 393).

In the captivities, Quentin Stockwell and Mary Rowlandson both deceive their Indian captors and are deceived by them repeatedly. The question of who is telling the truth, and the value of doing so, become central issues. Cotton Mather precedes his captivity narratives with a lengthy section in book 7, chapter 5 ("Wolves in Sheeps Cloathing: Or, An History of several Impostors pretending to be Ministers remarkably detected in the Churches of New England"), detailing the activities of various impostors pretending to be ministers. These reports so vividly describe the practices of these villains that the art of deception becomes the subject of the story, rather than the moral condemnation of deceitful practices. The focus on tricks and con artists underscores the necessity for concrete, detailed prose. (In the last two chapters I offer some examples of this precise prose, such as Mary Rowlandson's descriptions of her captors' makeup, clothing, and dancing.)

The battle over truth dominates these tales. John Williams upholds his faith against the "lies" of his French adversaries, the priests. In one of the central scenes of his narrative, Williams proves to his son that the French priest, Merial, has lied to him in order to convert him and many others. Williams's logic and careful reasoning here echo Henry More's philosophical treatises on the existence of the invisible world written fifty years earlier, but in Williams's narrative the philosophical debate has become part of a melodramatic scene. Williams uses common sense and everyday theology, rather than More's metaphysical abstractions, to construct his arguments. His accusations also resemble Glanvill's and

More's earlier warnings against most providence tales then in circulation, which they claimed were largely popish lies. The veracity of a providence tale was essential. A fascination with truth surfaces everywhere in them, and characters practiced in deception, con artists, impostors, and the like can be subjects of as much, if not more, fascination as such proponents of "truth" as John Williams. The art and ways of making people believe, of creating belief, lie just beneath the surface of many providence tales as a major subject of interest. Such a fascination led these providence tales further toward a more secular, scientific outlook, in which the moral qualities of the characters became less important than the impact they had on readers. The line between good and evil began to dim.[21]

Gothic action and settings constitute a second major convention common to all these tales. Violence and torture fill Cotton Mather's Indian stories. Murder and other deadly sins figure prominently in his accounts of criminals' confessions and last-second conversions on their way to their executions, and of demonic Quakers. Glanvill and Increase Mather also write about murder. Increase Mather specializes in clinical gore, minute descriptions of physical disfigurement and injuries, which his son rewrites in more dramatic style and adds to his own collections. Some of Glanvill's work features graphic sexuality and bawdy scenes; witches take power away from men's "genital members," or kiss Satan "on the breach" (Glanvill 470–71). In the earlier, anonymous witchcraft narrative about John Fian, whose trial was presided over by King James, the devil's disciples kiss their master's buttocks, "which being put over the Pulpit barre, everyone did as he had enjoyned them" (14). Another account, in Glanvill and reproduced by Increase Mather, tells of a witch discovered naked on the ground, groveling "globes upward" (Glanvill 388). Cotton Mather describes more overt forms of forbidden sexuality, such as adultery and bestiality. Savagery fills these tales, too. Hannah Dustan, Cotton Mather's most prominent captivity narrative heroine, kills ten Indians, including two women and six children, in their sleep, and takes their scalps. The crew in the English sea deliverance tale of their captain, Edward Gibbon, come close to acts of cannibalism three times. This tale was rewritten by both Mathers from a version in James Janeway. In addition, many tales depict Indian captives and shipwreck victims eating disgusting foods such as shark's blood and raw moose liver.

The motif of captivity itself is prominent, not just in captivity narratives, but also in Glanvill's and both Mathers' numerous tales of bodily possession. These tales include instances of ventriloquism (captive voices), for example, which was considered a preternatural occurrence in the seventeenth century (Mather, *Magnalia*, bk. 6, 67). Captivity tropes appear in tales where men are compelled to bark like dogs, or, "captivated" or possessed by demons, peoples' heads spin around three hundred and sixty degrees on their necks (*Magnalia*, bk. 6, 71). In other tales bodies and household articles fly through rooms at the bidding of unseen powers (Glanvill 425, 431). Figures of captivity become synonymous with the human condition when so many characters are controlled by outside forces.

The sensationalism of this unrelenting mayhem is deepened by a pronounced strain of sentimental melodrama, which frequently takes the form of images and accounts of dying children. Glanvill offers tales of the devil and other evil spirits luring children away from prayer (580), while Increase Mather's shipwreck deliverances have scenes of children dying in front of their parents (4–14). Both Mathers write tales similar to those in Janeway's *Tokens for Children*, as in the appendix to Cotton Mather's book 6, "A Token for the Children of New England, or Some Examples of Children in whom the Fear of God was remarkably Budding before they died . . . " (Mather, *Magnalia*, bk. 6, 84). Rowlandson describes in great detail carrying her five-year-old daughter through the snow without food for days. The girl dies in her mother's lap. Children also figure in more gruesome scenes. Indians bash out the brains of noisy children, those who cry or are unable to walk, or those whose mothers can no longer carry them. Rowlandson tells of another captive mother being tortured before being burned to death while her children are forced to watch. Rowlandson (or her editor Increase Mather only, in Mitchell Breitwieser's view) applauds the mother's fortitude in refusing to cry throughout the ordeal.

Another common motif then is the value of affliction. One accepts it stoically, as God chastises His chosen above all. Indeed, captives and other providence tale protagonists believe that they deserve much worse. Still, their suffering sometimes ends on a brighter note, in scenes of God extending His saving hand at the last minute. This motif repeatedly occurs in English sea deliverance tales. Fish fly into foundering boats and birds wait on masts for starving seamen to kill and eat them. Both Mathers feature scenes of food appearing miraculously to captives near starvation. Hannah Swarton's Bible keeps opening by itself to passages which so directly apply to her situation and to her despair that they save her soul. A similar remarkable deliverance occurs in *The Sovereignty and Goodness of God* and in the *Magnalia* when the Indians, at the height of their success both in King Philip's War and later in northern New England, are suddenly and for no apparent reason thrown into confusion and fear. All these wonders deepen the gothic atmosphere, in that preternatural powers are taking part in human affairs during extremely terrifying events.

The Indian captivity narratives, while sharing these providence tale characteristics, change the form in several ways. The most obvious additions are the Indians, those flesh and blood "devils" they add to the form. Along with physical devils comes a physical hell, the wilderness those devils inhabit. Captivity

Providence Tales and the Birth of American Literature

narratives bring the supernatural down to earth. Even more in this secularizing vein, these narratives, particularly a group of what I call unauthorized captivity tales which were not published until years, decades, or even centuries had passed, extend the boundaries of good and evil until, frequently, the line between the two becomes difficult to find. (Chapter 5 delineates both these borrowed and these original elements of the captivity narratives. It describes the literary result of New England captives, especially in these unauthorized texts, ending up, sometimes actually and sometimes just figuratively, in the wigwam.)

Current Critical Views of Indian Captivity Narratives

What critics have said about the Indian captivity narratives has varied widely over the past fifty years. At the same time, however, a striking continuity has persisted since the publication of Philip Carleton's 1943 article, "The Indian Captivity Narrative." Contemporary works by Mitchell Breitwieser, Nancy Armstrong and Leonard Tennenhouse, Annette Kolodny, and Lucy Maddox have added feminist and new historicist readings of captivities, but even these studies share aspects of Carleton's views.

The dominant critical position that has endured since Carleton's article consists of three main parts. Critics since Carleton have treated the early Indian captivity narratives as variations of an already established New England literary form, such as the spiritual autobiography, the sermon, the jeremiad, or the conversion narrative. A second, and the most widespread and dominant attribute of this fifty-year consensus, might be termed the declensionist view of the Indian captivity narrative. This view assumes an almost typological orthodoxy, demonstrating the seemingly universal critical notion of the Puritan fall, from Winthrop's vision of a "city on a hill" and Danforth's "errand in the wilderness" to "manifest destiny," from piety and righteousness to materialism and hucksterism. This view holds that the first Indian captivity narratives represented mythic piety and purity, while subsequent narratives fall, by 1700, into a depraved state of escapist entertainment or racist propaganda. Such a fall leads axiomatically to the third tenet of critical orthodoxy, that of the sanctity, superiority, and the chosenness of the original Puritan Indian captivity narrative, Mary Rowlandson's *Sovereignty and Goodness of God*.

Carleton charts a gradual decline, and establishes the conditions for later declensionists by invoking a nearly Edenic original phase of captivity narratives. He praises them for their "painful realism," for demonstrating "simple truth" with "simple, unaffected prose . . . vigorously written"; he calls the narratives a "revelation of a pioneer people" (169). They were, he says, "written . . .

by people who were not professional writers and who made no pretense of shaping their material or their work for any purpose other than that of the mere record" (176). Carleton goes on to deplore what he sees as an attempt of later writers to "imitate . . . or improve upon . . . the simplicity of the . . . captivity" (178). Of these attempts, he concludes that "conscious artistry applied to the captivity has only cheapened it" (180).

Roy Harvey Pearce, in his 1947 "The Significance of the Indian Captivity Narrative," steps firmly into the declensionist camp by writing that "the first, and greatest, of the captivity narratives are simple, direct religious documents" (2). He cites Williams, Stockwell, and Jonathan Dickinson as being "in the pattern of the best known (and deservedly so) of the narratives, Mary Rowlandson's *Sovereignty and Goodness of God* (1682)." He says of her work, "Here . . . is the fusion of immediacy and religious intensity . . . a certain aesthetic quality . . . freshness and concreteness of detail. . . . Here we have the captivity as a direct statement of a frontier experience" (3). However, Pearce modifies Carleton in citing the importance of what he also considers the later, depraved narratives. By the time of Cotton Mather's collections,[22] the captivity had become, for Pearce, equivalent to "Grub Street criminal biographies" (7), and had gone from being "religious confessional[s] to noisomely visceral thriller[s]" (1). He maintains that only these later captivities had any subsequent literary significance. For all its virtue, Rowlandson's text was a barren anomaly. It is as "the eighteenth century equivalent of the dime novel," Pearce says, "that the captivity narrative has significance for the history of our literature" (13).

Pearce believes that writers made different uses of captivity narratives according to the needs of the times. The captivity narratives, he writes, are "a popular form which shapes and reshapes itself according to varying immediate cultural needs" (1). In his view, the captivity narratives are a chameleonlike genre, capable of being transformed by writers and editors for a variety of social, political, or cultural purposes.[23]

Alden Vaughan is another staunch declensionist. He sees the earliest captivity narratives as typical of Puritan literature. They were spiritual autobiographies representing the soul's regeneration through a "day to day struggle with an alien culture, [which was] the mainspring of the experience" (Clark and Vaughan 11). He also calls them "lay sermons in the guise of adventure stories," explaining that the captivity narrative "owed much of its tone and content to jeremiads" (7). He does point out their dramatic and sensational sentimentality, their "pathos . . . in . . . descriptions of the forced rending of Puritan families" (10). Eventually, however, he agrees with Pearce that "Mather begins the transformation of the captivity narrative into a new sub-genre. By 1740, as

Pearce notes, 'religious concerns came to be incidental at most; the intent . . . was to register as much hatred of the French and Indians as possible'"(Clark and Vaughan 21).

Edward Clark and Alden Vaughan also ascribe a titillating quality to the narratives. Puritan readers could vicariously experience captivity "cut loose from . . . normal guideposts of language and social relationships [and then] entertain . . . ideas and values that colonial New England did not allow" (12). In all, Clark and Vaughan conclude, "From unpolished but intense religious statements in the Puritan period, captivity narratives evolved by the late eighteenth century into ornate and often fictionalized accounts that catered to more secular and less serious taste" (3).

James Levernier is another orthodox critic of Indian captivity narratives. In his 1975 *Indian Captivity Narratives: Their Function and Form*, he claims the earliest captivities had to be authentic and truthful, because Puritans distrusted fiction. He agrees in this with R. W. G. Vail who, writing in his 1925 "The Voice of the Old Frontier" (three 1925 lectures published in 1949), says captivity narratives were, "true tales of horror in the form of deathbed confessions, stories of shipwrecks, piracy, plague, disaster . . . as . . . [Puritans] did not believe in play acting or the corrupting influence of the novel (Vail 24–26). Vail and Levernier further imply that Puritans had to turn to such sensational but true accounts for their entertainment.

Because of their fear of fiction, a premium was put on truth in Puritan writing. This element disappeared quickly, according to Levernier, as the influence of religion faded and was replaced by the people's fear and hatred of the French and Indians. As early as Cotton Mather's 1690 captivity narratives, the narratives declined and became vehicles of racist propaganda. Levernier then goes on to agree with Pearce that the importance of the captivities resides in their variety of specific forms, literary treatments, and points of view they illustrate in narrating the same basic content. Levernier sees his basic project as classifying relationships between needs and forms in the captivities of different historical periods. His and Hennig Cohen's anthology, *The Indians and Their Captives*, is a fascinating work which traces how captivities from different historical periods reflect the political and cultural circumstances of their times.

Levernier discusses the captivities' affinities with spiritual autobiographies and jeremiads, but he is also aware of the relationship of providence tales to the captivities. In his 1975 study, he says the captivities were incorporated by the Mathers "into the conventional Puritan framework of the 'illustrious providence' to teach lessons about God's mercy." Rather than developing this relationship further, he tells readers to look at Perry Miller's *The Puritan Mind: The*

Seventeenth Century for more on the Puritan use of illustrious providences. Miller, in those pages cited by Levernier, presents a brief and disparaging picture of the Puritan providence tale, which must, I believe, be reexamined.[24]

In 1977, Levernier edited and wrote an introduction for a new edition of Increase Mather's *Essay*. Here he recognizes the providence tales' significance, calling them "some of the finest and earliest surviving examples of American narrative art" (xvi). He adds that Stockwell's captivity narrative in the *Essay* fits the providence tale mold, sharing with the providence tales "a unified point of view, a tragic hero, a suspenseful plot, and merciless villains" (xvii). Although he does not mention their most significant common elements, his introduction does seem to be an important step in unfolding the captivity narratives' relationship to providence tales.

In his 1993 work written with Kathryn Derounian-Stodola, *The Indian Captivity Narrative, 1550–1900*, Levernier writes of how the captivities were used to express God's mercy in letting people escape overpowering afflictions. Thus, he says, "Captivity narratives written during the religious phase [the earliest phase] often contain mention of any 'special providence' which befell captives along the way. An unexpected cup of broth, an act of kindness or courtesy, crossing a river without getting overly wet . . . in short, anything unusual that benefited the captive—were seen as signs of divine intervention and worth notice" (19). Here Levernier highlights more providence tale elements found in captivity narratives. He still subscribes, though, to the declensionist viewpoint in seeing these connections only in the early narratives. Also, in attributing the similarities between the two forms to the Puritans' "powerful . . . early tendency to use Indian captivity within a religious context" (22), he overlooks elements of the new science which both forms share.

Philip Carleton makes high claims for early Indian captivity narratives by citing structural elements they share with those found in Icelandic sagas. Richard VanDerBeets goes beyond Carleton in using myth and archetype theory to interpret the captivity narratives. Borrowing ideas from Joseph Campbell's *Hero with a Thousand Faces*, VanDerBeets says in "The Indian Captivity Narrative as Ritual" that the narratives represent "the wellsprings of humanity" (562). They describe, he says, the exile of a hero in the land of the dead, and his or her subsequent triumphant return. He shows how many ritual elements of captivity narratives, such as scalping and cannibalism, and the stages of ritual adoption, such as running the gauntlet, accepting Indian food, ritual weeping, having all one's hair cut off except for the scalp lock, face painting, taking a new name, and tattooing, are "elements of distinctly archetypal nature [which] have pervaded and informed the captivity narratives" (562). Such a concern with very old or mythic parallels also appears in Richard Slotkin's 1973 *Regeneration through Violence*, where Slotkin maintains that the captivity narratives depict an archetypal American belief in violent transcendence. Slotkin takes a largely psychological view of the captivity narratives. He shares some of Clark and Vaughan's sense of their titillating quality when he says they functioned as a means for the Puritans to vicariously experience their repressed desires to live as Indians and at the same time to assuage their guilt over those desires by seeing themselves, taken captive, as "forced" into such experiences (100).[25]

However, these broader Jungian and Freudian approaches do not radically alter the affinities these archetypal critics share with the traditional, declensionist outlook. Slotkin, for example, sees the Indian captivity narratives as "sermons [though] with profane concerns." He prefers Rowlandson's work, calling it, along with a few of the first captivity narratives, "genuine first person account[s] of actual ordeals . . . , natural, spontaneous product[s] of the New World experience" (95). He adds that Rowlandson's "greater degree of natural sensitivity and her experience as a captive made her more capable than her fellows of discovering and revealing the character of her soul . . . [which] mirrored the aspirations and anxieties of Puritan America" (112). Thus, for Slotkin, Rowlandson becomes the chosen exception to the tawdry rule.

Finally, the work of four critics, Tennenhouse and Armstrong, Kolodny, and Breitwieser, reflects some of the more prevalent perspectives in contemporary criticism. Kolodny calls the captivity narratives the "first indigenous new world narratives" which inscribe a "paradigm of woman's position" in the New World. She represents that position with a symbol Mather uses from an old Roman coin captioned "Judea Capta," which shows a crying, weak woman in need of the Lord. Kolodny believes this biblical image of "Judea Capta" was used to teach the Puritans about their vulnerability to Satan in the wilderness, and thus about their utter dependence on God. She also notes that editors such as the Mathers had trouble fitting the stories precisely into the figures of the biblical types they used (*The Land before Her* 21). Kolodny, along with these other contemporary critics, does notice more of the ambiguity of these texts in their challenges to orthodox Puritanism. Breitwieser's new historicist and feminist outlook presents a more powerful and subversive Rowlandson resisting the Puritan theocracy by insisting on her right to place mourning the loss of her daughter over orthodox ideas about the spiritual value of affliction. (Interestingly, where for Kolodny crying equals ideological conformity, Breitwieser sees it as subversion.) Breitwieser doesn't recognize that mourning and suffering aesthetically work together in synthesizing sentimentality, a form of sensationalism, with scientific objectivity, a product of asceticism in this case.

Tennenhouse and Armstrong also work from a new historicist perspective with a feminist turn, and elevate Rowlandson's text to being the originator of the English novel, specifically the model for Richardson's *Pamela*. Like Breit-wieser, though, they extend and greatly magnify the tradition of the singularity or chosenness of *The Sovereignty and Goodness of God*, and thus of the decline of all subsequent captivity narratives. Their effort to trace the impact of the captivity narrative beyond Pearce's penny dreadful tradition is a more full-blown exposition of a similar urge in several earlier works. Coleman Parsons's introduction to Glanvill's *Saducismus Triumphatus* discusses Glanvill's influence on Defoe, Scott, and Poe. Levernier's introduction to Increase Mather's *Essay* traces the impact of Mather's providence tales on Bartram, Brown, Poe, and the transcendentalists. All these views assign significant future roles mainly to the earliest captivities, particularly Mary Rowlandson's.

The Providence Tale Model of the Indian Captivity Narrative

The model against which we compare any object will obviously determine what we see of that object. Critics working without the providence tale model do not see the captivity narrative's deep roots in seventeenth-century English literary experiments. Rooting the captivity narratives in an English genre counters the notion of New England Puritan literature as anomalous and sub-literary, separate from and unequal to the literary productions of Restoration England. This view of the captivity narrative as a variant of an English form simultaneously illustrates distinctive and creative American inflections on English precursors. In establishing this transatlantic link, my work shares Tennenhouse and Armstrong's sense of the importance of demonstrating the interdependency between English and early American literature.[26]

Captivity narratives do not, as declensionist critics maintain, decline rapidly into mere propaganda. A providence tale model demonstrates how demonized Native Americans and sentimental portraits of dying English children were also being used to create a metaphysical model of the universe that has remained influential in American literature. This paradigm of innocent truth battling a gothic world with the help of God and scientific technology is an enduring trope in captivity narratives which seems to me to be of greater importance than the very important chameleonlike attributes of the captivities noted by other critics.

Clark and Vaughan do notice Cotton Mather's desire to compile a providence tale collection in *Magnalia Christi Americana*, but they find Mather's aim of demonstrating the "Wonders of the Christian religion . . . and the wonderful displays of [God's] infinite power, wisdom, goodness and faithfulness, wherein

His Divine Providence hath irradiated an Indian wilderness," to be "difficult to discern" (qtd. in Clark and Vaughan, 135). Their difficulty arises because they do not acknowledge that Mather's vivid and shockingly violent details, including his focus on the torture of children, typify the providence tales' imperative to shock readers' emotions and senses. In the light of the providence tale, Mather's collection of short and violent captivities in *Decennium Luctuosum* becomes more than simple propaganda. Instead it shows quite graphically God's power and ferocity, as well as his remarkable healing mercy in the face of the horrible demons he unleashes. Narrative features which seem merely sensationalistic have other dimensions when read in the context of the providence tale.

The providence tale model also foregrounds the importance of the various introductions, prefaces, and dedications that accompany these tales and collections. In introducing Rowlandson in their anthology of captivity narratives, Clark and Vaughan cite the preface by "Per Amicum" only to note their exclusion of it from their work, and to dismiss it by noting that it "chastises the Indians" and gives assurances of Rowlandson's credibility (32). I see such a token of credibility as an essential assertion of empirical truth, without which the tale would not be complete.

Studying captivities as providence tales also helps redress the neglect of tales other than Rowlandson's. Tennenhouse and Armstrong argue that Rowlandson's narrative, like *Pamela*, reconfigures Englishness in terms of a person's knowledge of both written discourse and Lockean rationality, but actually letters and rational debate constitute more important elements in John Williams's narrative than in Rowlandson's. Through these epistles, Williams, his captive son Samuel, and their papist adversaries enact a carefully reasoned theological struggle.

Breitwieser explores deviations from orthodox Puritanism in *The Sovereignty and Goodness of God*. He notes that "experience came to mean disconnection from enclosing contexts" for Rowlandson (6). In her narrative, he writes, "an anomalous textual ambience through which interdicted subjective pressure otherwise almost completely absent from seventeenth-century New England archives, moves" (9). Breitwieser argues that in Rowlandson's text there is an intrusion into prevailing ideology, a "break in the real . . . , raw and unremedied by the rehabilitated representation that was the major project of the postwar peacetime" (12). But many providence tales' preoccupations with the ambiguous line between truth and falsehood or good and evil highlight "subjective pressure," disconnections," and "breaks in the real." Stockwell acts as treacherously as his captors, who perform humanitarian deeds. Williams seems as crafty as his papist adversaries, and his children undergo drastic transformations, extreme "breaks in the real."

The captivity narratives' adherence to providence tale forms proves that none of these texts, including Rowlandson's, were really "raw and unremedied." Only the unauthorized or unedited texts approach that quality. Rowlandson's tears for her dead child Sarah, signs of subversion in Breitwieser's compelling view, also look different in a providence tale model. Mourning adds a sensational, sentimental note to Rowlandson's praise for another captive's stoicism under torture. Such ascetic suffering, in the context of the providence tale, is a sign of rationality and objectivity. Breitwieser sees these two reactions working only against each other.

The providence tale's connection to the Indian captivity narrative is so strong that all of the genre's critics have discussed aspects of the captivity narratives that are related to their providence tale origins. Such glimpses show that even without emphasizing, or sometimes without even recognizing, the providence tales' impact on Indian captivity narratives, the consequences of that impact are inescapable.

Carleton notices the captivity narratives' great concern with truth. He says, "The material is exciting enough in itself—but its chief value for the contemporaries who read it was its truth. Most of the captivities make painful attempts to be accurate; some of them are accompanied by affidavits" (169). Slotkin remarks on Rowlandson's emphasis on "sense perception" over "corrupted reason" (103), and the strong connection between apparition tales and the Indian captivity narrative: "Even the writings that emerged from the witch hysteria of 1692 derived images and narrative patterns from the captivities" (96). Breitwieser notes resemblances between Rowlandson and Melville, owing to the former's "literary realism" (6).

Tennenhouse and Armstrong describe distinct providence tale characteristics in their discussion of Rowlandson, even though they never refer these traits to their providence tale origins. They argue the captivity narratives were precursors of a later gothic mode, and remark on Rowlandson's innocence in the face of the gothic horror she is forced to inhabit. They also see the sentimentality in her tale, and state that "the captivity narrative [makes us care] about what Rowlandson calls the English 'heart', which introduces some of the language of the later Gothic romance into the Puritan narrative" (206).

The critic with the clearest sense of the close and meaningful relationship between the two forms, even though he finally fails to recognize their family kinship, is Richard Dorson, the editor of the 1950 anthology *America Begins: Early American Writing*. Dorson includes providence tales, which he calls "judgements, deliverances, prodigies and accidents," with captivity narratives, natural wonders, witchcrafts, voyages, Indian conceits and antics, Indian treaties, and accounts of forest wars as among the most exciting examples of early American

Providence Tales and the Birth of American Literature

writing. He says these forms share a "vivid, stark and fresh" (15) style, a lack of "posturing" and "earthy, post-Elizabethan English" (5), and a "graphic and salty nature" (1). These are all aspects of seventeenth-century providence tales. Dorson does not realize that most of the genres he mentions were written as providence tales, but he does illustrate many important characteristics of the genre and its writers. Dorson sees in Cotton Mather, not the harsh fanatic so commonly described, but rather a "master reporter with an eye for the sensational" (3). Mather's tales exhibit, for Dorson, "on the spot reporting of sensational events" (114). The *Magnalia* he calls a mixture of fact and romance. In all these insights, Dorson shows a keen intuitive awareness of how providence tales and captivity narratives produced a new synthesis of scientific reasoning and religious faith, of physical facts and supernatural occurrences.

Several critics have noted the influence of providence tales and captivity narratives on later authors. Coleman Parsons wrote introductions to both Sinclair's *Satan's Invisible World Discovered* and to Glanvill's *Saducismus Triumphatus*. In the latter he writes, among other statements showing his recognition of the importance of providence tales, that, "these collaborators [of Glanvill and More] and many more unnamed were joined in an effort to sting and startle spiritual drones with 'fresh examples of Apparitions and Witchcrafts' for their souls' welfare. What they did not realize was that they were making a very secular contribution to entertainment in the form of the short story" (Glanvill, *Saducismus Triumphatus*, xix).

In this essay introducing *Saducismus Triumphatus*, titled "Glanvill's Witch Book and Its Influence," Parsons mentions Defoe, Scott, and Poe as the most prominent beneficiaries of Glanvill's work. Of the connection to Poe, he writes, "The method by which Henry More [and] Joseph Glanvill . . . intensified interest by linking comment to gruesome action, the rational to the irrational, is similar to Poe's ratiocinative approach to abnormality and crime" (xvi).

Matthew Arnold, he claims, "renew[ed] to immortality" (x) Glanvill's scholar gypsy story. Of Glanvill's "Drummer of Tedworth," Parsons wrote that it "has stimulated diarists, journalists, balladmakers, pamphleteers and propagandists, satirists, writers on the psychic, scholars, playwrights, and poets, from Samuel Pepys to Edith Sitwell" (xi). Parsons also argues that Hogarth and Joseph Addison used the Tedworth story, and describes George Sinclair's influence on Robert Louis Stevenson. Finally, in showing the close relationship between Defoe's "True Relation of the Apparition of One Mrs. Veal" and Glanvill's work, Parsons proposes the latter as an important source for and influence on what he calls the first modern short story (xv).

Levernier also notes, in his introduction to Increase Mather's *Essay*, some subsequent influences of the providence tales and captivity narratives. He says the *Essay* "can be seen as the progenitor of the more secular compendiums of unusual natural phenomena compiled by such writers as Bartram, Franklin, Thoreau and Muir, and the symbolic fascinations which characterize the American romantics, particularly the Transcendentalists, owe their origin in part to the Puritan practice of extracting spiritual meaning from the environment" (viii-ix). Levernier later notes the persistence of the captivity story in Cooper's Leatherstocking tales, and in works by William Gilmore Simms, Robert Montgomery Bird, and others.

A full analysis of the captivity narrative as a providence tale broadens our sense of the importance and future impact of these tales. The evolution of the form from apparition tale to captivity narrative tells us a great deal about the development of prose narratives into a powerful and immensely popular literary form. The transmutation of the supernatural into the imaginary, and the casting of the imaginary into a viable and rational form, is another story that the present analysis seeks to unfold. The confluence of Enlightenment empiricism and the Reformation's religious passion can be viewed microscopically in the development of the captivity narrative from providence tales. Most important, finally, the recurring apparition tale and captivity narrative figure of an innocent or truthful narrator or protagonist confronting or captivated by a world of gothic hellishness suggests that a major source of R. W. B. Lewis's "American Adam" (often thought of as an American Eve) can be found in these texts. Such a genealogical line would extend forward at least to *Moby Dick*. In that book, Ishmael the innocent and Ahab the tormented seeker of truth are captivated while out on the wild ocean by the monstrous and inexplicable white whale. In the confrontation that ensues, we see the captivity narrative as providence tale inscribed in perhaps its most ambiguous, sensational, and scientifically realistic American form.[27]

2

The Providence Tale in England,
1597–1697

In the middle of the seventeenth century in England, the providence tale changed dramatically. A focus on morality and God's judgments became less dominant as authors created longer and more realistic narrative "proofs" of the existence of an invisible world of spirits and divine agents. Ironically, while attempting to demonstrate the presence of God to the skeptics, atheists, and materialists of the age, providence tale writers developed a literary form that enmeshed the spiritual with the physical world. Thus, they helped bring spiritual beings into the material realm they were contesting.

By the latter half of the seventeenth century, "true relations" about apparitions, witches, sorcerers, and haunted houses became the most popular type of providence tale in England. The "inexplicable" became the literary domain of the providence tale writers. Authors also told of unusual effects of thunder and lightning, miraculous cures of birth defects and gruesome injuries, and of inconceivable deliverances from shipwrecks and pirates. Readers could still hear about the sudden deaths of the mighty, and often in these tales good was rewarded and evil punished. Nevertheless, by 1650, the major writers of providence tales were concentrating on stories that illustrated, in a style both scientific and sensationalistic, the activities of an invisible, spiritual world in human affairs. These activities did not always present a clear message about good and evil.

Five immense historical forces influenced the creation of these tales: the English Civil War and its political reverberations, Renaissance humanism, the emphasis on reason in the theological outlook of the Reformation, the Scientific Revolution, and the growth of atheism. In this chapter, I trace some relationships between these intellectual movements and the ministers who collected, edited, and wrote the providence tales which so influenced the Mathers and the other writers of Indian captivity narratives. In the succeeding chapter I examine the effects of these movements in a variety of individual providence tales.

THE THEATRE OF GOD'S JUDGEMENT: THE NEW
PROVIDENCE TALE EMERGES

The Theatre of God's Judgement, compiled by Thomas Beard, appeared in 1597. In some ways a collection of traditional providence tales, it also contains elements typical of the providence tales of the second half of the seventeenth century. The first edition is subtitled *A Collection of Histories out of Sacred, Ecclesiastical and Prophane Authors, Concerning the Admirable Judgements of God upon the Transgressors of his Commandments*. A second edition's 1612 subtitle more accurately illustrates this collection's direct relationship to the long medieval tradition exemplified by works such as John Lydgate's *Fall of Princes*. The subtitle reads, *Wherein is represented the admirable justice of God against all notorious sinners, both great and small, but especially against the most eminent persons of the world, whose transcendent power breaketh through the barres of human justice*. This emphasis on the powerful is one element that changes with the seventeenth-century providence tale, where the focus shifts to the new mercantile and the lower classes. Beard, however, retains the traditional medieval focus on the mighty.

Another traditional element in Beard's work is its prominent moral purpose. The work depicts, generally in brief accounts, the evil deeds of mighty rulers and the fitting punishments they eventually receive. The purpose is clearly stated by Beard: "to give examples to drousie consciences . . . of God's judgements." The reader is told in the 1597 epistle dedicatory that "if to avoid and eschew vice (according to the saying of the Poet) be a Chiefe vertue . . . [then it is a] necessarie point to know what vice and vertue is." Beard also presents these exempla of retribution, as opposed to models of virtue, so that "whome the promises of life and salvation could not allure, and persuade to do well, them the feare of punishment (which followeth sinne as a shadow doth the body) might bridle and restrain from giving them over to impiete." Obviously, Beard believed he could frighten his audience into obedience.

The influences for such a project extend back to *The Mirror for Magistrates* (1559), on back to Chaucer's "Monk's Tale" and Lydgate's *Fall of Princes*, all the way back to Lydgate's source, Boccaccio's *The Fate of Illustrious Men* (1358). In

Providence Tales and the Birth of American Literature

the introduction to his work, Boccaccio writes, "From among the mighty I shall select the most famous, so when our princes see these rulers, old and spent, prostrated by the judgment of God, they will recognize God's power, the shiftiness of fortune, and their own insecurity" (2).

To the extent that Beard's work continues the tradition of the exemplum, his work looks back to previous providence tales. However, Beard's work also contains elements which were to be more fully developed in the seventeenth century. "Besides," he briefly adds near the end of the preface, "here is ample matter and argument to stoppe the mouthes of all Epicures and Atheists of our Age." This direct attack on atheism is what joins *The Theatre of God's Judgement* to later seventeenth-century providence tale collections, in which such a motive becomes paramount.

The Rise of Atheism in Sixteenth- and Seventeenth-Century England

The audience aimed at by providence tale writers had already begun to change by Beard's time. This new audience had been partly created by the fifteenth- and sixteenth-century revival of classical literature. Medieval and early Renaissance providence tales were directed at sinners in general, many of whom were still considered to be believers of some sort, and thus subject to persuasion through emotional terror. As the seventeenth century progressed, the Protestant providence tale was aimed more directly at increasingly literate laymen and intellectuals who had been influenced by translations of the ancients. Some of these new intellectuals had become atheists, who were called Sadducees,[1] materialists, Nullibists, and Holenmerians, among other epithets.

The word *atheist* had a broad definition. It could refer to the skeptical proponents of the new science, with their insistence on making direct, concrete, tangible observations part of discovering truth. Rationalists reading works such as Thomas More's and Erasmus's translations of Lucian and Lucretius espoused views considered "atheistical." An atheist could also refer to any member of the dissenting sects proliferating by the middle of the sixteenth century. Generally, the atheists addressed in these Protestant providence tales were the nonbelievers and materialists, the followers of Descartes, Spinoza, and Hobbes. Such an audience of rationalists and philosophers, of educated, skeptical thinkers, and of scoffing "wags and drolls" demanded higher standards of proof, logic, argumentation, and evidence from those who wished to rebut their arguments. The providence tales directed at these skeptics and atheists needed to be more believable, to prove that the events they were describing could not be explained by natural causes or by "juggling," deception, or melancholy. Accordingly, providence tales became more detailed, and contained more attestations of their truthfulness as the century progressed. These stories of the invisible world were told in increasingly convincing ways.

Atheist and agnostic ideas had grown steadily in sixteenth-century England. George Buckley attributes this growth to the humanists' belief that "the world itself . . . and man . . . are worthy of the attention of the best men." The minds of thinking men and women focused more and more on the world and less on God. Scholars began to read the classics as literature and history, rather than for the purpose of rationalizing those works with Christianity. In this new light, Buckley says, it became clear that "Plato and Aristotle were not forerunners of Christ, but representatives of a religion and culture in which Christ and his Church had no part" (2). The works of Pliny, Lucian, Lucretius, and other classical Epicureans and "active rationalists" went through numerous editions in sixteenth-century Europe, and English translations were also published. Erasmus, who said, "Remain good Christians but profit by ancient wisdom" (Buckley 17), was the foremost translator and popularizer of *Dialogue of the Gods* and other satirical works by Lucian. Pliny, Lucretius, and Lucian's Epicureanism included the non-Christian beliefs that the world had been created more for the wild beasts than for mankind, that the Gods exist but are unconcerned with man, and that the soul dies with the body, among others. Christian divinities were soon exposed to the same satirical light that the Epicurean dramatists used on their pagan gods.

Stoic ideas also undermined Christianity. "From 1481, when Caxton printed Cicero's *De Amicitia*," Buckley writes, "the ideas of the Stoics appeared in [translations of] works by authors such as Seneca, Plutarch, and Cicero" (17–18). These ideas demonstrated that there were other valid systems of thought besides Christianity, and thus served to undermine its absolute dominion. Cicero, the Stoic popularizer, furthered this relativizing trend by using the arguments of one character in *De Natura Deorum* (The Nature of the Gods) to attack two Stoic arguments commonly praised by Christians: "that natural order in the universe proclaimed a divine ruler, and that his existence was proved by the universal consent of mankind, savage as well as civilized" (Buckley 12). Cicero and Plutarch, in *De Divinatione* and *Cessation of the Oracles* respectively, also argued that miracles have natural causes and that atheism was at least ethically superior to a belief in superstition. The former idea influenced David Lloyd's *Wonders No Miracles* and Valentine Greatrakes's 1666 answer to Lloyd's charges, *A Brief Account of Mr. Valentine Greatrak's, and Divers of the Strange Cures By Him Lately Performed*. Greatrakes's work contains many providence tale tropes, particularly the many eyewitness testimonials he adds to his own narrative account and explanation of his healing feats. King James's 1597 *Daemonologie*, which has close affinities with the more philosophical works of providence tale writers, was written in response to skeptics such as Reginald Scot and Johan Wier. *Daemonologie*, however, shows its more traditional approach in its concern with punishing witches. By the mid-century writers are so focused on atheists and on proving that witches exist that punishing them becomes secondary. In a sense, the witches become the heroes and heroines of the tales. Even as the providence tale writers were trying to reverse the "new" relativity, they were advancing it by becoming the witches' allies, rather than their judges and executioners.

Buckley notes how Cicero described another characteristic of religion in his day which also reflects the situation in seventeenth-century England. According to Cicero, "there is no subject []on which the learned, as well as the unlearned, differ so strenuously as this [religion]; and since their opinions are so various, and so repugnant one to another, it is possible that none of them may be, and absolutely impossible that more than one should be right" (Buckley 12). Buckley, echoing Cicero, points out that quarreling among the various Protestant sects spawned by the Reformation also contributed to the rise of atheism. These groups included Anabaptists, Socinians, Familists, Brownists, and many others. Their varied conceptions of truth contributed to a sense of relativity about religious doctrine. Some of the sects propounded ideas that bordered on atheism. Some groups denied the Trinity, others the divine origin of Scripture, still others the immortality of the soul. Some believed that Scripture should only be interpreted allegorically, or that heaven and hell were here on earth alone.

Many political figures and Anglican leaders equated these "atheistic" concepts with sedition, since, from the Tudor reign of Henry VIII, criticism of the church was considered an attack on the crown. Thus many staunch Church of England men such as Bacon, in "Of Atheism," and Hooker, in *The Laws of Ecclesiastical Polity*, attacked the wave of atheism and divisive sectarianism. "A strong influence for religious unbelief in England during the last half of the sixteenth century was the warfare of the various religious sects" (43), Buckley writes. He quotes Thomas Nash's *Pierce Penilesse* (1592), among other works, to show how Church of England men attributed atheism to both the influence of classical authors and to contemporary sectarians including, apart from those already mentioned, the Unitarians and Puritans:

> Whence, a number that fetch the Articles of their Beleefe out of Aristotle, and think of heaven and hell as the Heathen philosophers, take occasion to deride our Ecclesiastical State, and all Ceremonies of Devine worship as bugbeares Scarcrowes, because (like Herodes soldiers) we divide Christ's garments among us. . . . Hence Atheists triumph and rejoyce, and take as prophanely of the Bible as of Bevis

of Hampton [characterized by McKeon as a "mob romance" (au.)].(qtd. in Buckley, 83)

Beard responded to the spread of atheism by compiling his collection of translations of French providence tales and English tales. Producing these anthologies became, by the end of the seventeenth century, the dominant response to atheism of many moderate, Nonconformist, Puritan, and Presbyterian ministers. Gathering providence tales also became important to those Anglican ministers and philosophers known as the Cambridge Platonists for their interest in the ideas of Plato, Plotinus, and Porphyry. Among the Nonconformists who wrote providence tales were Beard, Thomas Taylor, Matthew Poole, James Janeway, Samuel Clarke, William Turner, and Richard Baxter. The Cambridge Platonists included Joseph Glanvill,[2] Henry More, Ralph Cudworth, and Benjamin Whichcote. Although these two groups differed politically, they still had much in common. These Nonconformists were political moderates and opposed the sects and religious enthusiasm. Similarly, the Cambridge Platonists criticized sectarianism and religious enthusiasm. Both groups believed that reason could and should be used to justify and explain religious belief. Reason as an intellectual tool and moderation as a sensibility contributed to the evolution of the more detailed and realistic seventeenth-century providence tale.

The complete transformation of the providence tales did not occur until nearly fifty years after Beard first published his collection, meaning around the time of the English Civil War. The changes became much more evident in works by Richard Baxter and Samuel Clarke among writers from the Nonconformist group of ministers and in the works of Joseph Glanvill and Henry More from the Cambridge Platonists.

The Politics of Moderation and the Providence Tale

Thomas Taylor (1576–1633) edited a fourth edition of Beard's *Theatre*, published in 1648. Both men's careers seem consistent with moderate Nonconformity. Beard, who died in 1632, taught Oliver Cromwell at Huntington, where Beard also held a lectureship and preached for many years. That Beard was at least somewhat of a dissenting, Nonconformist nature is clear from his testifying, in 1628, against Bishop Neile[3] in the House of Commons. Beard accused Neile of "anti-Puritan practices" (Lee 2:15), claiming Neile had denounced him for not delivering a sermon first spoken by another minister which Beard said contained "tenets of popery" (Lee 2:15). Nevertheless, Beard was prebendary at

Lincoln from 1612 until his death, and in 1630 was "made a justice of the peace for the county" (Lee 2:15). His connections to the establishment, as well as his challenge of the Arminian[4] reforms of Charles I suggested by his refusal to preach the "popish" sermon, indicate a pattern of moderate dissent similar to Baxter's.

Taylor preached against Archbishop Bancroft's[5] harsh treatment of Puritans as early as 1608, was afterwards silenced, and did not receive his degree until 1630, despite having "distinguished himself at Christ's College, Cambridge, [and] graduated there (B.A. 1595 and M.A. 1598)" (Lee 19:465). Nevertheless, he maintained his living, was vicar at Walford in 1612, and in 1625 was "chosen minister of St. Mary Aldermanbury, London, in 1625" (Lee 19:465). Baxter, the most prominent Nonconformist minister in this group, wrote a biography of Taylor, entitled *Truth, Innocency, and Simplicity shining through the conversion, gospel ministry, labours, epistles of love, testimonies and warnings to professors and profane (with the long and patient sufferings) of that ancient and faithful minister and servant of Jesus Christ, Thomas Taylor.* Baxter's description of Taylor in this title suggests Taylor's use of the plainer style of expression and more moderate arguments that these Nonconformists sought in their providence tales. This plain style was a reaction against the ornate and metaphysical imagery of John Donne, Launcelot Andrewes, and other Anglican ministers, as well as a response to Bacon and the new science's call for a simpler writing style. William Haller describes Taylor's *Pilgrim's Profession* as a significant move away from the sermon toward symbolic narrative, calling it an early version of the wayfaring Christian, a precursor of Bunyan's *Pilgrim's Progress.* Such plain style and narrative propensities further propelled these writers' providence tales in the direction of a dramatic, narrative prose form that became a springboard for American and British fiction.

Of all the ministers discussed here, Richard Baxter (1615–1692) was the most influential. He played a leading role in several major political and theological controversies and published approximately 160 treatises during his lifetime. Baxter grew up in a solidly conforming family, but by 1640, when he began preaching at Kidderminster, Worcestershire, he had already begun advocating such Nonconformist positions as not wearing surplices, not using the cross in baptisms, and stricter discipline in deciding who could receive the Lord's Supper. In 1640 he refused to "subscribe 'ex animo' that there was nothing in the Articles, Homilies, and the Liturgy contrary to the Word of God" (Lee 1:1352). Thus he did not sign the "et cetera" oath[6] in 1640. Throughout his life Baxter refused oaths and subscriptions that denied free discussion or appeals to reasoned debate or compromise. At times he sided with Conformist positions, at others with Nonconformist ones. What remained constant was his insistence on independent, rational thought, as well as his constant effort to find moderate compromises which would include various contending positions.

Despite his early conforming background, and despite the support of many of his parishioners for the king at the start of the Civil War, he served as chaplain in the regiment of Whalley (who would take part in the future regicide) when the war broke out. Nevertheless, in 1647 he opposed regicide at the risk of his life, just as in 1641 he had opposed the "Root and Branch"[7] extirpation of the episcopacy, and just as, in 1660, he would oppose setting aside Charles II. Baxter refused to subscribe automatically to any one position. During the Civil War he stated, "I make no doubt that both parties were to blame, as it commonly falleth out in most wars and contentions, and I will not be he that will justify either of them. I doubt not but the headiness and rashness of the younger inexperienced sort of religious people made many parliament men and ministers overgo themselves to keep pace with those Hotspurs . . . these things came chiefly from the sectarian, separating spirit, which blew the coals among foolish apprentices" (Lee 1:1353).

Baxter tried to reconcile various Nonconformist views with those of the Church of England by participating in the Savoy Conference[8] of 1661–1662. Still, after its failure, he refused to sign the Act of Uniformity.[9] His refusal, and that of others, resulted in the "church outing" of him and some two thousand other Puritan Nonconformists, including providence tale writers Matthew Poole, Samuel Clarke, and James Janeway. Despite this act of resistance, he was "said to have been in the most intimate contact with the leaders of the Restoration," was appointed a Royal Chaplain to Charles II, and offered the bishopric of Hereford, both of which offices he declined. Baxter could not be easily defined. "It was nothing to him who were his friends or foes. He was obedient only to his own conscience" (Lee 1:1354). So again, in 1643 he sided with the Presbyterians who were in favor of the Solemn League and the Covenant,[10] whereas in 1647, opposing Engagement, he opposed in turn the same two oaths he'd taken in 1643.

Though he was "outed," the technical term for being stripped of his living or position, Baxter's popularity as a lecturer and his prolific writing continued, even through periods of ill health which sent him into near retirement. A spirit of compromise and moderation entered all his activity. In 1670 he wrote *A defense of the principles of love, which are necessary to the unity and concord of Christians, and are delivered in a book called The Cure of Church Division . . . I. Inviting all sound and sober Christians to receive each other in communion in the same churches . . . II. And where that . . . cannot be attained, to bear with each other in their distinct assemblies . . . Written to detect and eradicate all love killing, dividing, and church dividing principles.* In 1675 he again tried to effect a compromise between Conformists and Nonconformists after the passage of the Test Act,[11] by negotiating for a "Bill of Comprehension,"[12] which would have eased restrictions on Roman Catholics and Protestant dissenters alike. This bill never passed. Despite his popularity and fame, he suffered greatly because of the Conventicle Act of 1685 and was imprisoned for eighteen months after a trial before Lord Jeffries. In 1688, he joined a national coalition of Protestant dissenters and National Church members against James II and agreed with the terms of the Toleration Act of 1688 of William and Mary, indicating that in the final analysis he placed unity and comprehension above doctrinal purity.

These political milestones in Baxter's career underline his connections with other providence tale writers. His independent, complex positions on different sides of the political spectrum and the moderate and intellectual quality of his decision making were qualities also reflected in his providence tales. Christopher Hill, in his *Society and Puritanism in Pre-Revolutionary England*, has pointed out the "Protestant theological emphasis [from Wycliff] to elevate teaching, discussion, the rational element in religion generally, against the sacramental and ceremonial aspects" (55).

Nonconformity, the New Science, and Popular Narratives

Baxter's last work (1691) was also his major providence tale collection. It is called *The Certainty of the World of Spirits, and Consequently of the Immortality of Souls. Of the Malice and Misery of the Devil and the Damned, and of the Blessedness of the Justified. Fully evinced by the Unquestionable Histories of Apparitions, Witchcrafts and Voices. Written as an addition to many other treatises for the Conviction of Sadducees and Infidels.* In the work's introduction, Baxter describes the tales as "most helpful for atheists, that have sinned themselves into an incapacity of more Rational and Excellent Arguments." Baxter's concern with atheism again is paramount, and had been evident in his work since the 1650s, when he started reading providence tales and adding some to his own works; part 2 of *The Saints Everlasting Rest* (1650), *The Unreasonableness of Infidelity* (1655), *The Reasons of the Christian Religion* (1667), and *More Reasons of the Christian Religion* (1672) all have providence tales in them.

Mention in *The Certainty*'s introduction of atheists' "incapacity of more Rational Arguments" refers to another significant trope these providence tales were developing. Baxter demonstrates this trope more fully when he writes in *The Certainty* that "these confirmations of spirits and immortality . . . [are] . . . of the lower sort. . . . [These tales of] apparitions [and] other sensible manifestations of the certain existence of spirits of themselves Invisible [are for] such as are prone to judge by Sense. . . . I write it [the collection] for Practice, and not to please Men with the Strangeness and Novelty of useless stories" (4).

By 1691 such apologies had become standard fare in the introductions to collections of apparition tales. Where at one time Baxter and the other writers had rebutted atheists in sermons or theological treatises, they were now condescending, out of their ministerial sense of duty, to present stories, the better to have an effect on what they saw as the debased faculties of mankind. The Cambridge Platonist Henry More explained that the discrediting of superstition, beneficial in itself, had led to an equally harmful tendency toward scoffing at everything that concerned religion. Religion's decline, in More's logic, naturally led to the lowering of mankind's reasoning faculties; for him, to deny God was to deny reason. Great tension developed between these writers' attraction toward reason and moderation and their need to write sensational narratives to have an effect on their "irrational," disbelieving audience.

Resolving this tension produced further advances in the providence tales. Proofs of God's existence now had to be sufficiently shocking to awaken the "drousie," as Beard had said, as well as convincing enough to overcome skeptics. The tales also had to conform to the scientific standards Royal Society members such as Glanvill, More, and Increase and Cotton Mather had inherited from Bacon, particularly that truth had to be established by direct physical observation. Haller points out a general Puritan inclination toward empirical analysis, because of their view of nature as a revelation of divine providence. An interest in observation and proof pervaded these providence tales. Baxter writes of the "*certain* existence of spirits" and the "*unquestionable* histories of apparitions" (my italics). When discussing other books on witchcraft, he cites Cotton Mather's *Wonders of the Invisible World* as having, "the most convincing evidence" (80). Baxter and the other ministers were concerned with amassing evidence from many different sources. Each source's credibility is painstakingly asserted. Furthermore, the testimony itself, as a further proof of its veracity, is filled with as many sharp details as possible. Out of this mixture of sensationalism, narrative drama, and scientific verisimilitude developed an early form of popular imaginative literature.

Certainty of the World of Spirits illustrates another important element that made these providence tales so important in the future development of English and American narrative literature. Baxter heads the longest section of the work "An Historical Discourse of Apparitions and Witches." This narrowing focus on stories of the invisible world, which was begun by the Cambridge Platonist Henry More, in his 1652 *Antidote to Atheism*, furthered the progress of dramatic narrative elements in the providence tales. Most of these apparition stories were contemporary. Therefore, several sources of testimony could often be found for each tale. At times the authors or editors themselves were eyewitnesses to the apparitions, as Joseph Glanvill was at the home of Mr. Mompesson in his signature tale "The Drummer of Tedworth," first published in 1668, and as Baxter was in the possession case of Mary Hill. The contemporary nature of these tales also meant that highly specific details could be included in the tales. More socially diverse characters could be found in them once the moral purpose in Beard had been replaced by a scientific one, and the former villains were now the protagonists, some of the first fictional antiheroes. These new features produced narrative texture and complexity. The need for physical evidence, so intensified by the writers trying to prove that something invisible was, in fact, present, pushed these tales into being early examples of literary realism. Moreover, by making invisible spirits the protagonists of their tales, providence tale writers were unconsciously defending and supporting the imaginary in an increasingly scientific and materialistic age.

Certainty of the World of Spirits is not limited to narratives. Like most other writers of providence tales and like writers of witchcraft tales for two hundred years before him, Baxter inserts theoretical, or more metaphysical sections into his work. However, when compared to some of the lengthy and encyclopedic providence tale collections from this period, Baxter's is a slim and tightly focused example of the form. He moves closer to pure storytelling and toward a reliance on contemporary and English tales over biblical, classical, and continental stories. These were two more important steps in the development of this genre. However, more encyclopedic writers such as Turner, Clarke, and More, who combined with their contemporary stories either sections of dense metaphysics and logic or pages of classical and biblical tales, were also quite capable of writing dramatic and colorful narratives themselves.

These writers' encyclopedias did not classify all knowledge into innumerable unrelated categories like their modern counterparts. Rather, they were attempts to assert or "essay" one single idea by using many different examples. Cotton Mather in *Magnalia Christi Americana* also illustrates this method. In addition to their authors' evolving narrative skills, the encyclopedic providence tale collections have a broad reach which seems similar to later American works such as Melville's *Moby Dick*, works which in fact reproduce the providence tales' variety of interests and narrative forms.

The Nonconformist minister and writer Samuel Clarke (1599–1683) was perhaps the greatest storyteller of either group of providence tale writers. His encyclopedic providence tale collection first appeared in 1646. Though Clarke is mainly known for his various editions of mostly ecclesiastical "lives," including his *English Martyrologie* (1652) and *General Martyrologie* (1657), he also wrote *A Mirrour or Looking Glass both for Saints and Sinners, held forth in some thou-*

sands of examples, which went through several editions. This is a long work which contains stories (some two thousand by the 1654 edition) of God's "severe judgements" and his "wonderful mercies" toward a long list of people exemplifying all manner of virtue and vice. Clarke used examples from "the most classique authors, both ancient and modern," as well as "some late examples observed by myself." To these he also included *A Geographicall description of all the countries in the known world; as also the wonders of God in nature; and the rare, stupendous, and costly works made by the art, and industry of man.*

Clarke's collection illustrates the encyclopedic form, including, in addition to mercies and judgments, a section on geography and one devoted to descriptions of the wonders of God in nature and in the works of man. These two sections demonstrate the seventeenth-century providence tale's dual purpose of gathering scientific knowledge while spreading religious faith. Prodigies of all sorts, as well as geographical data from the previously unknown world, interested natural historians and philosophers. Inexplicable wonders were thought to reveal the direct hand of providence. Nature's marvelous design seemed to show unmistakably that the hand of a Creator orchestrated events on earth, not the fortuitous interplay of Democritus's atoms advanced by Hobbes. It seemed inconceivable to the providence tale writers that the intricate design apparent in mankind's and nature's wonders could have occurred without conscious direction. If the wonders could be explained by natural causes, their intricate order and design still "proved" that mere chance and random coincidence could not have created them. Cicero's *De Rerum Natura* and *De Divinatione* and works by other classical writers made similar arguments. Translations of Pliny's *Natural History* and of other ancient works of natural history and philosophy also inspired new collections of wonders. Pliny "went through thirty-eight editions on the Continent between 1463 and 1532" (Buckley 4). In detailing manmade, natural, and supernatural wonders, Clarke and his cohorts were both glorifying God and engaging in the work of natural history. All these efforts, in writers ostensibly defending God from his materialist enemies, promoted an increasingly greater focus on the physical world. Such a focus naturally produced stories of greater realism.

Indeed, despite Clarke's vast and encyclopedic reach, many of his tales are quite detailed. One of these tales, the story of Mrs. Teate, in a chapter titled "Providences of Mercy," is startlingly similar to many New England Indian captivity narratives. Several of its major tropes, including images of dying infants, naked, innocent wives separated from their husbands, an initial and surprise attack by "heathenish," "wild" men, and the miraculous discovery of food at the brink of starvation, recur in the Indian captivity narratives. In this story, Clarke tells of the minister Mr. Teate, who at the start of the Irish rebellion in 1641 is persuaded to leave for Dublin, forty-seven miles away, leaving his wife and children behind. Eventually Mrs. Teate, or Tate as later writers call her in abridged versions of Clarke's tale, is attacked by and forced to flee from the "savage" Irish rebels. Finally, "stript naked" and wandering in the winter across snow-covered "commons,"

> They sat down together under the lee of an Irish mountain . . . for it was frost and snow. The minister's wife had a young child named John Teate hanging upon her breasts, which were become dry through her manifold feares, griefs, and want of sleep three nights together [one recalls Mary Rowlandson's own struggle to save her five-year-old daughter in the wintry forest, as well the absence in Boston of her husband, the minister Joseph Rowlandson, at the time of the Indian attack on Lancaster]. The child cried and groaned, and for want of nourishment was ready to dy, in such sort that the said mother not being able any longer to endure the groans and cries of her babe arose up from the company (who sat altogether as close as they could with children in their laps to keep one another warm) and she thought to leave her child by himself to cry and dy, that she might be freed from those his heart piercing sobs and wailings. (Clarke 1:507)

She goes off with the child, but miraculously finds a bottle on a rock, without any footprints nearby, filled with "bonny clabbe," which, though the child has never had a bottle before, he drinks eagerly. Eventually, they return safely to civilization. Clarke devotes much of the rest of the tale to comparing these events with those in the story of Hagar and Ishmael in *Genesis*, in which Hagar, sent away because of Sarah's jealousy and her own pride, tries to abandon Ishmael in the same fashion before she miraculously discovers water. Clarke's method of synthesizing domestic realism with melodrama and biblical typology illustrates another quintessential characteristic of the new providence tale.

The Teate story clearly demonstrates many important elements of English providence tales which Indian captivity narratives shared. It is fitting too that Teate's is an Irish tale, since the sixteenth-century English invasion of Ireland had served as a training ground for the soldiers and sailors who eventually helped to conquer the New World, such as Martin Frobisher and Humphrey Gilbert. Many other stories, however, also contain elements that were carried over without much alteration into the New England providence tales and particularly the Indian captivity narratives.

Politically, Clarke had much in common with Baxter. In fact, in 1642, as the battle of Edge Hill began, Baxter was preaching for Clarke at Alcester, where Clarke had been rector and lecturer since 1633. Like Baxter, he had refused to take the "et cetera" oath in 1640. Earlier he had gained some notoriety for attacking James I's *Book of Sports*, and after receiving a lectureship upon graduating from Emmanuel College, Cambridge, he had found himself attacked for his omission of certain Anglican church ceremonies. Still, he argued alongside Baxter against regicide in 1649. In 1661 Baxter and he both participated in the Savoy Conference, and finally Clarke found himself outed from his position in 1662. In September of that year he married Baxter to Margaret Charlton. He was, however, no "Baxterian," and wrote in 1660 "A Discourse Against Toleration." Also unlike Baxter, Clarke "took an oath against resistance imposed by the Five Mile Act,"[13] but afterwards retired from his new position rather than appear on too close terms with the Anglicans, and he devoted much of the rest of his time to writing. He also opposed sects and religious enthusiasm. After the Civil War he resigned his position at Alcester, which he found "pestered with sectaries," in order to retain the curacy of Bennet Finks. A quite conservative Nonconformist, Clarke, through his ordination from Emmanuel, is also connected to the Cambridge Platonists as well as to another important Nonconformist minister involved in the development of the providence tale, the Emmanuel graduate Reverend Matthew Poole (1624–1679).

Nonconformity, the New Science, and the Cambridge Platonists

Poole enters this story most dramatically in the preface to Increase Mather's providence tale collection *An Essay for the Illustration of Remarkable Providences*, published in 1684. Mather writes that his inspiration for the *Essay* came from Poole during a trip to England in 1657/8. William Turner corroborates Mather's claims about Poole's impact on the providence tale in the title to his own collection, one of the most extensive seventeenth-century encyclopedias of providence tales, which appeared in 1697. It is called: *A Compleat History of the Most Remarkable Providences Both of Judgement and Mercy Which Have Hapned in the Present Age. Extracted from the Best writers and the Authors own Observations, and the Numerous Relations sent him from divers partes of the Three Kingdomes. To Which is added whatever is Curious in the work of nature or Art. The Whole Digested into One Volume under Proper Heads being a work set on foot nearly thirty years ago by the Rev. Mr. Pool*. It is possible that Turner wrote this introduction well before the work's publication date of 1697, or that he was not aware that Poole had actually initiated the project well before 1667. In any case, this discrepancy in dates between Mather's and Turner's accounts does not cast doubt on one central fact; Matthew Poole was a major figure in the development of seventeenth-century providence tales.

Providence Tales and the Birth of American Literature

Mather does not say exactly how Poole influenced him, but someone, he writes, did produce a manuscript at that time in England: "The composer whereof is unknown to me, wherein the subjects proper for this Record, and some Rules for the better managing a design of this nature, are described" (Preface, *Essay* A4). Those who were to have produced or managed the enterprise, however, had their "thoughts diverted another way." Mather also seems to have forgotten about the project when he left England. Twelve years later, in 1670, while going through the papers of the recently deceased John Davenport, he again came across the manuscript he had seen in 1658. This manuscript, he claims in the preface, had been brought to Davenport by Samuel Hartlib.

According to James Levernier in his introduction to Mather's *Essay*, Hartlib was a friend of John Milton. A Polish immigrant and refugee from Jesuit persecution, Hartlib had many educational plans, including some for poor scholars, and ran the first "general news agency."[14] Moreover, according to the Cope and Jones appendix to Sprat's *History of the Royal Society*, Hartlib, along with Theodore Haak, was a foremost English Comenian. Followers of Comenius, the Cope appendix notes, constituted one of the three main groups whose convergence in the 1650s evolved into the Royal Society, chartered in 1662. Comenius's plans involved the unification of all knowledge and an international language developed by a worldwide exchange organization of learning and research. Not unlike those projects, the design for managing the creation of a providence tale collection involved organizing a widespread group of ministers and scientists to collect data and send it to an editor or compiler. Poole, Hartlib, and Comenius shared an interest in the collection and dissemination of knowledge. Hartlib's interest in Poole's plan more directly links Poole, the Nonconformist divine, with the new science and the Royal Society.

Poole received his M.A. from Emmanuel in 1654. In 1658, two of the most prominent Cambridge Platonists, Benjamin Whichcote and Ralph Cudworth, approved of a plan of Poole's for a permanent fund to maintain "young men of promise for the ministry during their university courses" (Lee 16:99). This was one of the earliest schemes for supporting the training of a Nonconformist ministry and a day school. It also recalls Hartlib's interests in helping poor scholars. Cudworth and Whichcote also appear as collectors and transmitters of several of the most well known apparition tales. According to a modern editor and critic of the Cambridge Platonists, C. P. Patrides, the only one of these Platonists who had anything to do with tales of the occult was Henry More. Patrides's oversight suggests that he held the Platonist's storytelling in such contempt that he did not read Glanvill and More's apparition stories, in which Cudworth's and Whichcote's involvement is made explicit in the advertisements. Thus it is also not surprising that none of More's occult tales appear in Patrides's anthology of

Cambridge Platonist writing (nor in Gerald Cragg's anthology nor in Campagnac's 1901 anthology). Patrides lauds the Platonists as philosophers and even as literary stylists, but the apparition stories More told were, in Patrides's view, an "indulgence in perversities [which] sets him quite apart from the other Cambridge Platonists" (321).

We see this neglect again in the comments of another Cambridge Platonist editor and critic, Gerald Cragg. In *From Puritanism to the Age of Reason*, he wrote that for many of the "new thinkers" of the seventeenth century "Copernicus might never have lived, and even fellows of the Royal Society could retain strange fragments from the older thought." Cragg adds a footnote that reads, "Note the views of Henry More and Joseph Glanvill on witchcraft and necromancy" (91).

Cudworth's and Whichcote's involvement with the occult connected them closely with More and with More's chief cohort in psychic and occult research, another major figure in the development of the providence tale and of the Royal Society, Joseph Glanvill. Patrides's neglect of Cudworth's and Whichcote's occult interests and of More's apparition tales points to a general critical neglect of the seventeenth-century providence tale. Such neglect helps explain how a major source for the Indian captivity narrative, as well as other types of early English and American narrative fiction, has been so overlooked.[15]

Clearly Poole, Hartlib, and other Royal Society members shared with the Cambridge Platonists a concern with the support and education of ministers and scholars, and with the collection and reproduction of knowledge. These communities of learning resembled the loose-knit organizations Glanvill, More, and both Increase and Cotton Mather created to collect their providence tales. For these ministers, collecting evidence of God's acts on earth, certifying that evidence to be true, and finally publishing it to the world were actions blessed by God.

Early American providence tale writers influenced their English counterparts also. Turner says it was "a small essay by Increase Mather [which] invited some others to continue [Poole's unfinished project]." Turner probably referred to Mather's election day sermon of 1677, "A Discourse Concerning the Danger of Apostasy . . . ," which Mather published in 1679, in a treatise titled *A Call to Heaven*. In this sermon Mather, who also belonged to the Royal Society, calls for the production of a New England providence tale collection. He also recommends a centralized agency for licensing and educating ministers. This organization of education and knowledge seems motivated too by a desire for political and religious control, and suggests some of the political purposes behind the collection and production of providence tales. Mather writes, "Though the just liberty of Churches should not be infringed, yet that every plantation in the country should have allowance to chuse, whome they please to labour in the publick dispensation of the world, may be in time a great inlet to ignorance, error and profaness. Therefore let me humbly propound to you, that you would think of some expedient, respecting the approbation of such, as shall be under a constant improvement as Publick Teachers." (73)

Poole's moderate Nonconformity is apparent in certain of his actions and in his relationship with Richard Baxter. Poole resigned his living in 1662, apparently out of his opposition to "curiosity of voice and musical sounds" (Lee 1:99) in church, and retired to write on a patrimony of one hundred pounds. In 1672 he did present to the king a "cautious and moderate thanksgiving for the indulgence" which Baxter had refused to accept (99). In 1675 he sided with Baxter in the negotiation for Comprehension, but by 1678, fearing assassination during the Popish Plot, he fled to Amsterdam. He died there in 1679, and thus was not restored as Baxter was after the Toleration Act of 1688.

Poole never carried his providence tale plans through, perhaps in part because of the dislocations of the Restoration and the 1662 Act of Uniformity which displaced over two thousand Puritan ministers. He remains best known today for his *Synopsis Criticorum*, a summary of biblical commentary, in itself another Comeniuslike project in its encyclopedic vastness and educational intent. Still, all the evidence does make a case for his having been instrumental in the creation of Increase Mather's providence tale collection. Another moderate Nonconformist, Poole was an important conceptualizer behind the development of the providence tale, balancing religious and scientific elements in all his schemes.

OTHER NONCONFORMIST PROVIDENCE TALE WRITERS

The man who completed Poole's work in 1697 was William Turner (1653–1701), vicar of Walberton from 1682 and then, in 1687, rector of Barnstead. His introduction to *The Compleat History of the Most Remarkable Providences* demonstrates both his antiatheist orientation as well as his Baxterian, moderate values. He proclaims that his main purpose is to combat "the abounding atheism of the Age." He also recommends Baxter's *Saints Everlasting Rest* as a good book for overcoming schisms. "Be not transported with passion against the Conformists, who are more sober than many others" (62), he advises, and declares later , "I am no favorer, as I said before, of Enthusiasme, or Wild Fanaticall Rapture (the common denominator of giddy brains and distemper'd minds) but certainly our Religion doth not abandon all Inward Motions for Meer Fancies, but only such as are rash, groundless, inconsistent with Sobriety,

Order and Orthodoxy. Let all these Properties meet together, and it will be hard to censure Impulse" (ch. 9, 54). Although this statement appears to set him closer to the Conformist camp, his yoking of antiatheist passion with sobriety and order is duplicated by most seventeenth-century providence tale writers. His title alone reflects many other providence tale themes and states the work's encyclopedic reach. It mentions judgments and mercies and that the collection draws from Turner's own experience. The title also cites the scientific method used to gather the information and then edit it. Providence tales were "sent to him [Turner] from divers partes of the three kingdomes . . . [and] the Whole [was] Digested into One Volume under Proper Heads."

Two additional Nonconformist Puritan writers of providence tales need to be mentioned. One is James Janeway (1636?–1674). He specialized in two particular types of providence tales, examples of which were commonly rewritten by other writers or used as models in New England for more local versions. His 1671 *Tokens for Children* contains accounts of conversions and of "the holy and exemplary lives and joyful deaths" of many young children, while his 1674 *Legacies to his friends . . . Instances of Sea Dangers and Deliverances* is a collection of vivid and melodramatic accounts of contemporary shipwrecks, which Levernier criticizes for being overwritten. This seems another example of the common critical disdain for popular literature in this period.

Janeway wrote in a sentimental and melodramatic style which, with his focus on stories of dying religious children and shipwrecked families and crews, increased the dramatic impact of his narratives. Politically, he claimed to have been converted to Nonconformity by reading Baxter's *Saints Everlasting Rest*. Baxter, in turn, prepared an introductory epistle to a book Janeway wrote regarding his brother John, *Invisibles, Realities demonstrated in the holy life and triumphant death of Mr. John Janeway, fellow of Kings College, Cambridge*. There is no evidence of his ever having entered the ministry prior to the Uniformity Act of 1662,[16] but Baxter lists him among the outed ministers in Edmund Calamy's 1702 *Abridgement of Mr. Baxter's History of His Life and Times*. Janeway did preach in London in 1665 during the plague when several conventicles[17] were opened there, and even had his own meeting house for a brief period during the indulgence of Charles II in 1672.

The Scottish professor George Sinclair (d. 1698), who wrote *Satan's Invisible World Discovered*, published in 1685, is another example of a writer more interested in melodrama than theory and encyclopedic inclusiveness. Sinclair's career, more than his uneven narratives of apparition tales, illustrates providence tale writers' association both with the new science and with the occult. He was a professor of philosophy and mathematics at Glasgow and "one of the first in Scotland who devoted attention to the study of physics" (Lee 18:294). He helped in the development of the diving bell and was among the first to use a barometer. Coal mine owners employed him "to report on the extent and dip of the various beds of coal in their neighborhood," and he published an account called *Hydrostaticks* in 1672, "where he suggested the best methods of draining off water from the coal seams" (Lee 18:294). In 1673 he superintended the laying of water pipes in Edinburgh. Even during this period the occult interested him, and he included one of his most famous apparition stories, "The Devil of Glenluce," in an appendix to *Hydrostaticks*. Sinclair, once again like many other providence tale writers, was also a Nonconformist, and in 1666 he had had to resign his professorship for refusing to accept the episcopal form of church government.

Sinclair's narratives of 1685 were extremely popular, and his book was frequently reprinted. All his stories were about apparitions and witchcraft. He wrote to "vindicate" the existence of devils, spirits, witches, and apparitions "against those who would assault one of the outworks of religion." Although some of his stories were of his own collecting and writing, most of them were rewritten versions from Joseph Glanvill and Henry More's 1681 edition of *Saducismus Triumphatus*. Sinclair admits in his introduction that his aim was to produce a version of Glanvill's work that, because of its shorter length, would be more widely affordable. Sinclair then, less self-consciously than anyone else, proclaimed himself as an originator of popular prose narratives, without the guilt expressed by his storytelling peers over having written mere stories.

JOSEPH GLANVILL AND THE CAMBRIDGE PLATONISTS

Joseph Glanvill (1636–1680), whom Sinclair emulated and abridged, was the posthumous co-author with Henry More of the 1681 and subsequent editions of *Saducismus Triumphatus*, the providence tale collection that most fully represents the union of the scientific method, encyclopedic form, and more dramatic narratives. Glanvill himself is a good example of a minister who held strong religious beliefs while he simultaneously wrote from a scientific and skeptical perspective.

Saducismus Triumphatus; Or, A Full and Plaine Evidence Concerning Witches and Apparitions evolved from its first appearance in 1666 as *A Philosophical Endeavor towards the Defense of the Being of Witches and Apparitions* in ways illustrative of the overall movement in providence tales toward dramatic and sensational narration. The 1666 edition contains logical, "philosophical" refutations of those who had denied the existence of invisible spirits, witches, and apparitions. In 1668 Glanvill added his most famous story, "The Drummer of

Tedworth." This edition includes a satirical attack on atheists and skeptics, whom he calls "whips and drolls." It also contains some additional "proofs" of and commentary about the apparition stories. It includes material from the Bible along with contemporary accounts of the famous healer, the "Irish stroker" Valentine Greatrakes, who claimed to be able to cure people of, among other illnesses, the "kings sickness" (scrofula) by rubbing them with his hands. After Glanvill died, his friend and close associate Henry More edited a new edition in 1681 which contains, along with some of More's own philosophical writings, a large number of additional apparition and witchcraft stories taken from Glanvill's notes. *Saducismus Triumphatus* (1681) displays all the major providence tale elements, from the most abstract and theoretical treatises to the most sensational ghost stories. The most substantial change in *Saducismus*'s content over the years was the addition of scores of stories.

Glanvill was the most uneasy of all these ministers about writing stories. In the preface to part 2 of *Saducismus Triumphatus* he writes, "I know it is matter of very little Credit to be a Relator of stories, and I of all Men living, have the least reason to be fond of the Imployment" (257). However, relate stories he did, under More's prodding, for the reasons he gives in the following dedicatory epistle to part 1, written to Charles II, for whom, in 1672, he had become chaplain in ordinary:

> And that our expectations of a future Being, are not imaginary and fantastick, we have reasonable evidence enough from the Attributes of God, the Phaenomena of Providence and the nature of our Souls, to convince any, but those who will stupidly believe that they shall dye like beasts, that they may live like them. I confess the philosophick Arguments that are produced for the desirable Article, though very cogent, are many of them speculative and deep, requiring so great a attention and sagacity, that they take no hold upon the whistling spirits, that are not used to consider; nor upon the common sort, that cannot reach such heights of Argument: But they are both convinced by the proofs that come nearest the sense, which indeed strike our minds fullest, and leave the most lasting impressions, whereas high Speculations being more thin and subtile, easily slides off even from understandings that are most capable to receive them. For this reason, among some others, I appear thus much concerned for the justification of the belief of Witches, it suggesting palpable and current evidence of our Immortality, which I am exceedingly sollicitous to have made good. (58–59)

To counteract his guilt over storytelling, he and More struggled to make their stories convincing. One way to do this was to follow advice about prose style promulgated early in the century by Francis Bacon. Glanvill's prose evolved in the direction of Bacon's "plain style," which was also in favor among Puritan lecturers. William Wimsatt and Cleanth Brooks compare the same passage from the first edition of Glanvill's *Vanity of Dogmatizing* and a 1676 version. Their juxtaposition dramatically illustrates this shift in style and clearly demonstrates why the later style is more suitable for narration:

> 1661: If after a decoction of hearbs in a Winter night, we expose the liquor to the frigid air; we may observe in the morning under a crust of Ice, the perfect appearance both in figure, and colour, of the Plants that were taken from it. But if we break the aqueous Crystal, those pretty images dis-appear and are present[ly] dissolved. Now these airy Vegetables are presumed to have been made, by the reliques of these plantal emissions whose avolation was prevented by the condensed inclosure. And therefore playing up and down for a while in their liquid prison, they at last settle together in their natural order, and the Atomes of each part finding out their proper place, at length rest in their methodical Situation, till by breaking the Ice they are disturbed, and those counterfeit compositions are scatter'd into the First Indivisible.

> 1676: . . . after . . . a decoction of Herbs in a frosty Night, the shape of the Plants will appear under the Ice in the Morning: which Images are supposed to be made by the congregated Effluvia of the Plants themselves, which loosely wandring up and down in the water, at last settle in their natural place and order, and so make up an appearance of the Herbs from whence they were emitted. (Wimsatt and Brooks 227)

Another method of proving credibility was to introduce accounts of a variety of witnesses to corroborate each other's stories. Indeed, the additions to *Saducismus Triumphatus* beginning in 1672 often consist of various attestations, such as letters from Glanvill and others, and "advertisements" by Henry More introducing or concluding each tale, establishing its veracity. Such a scientific "apparatus" was natural for Glanvill to compile, since he was a member of the Royal Society and even wrote one of the foremost apologies for that organization and one of the first histories of science, the 1668 *Plus Ultra; or, The Progress and Advancement of Knowledge since the Days of Aristotle.* This work celebrates the major achievements of Royal Society members, and was modeled on George Hakewell's 1628 *Apologie and Declaration of the Power and Providence of God in the Gov't of the World.* Glanvill sought "empirical grounds for a belief in the Supernatural" and is said to have formed a "virtual study center for psychic research with Henry More." For Glanvill, the psychic world was a "land of spirits . . . a kinde of America" (intro., xvi), the study of which he advocated to the Royal Society.

Glanvill's occult interests involved him with other Cambridge Platonists. Cudworth and Whichcote, for example, also played significant parts in the controversies swirling around Valentine Greatrakes and other occult healers such as Francis Mercury Van Helmont, who had written books about hypnotism among continental gypsies. Van Helmont called the gypsies' abilities their "wonders by the powers of the imagination, their fancy binding that of others" (Nicolson, *Conway Letters*, 309). Robert Boyle also admired Greatrakes and Van Helmont. Many kinds of psychic and occult phenomena were of great interest to members of the Royal Society. This area of study was the most significant point of intersection between the religious and scientific communities of seventeenth-century England. Greatrakes's main work, first issued in 1666, *The Great Cures and Strange Miracles of Mr. Valentine Greatrakes*, was written, the reader is further informed in the title, *. . . by himself, in a letter addressed to the Honorable Robert Boyle. Whereunto are annexed the testimonials of several eminent and worthy persons of the chief matters of fact therein related*. Several of these testimonials, written in 1665, came from Ralph Cudworth and Benjamin Whichcote, while among Greatrakes's patients were both Cudworth's "little son Charles" and Whichcote himself. Greatrakes cured him, Whichcote testified, of "pain and inflammation of . . . [a] . . . tumours fungous and superfluous flesh," by the "application of his hand and spittle" (Greatrakes 53).

Glanvill was not a Cambridge Platonist, having been ordained at Oxford, in 1660. Still, he wished he had gone to Cambridge and admired the Platonists there. He also respected Richard Baxter, whom he went to hear preach at Kidderminster in 1660.[18] He regretted being unable to obtain a personal interview with him there but sent Baxter a copy of his first treatise, *The Vanity of Dogmatizing*, in which he "attacked the scholastic philosophy dominant at Oxford" (Lee 7:1287). In this work we see him in agreement with Baxter's aversion to sectarian enthusiasm. Unlike Baxter, however, Glanvill conformed in 1662, and during the Popish Plot he wrote a tract against the Nonconformists, "making a complimentary exception" for Baxter. Baxter still protested the tract's intolerance. He added, however, that Glanvill was opposed to the persecution of Nonconformists. In his autobiography, Baxter said that Glanvill had offered to defend him when he was silenced. Glanvill, the Cambridge Platonists, and other moderate Nonconformists such as Baxter all opposed religious enthusiasm and doctrinaire, divisive platforms, but the widespread urge after 1660 toward uniformity and an end to all religious disputes seems to have affected Glanvill more than it did Baxter. Glanvill did not fit in precisely with any one group, but he seems to have been at the center of the various ideas which together transformed providence tales.

HENRY MORE AND THE CAMBRIDGE PLATONISTS

Like Glanvill, More remained loyal to the king throughout his career. Along with his fellow Cambridge Platonists and the moderate Nonconformists, he opposed sectarianism and enthusiasm. The Cambridge Platonists represented a substantial departure from the rigorous Calvinism and strict, doctrinaire Puritanism of pre-Restoration England. They sought to pare down religious practice to a few essential ideas, leaving liturgical and theological matters which had proved so divisive for decades to each individual to decide privately. Opposed to predestination, and with an optimistic, idealistic view of man's perfectibility if he could but nourish the "Christ within," the Cambridge Platonists are usually seen along a continuum extending from the Latitudinarians, to John Toland and the Deists, and even as far ahead as the principles of John Locke (Cragg, *From Puritanism to the Age of Reason*). What made the Cambridge Platonists unique was their belief that religion and revelation were consistent with reason. To advance this idea, they at first wrote dense philosophical works in which they attempted to produce clear definitions of spirits—sharp descriptions of what they were made of and explanations of their operations in the physical world. One such work is Cudworth's massive 1678 *True Intellectual System of the Universe and Eternal and Immutable System of Morality*; another example is More's *Enchiridion Metaphysicum*. As the century progressed, however, the Cambridge Platonists increasingly turned to producing their factual and sensational providence tales to make the same points in a more broadly accessible fashion.

The Cambridge Platonists are praised for their complex philosophical thought and their clear and simple style by critics such as C. A. Patrides, Gerald Cragg, Basil Wiley, and Ernest Cassirer. They are credited with being among the first to introduce the ideas of Descartes in England. But by the 1650s, More had come to see Descartes as nearly as big a threat to religion as the philosopher who became the main focus of his wrath, Thomas Hobbes. As Marjorie Hope Nicolson writes in *Mountain Gloom and Mountain Glory*, Hobbes's ideas were circulating in manuscript by 1640. *Leviathan* appeared in 1651, with its pessimistic argument that the universe had developed through the chance interplay of matter, without the direction or intervention of any spiritual force. More published his *Antidote to Atheism* one year later, and according to Nicolson, "it was recognized as one of the early important replies to Hobbes. . . . The Cambridge Platonists were as much united by their opposition to Hobbes as by their Platonism" (117).

Antidote to Atheism is written in three main sections and a long appendix. The anthologies of Cambridge Platonists never print any more than the table of contents of the third section, which is, in fact, the first seventeenth-century providence tale collection to synthesize the various elements I have been discussing. It includes numerous apparition stories among sections of theoretical commentary on the nature of these apparitions, witches, and ghosts. Taken as a whole, the book does have a vast, encyclopedic reach, reflecting More's intense philosophical interests. Even so, in part 3 he focuses mainly on apparition stories. His inclusion of so many narratives, the characteristics of these, and the theoretical ideas he propounds about the stories all reflect the path-breaking nature of this work.[19]

The work is subtitled "An Appeal to the Naturall Faculties of the Mind of Man, Whether there be not a God." In the preface he declares he will employ a simple style, with "Reason over Rhetoric." He pares away at the tradition of retelling miracles from holy writ, because these miracles are too easily refuted by atheists. Similarly, at the beginning of book 3, he explains why examples of divine vengeance on the wicked are not persuasive either: "they don't convince the obstinate and refractory Atheist who will cite examples of evil ones who got away and good ones who didn't." He promises to tell no stories in which "either the avarice of the Priest, or the credulity and fancifulness of the Melancholist many readers suspected." Instead, More turns to "effects discovered in the world as are not deemed Natural, but Extraordinary and Miraculous," and he plans to "bring only those [arguments or effects] that cannot be resolved into any Natural Causes, or be phansied to come by Chance, but are so miraculous, that they do imply the presence of some free subtile understanding essence distinct from the brute Matter and ordinary power of Nature" (More, "Antidote Against Atheism," bk. 3, ch. 1, pp. 86–97).

Despite the miraculous effects his stories describe, More never stops theorizing about how invisible, supernatural spirits operate on the physical world, what they could be made of, and what powers they must, according to reason, possess. He attempts to establish rational, scientific criteria for his stories of apparitions and young women vomiting out pins and unlearned maids speaking fluent Greek. He sometimes reverts to older, scholastic ways of thinking too, and will argue, for example, through analogy. He writes that the untrue apparition stories in circulation prove there must be real ones, just as fool's gold can only exist because there is real gold. Atheists, he says, claim that there is the touchstone to verify the presence of real gold, but More, always ready with a logical reply, says there are similar touchstones to verify the presence of spirits. These are:

1. If the spirits are avouched by persons with no interest in so doing;
2. If there are eyewitnesses; and,
3. If miracles leave behind sensible effects. (*Antidote*, bk. 3, ch. 1, p. 88)

More employs a more abstract and metaphysical style in other parts of the *Antidote*, where he draws detailed and imaginative maps of the nature and operations of spirits. More is a seventeenth-century Renaissance man, a story-teller, philosopher, scientist, and theologian. It is easy to say his theories were narrow-minded delusions. However, in his own time, the inexplicable prodigies reported by Glanvill, More, and the other ministers were highly regarded by leading scientists and were spurs to some of the most important scientific research of the day. As Margaret Murray writes in *The Witch Cult in Western Europe*, among those " who believed in the reality of the facts confessed at the [witchcraft trials] . . . [were] . . . the . . . most brilliant minds . . . [such as] . . . Bodin, Lord Bacon, Raleigh, Boyle, Cudworth, Selden, Henry More, Sir Thomas Brown, Matthew Hale, [and] Sir George Mackenzie . . . [while] . . . the sceptics were . . . Reginald Scot, a Kentish country squire . . . Wagstaffe, who went mad from drink; and Webster, a fanatical preacher" (10–11).

More verified his accounts with the testimony of many witnesses. He suc-ceeded in describing sensational and inexplicable phenomenon in plain, simple language. Although some providence tale writers introduced more melodra-matic language, with the scientific and objective elements fading into the back-ground, More's plain, rationalistic prose clearly influenced Baxter, Glanvill, and Increase Mather's providence tales. More's objective and legalistic way of de-scribing the supernatural eventually appears in the work of Charles Brockden Brown and Edgar Allan Poe.

By the end of the seventeenth century, moderating turns in Reformation thought combined with the age's growing scientific spirit to produce a new prose form. These providence tales united the clarity of scientific discourse with the emotional force and imagination of sensational and melodramatic tales of the supernatural. Trying to put God back up on his heavenly throne, providence tale writers were making him and his minions integral parts of the material world these writers were simultaneously resisting. The infusion of the spirit world into a discourse of scientific and legalistic objectivity was the spark that enabled the production of this early and unrecognized imaginative prose.

3

Witchcraft Relations in England and on the Continent, 1484–1697

The most important seventeenth-century providence tale form was the witchcraft relation. Witchcraft discourse in general had proliferated since the publication of Pope Innocent VIII's papal bull of 1484. This proclamation, addressed primarily to three north German Dominican friars who had already been empowered to act as inquisitors there, declares that "heretical depravity should be driven from the frontiers and bournes of the faithful" (qtd. in Kramer and Sprenger, xliii). It describes a crisis in which people had "abandoned themselves to devils, incubi and succubi . . . , slain infants yet in the mother's womb . . . [and where these devils] hinder men from performing the sexual act and women from conceiving . . . and at the instigation of the Enemy of Mankind they [the people] do not shrink from committing and perpetrating the foulest abominations and filthiest excesses" (xliii).

The bull tried to overcome various hindrances and objections that were keeping these inquisitors, two of whom were Jacobus Sprenger and Henry Kramer, from executing their commissions. Similar conditions of demonic chaos also characterize descriptions of England during the witchcraft manias of the sixteenth and seventeenth centuries, and of New England during the Indian wars from the 1630s through those of the 1670s, 80s and 90s (including descriptions found in Indian captivity narratives and in witchcraft relations of the 1690s). One of the precursors for the captivity narratives' relations of demonic chaos, then, can be found in works such as Pope Innocent's bull and in the witchcraft literature that grew out of its directives. These accounts of diabolical prodigies helped justify the persecutions by the inquisitors and other authorities from the

1480s until the late 1600s. In New England, captivity narratives promoted continued warfare against the Indians, just as witchcraft relations justified the persecution of witches.

The bull was effective. It led to an increase in the discovery, apprehension, and execution of witches throughout the Continent. It also preceded by only two years and surely provoked the publication of the foremost of the many witchcraft treatises that appeared over the course of the next century, Kramer and Sprenger's *Malleus Maleficarum*.

The authors of witchcraft treatises were primarily inquisitors themselves. Their works contain definitions of witchcraft, its different manifestations, explanations of its operations, arguments of those who denied its existence, refutations of those arguments, and stories, usually in the form of short anecdotes, of actual cases of witchcraft the judges had heard or read. These judges were trying to systematize their legal labors, as well as justify their pronouncements. The treatises include Bodin's *Demonomanie des Sorciers* (1570), Remy's *Demonolatry* (1595), Guazzo's *Compendium Maleficarum* (1608), and Delrio's *Disquisitionum magicarum libri sex* (1599). Kramer and Sprenger's *Malleus Maleficarum* appeared in 1486 and drew on the judges' own observations, as well as on earlier witchcraft accounts and treatises. Jon Nider's (1380–1438) *Formicarius* was one of their favorite sources. They also took stories from works by Nicolas Eymeric (1320–1399), Nicolas Jaquer ("On the Treading Underfoot of Demons"), Michael Psellis, the nun Hrotswitha, Vincent of Beauvais, Caesarius of Heisterbach, and various church fathers, John of Damascus, Augustine, Gregory, and Aquinas. Pagan stories of witches and their operations by Lucian and Apuleius also appear in this collection.

The main purpose of *Malleus Maleficarum* (The Witch's Hammer) was to justify the punishment of witches and to make witchcraft a capital offense in all cases. Although there had been stories told about witches since pagan times, the upheavals of the Reformation caused the Catholic Church to pursue any people it could brand as heretics, and thus to extend its search for and punishment of witches. A sharp rise in the number of witches caught and executed, along with an increase in works written about those discoveries and executions, ensued. Kramer and Sprenger devote the third and last part of their work to "the Judicial Proceedings in Both the Ecclesiastical and Civil Courts Against Witches and Indeed All Heretics." This segment contains "XXXV Questions in Which Is Most Clearly Set Out The Formal Rules for Initiating a Process of Justice, How It Should Be Conducted, and The Method of Pronouncing Sentence" (iii). Throughout their work, Sprenger and Kramer cast all their ideas, theories, and anecdotes in the context of punishment. After a page-long relation of a count who discovers, by very devious means, the location of a charm placed in his yard by an ex-mistress to keep him from being able to have sex with his wife, Sprenger and Kramer advise the reader that "for the sake of the Count's reputation it is not expedient to name that castle and estate; but we have related this story in order that the truth of the matter may be known, to bring so great a crime into open detestation" (98). Sprenger and Kramer's focus, then, was not primarily to glorify God's mercy or judgment but to prosecute a witch. Their meticulous and punitive approach was an attempt to silence those who opposed these judicial measures. Their enemies were primarily Protestants but also included rationalist inheritors of the ideas of Avicenna, Averroës, and Abelard, and Renaissance philosophers rediscovering Democritus's theory of chance, Lucretian and Epicurean atheism, and other classical ideas.

The comprehensive and systematic nature of *Malleus Maleficarum* represents a new level in the development of witchcraft literature and adds a scientific character to the relations it contains. The science in *Malleus*, a systemization of centuries of received opinions, is still more scholastic than empirical in nature and does not follow the methods of the new science that are evident later in the works of members of the Royal Society. Still, *Malleus Maleficarum* is an interesting text with which to start this close inspection of the later witchcraft relations because it illustrates several important tropes, principally a demon-filled environment, which appear in the Indian captivity narratives. Features of *Malleus Maleficarum* that are no longer prominent by the 1650s, such as the emphasis on punishment, highlight the most important changes that become evident by then in providence tales in general, in witchcraft relations especially, and finally in Indian captivity narratives. Such changes contribute to the increasing complexity and power of the later providence tale narratives.

Malleus Maleficarum is divided into three major sections. The first, "Treating of the Three Necessary Concomitants of Witchcraft, Which are the Devil, a Witch, and the Permission of Almighty God," is largely theoretical. It attempts to establish theological grounds for the existence of a wide assortment of powers wielded by the devil and witches. It describes the various demonic forms at the devil's command, and how those spiritual forms manipulate the humans who make compacts with the devil, the witches, wizards, sorcerers, and hags whose execution is the ultimate goal of this treatise. Question 13 of part 1 explores, for example, "the Question concerning the Two Divine Permissions which God justly allows, namely, that the Devil the Author of all Evil, should Sin, and that our First Parents should Fall, from which Origins the Works of Witches are justly suffered to take place." Section 1 also asserts God's ultimate control over both the earthly and supernatural realms. Section 2, "Treating of the Methods by which the Works of Witchcraft are Wrought and Directed, and How They May Be Successfully Annulled and Dissolved," contains short anecdotal accounts of witchcraft heard by the inquisitors, while part 3 describes the step-by-step procedures that should be taken in examining, torturing, judging, and finally executing a witch. One structural element in *Malleus Maleficarum* that does persist through the mid-seventeenth-century work of Glanvill and More to the end-of-the-century providence tale collections of Turner, Baxter, and the Mathers, is the combination of theoretical commentary with sections of relations or narratives.

The joining of commentary to tale was not new in witchcraft discourse and can be seen, to choose one example, in the *Dialogue on Miracles* of Caesarius from around A.D. 1200. This collection offers visions (for example, of saints and their holy relics), miracles wrought by the sacrament of the body and blood of Christ and other relics and rites of the church, and tales of many other miraculous events. Brief dialogues between a novice and a monk, in which theological issues in the narrative are discussed, often follow the tales. *Malleus Maleficarum* focuses more narrowly and theorizes at greater length solely on witchcraft. But Joseph Glanvill, Henry More, Richard Baxter, and both Increase and Cotton Mather also fuse commentary with narrative in their seventeenth-century collections of witchcraft stories. As in *Malleus Maleficarum*, theoretical issues wrap themselves around the tales, forming an apparatus that becomes an integral part of the narratives, a kind of metanarrative.

In *Malleus Maleficarum*, this metanarrative focuses on Scripture or commentary on Scripture by patristic fathers. In Glanvill and More's works, the Neoplatonism that arose in Italy with Marsilio Ficino and Pico Della Mirandola, and then was introduced in England by such works as Cudworth's massive *The True Intellectual System of the Universe* and More's *Enchiridion Metaphysicum*, overshadows scriptural rationales. The surrounding commentary also becomes legalistic and describes the motives and backgrounds of the witnesses in each case. Theological questions in *Malleus Maleficarum* focus on scriptural questions: "Whether the Belief that there are Beings as Witches is so Essential a Part of the Catholic Faith that Obstinacy to maintain the Opposite Opinion manifestly savours of Heresy" (question 1 of part 1). By the seventeenth century more technical debates occur between papists and Puritans over, for example, the merits of each other's methods of dispossession. To these are added Neoplatonic arguments against atheistic, Hobbesian, and Cartesian denials and doubts that there even is a spirit world acting on earth, and legalistic, empirical probes into the credibility and honesty of narrators and witnesses. Still, though the contents of the metanarratives change, structurally the combination of commentary with stories persists. Whether that content is scriptural, Neoplatonic, more secular and legalistic, or some combination thereof, questions about the existence and operations of God's providence are raised and overcome, both explicitly and structurally, in the narrative-plus-commentary form from *Malleus Maleficarum* to *Saducismus Triumphatus*.

For Sprenger and Kramer, the motivation for establishing the existence of witches is to justify punishing them. Witches' reality is not problematical. As the secularization of the Enlightenment continues, metanarratives become increasingly concerned with proving the truth of the stories they surround. Punishment is forgotten, and the existence of a witch becomes an emblem of the existence of God. The subject of these later tales, whether witchcraft, sea deliverance, or captivity narratives, becomes their own credibility. Rather than trying to punish and eliminate witches and demons, they seek to prove the certainty of their existence. Punishment becomes unnecessary and irrelevant. From a postmodern perspective, these later tales of the invisible world read like self-reflective analyses of themselves, defenses or apologies of their own claims to representing reality.

One theological question in particular remains prominent from *Malleus Maleficarum* to the seventeenth-century witchcraft tale. This is Sprenger and Kramer's explanation of why God allows afflictions to occur to innocent children and just men and women, who are precisely those, they say, who suffer most from witchcraft. They explain that God permits their suffering "for the perfecting of the universe, as through the persecution by tyrants came the patience of the martyrs, and through the works of witches comes the purgation or proving the faith of the just" (68–69). This same idea is evident, as many critics have pointed out, in Mary Rowlandson's captivity narrative written nearly two hundred years later.[1] Sprenger and Kramer say, "God scourges man with witchcraft [or with any calamity such as captivity, they might have said] so He may be glorified when the spell is removed, and so man may acquire merit through patience, see his virtue preserved through humiliation and castigation and be purified through the expulsion and obliteration of scourges" (69). Both captivity tales and early witchcraft stories, then, seek to present affliction in a positive light. Moreover, they both glorify God, though by the time of the captivities the anxiety over proving his existence had grown tremendously.

Several important features of the anecdotes in part 2 of *Malleus Maleficarum* also persist in later providence tales. Two of these features involve narrative persona, while a third involves the stories' content. An apologetic, embarrassed, or self-conscious narrative voice which serves to remove the taint of self-interest from the narrators, and thus raises their credibility, appears in many of these tales. The reliability of narrators and other witnesses to the stories' events become analogues for God's existence. Finally, sensational content, which constitutes a form of early modern low realism or early modern gothic, colors every tale. Their authors believe such content can best penetrate the thick, irrational minds of their heretical or atheist opponents.

Kramer and Sprenger, judges as they were, were not as embarrassed to be retailing stories as later providence tale writers were. Still, before telling their stories, they do put some distance between themselves and these tales by admitting their hesitations about relating them. At the beginning of part 2, they discuss people immune from witches' power, who include inquisitors. After one brief anecdote about one such inquisitor, they say, "And many more such experiences have happened to us Inquisitors in the exercise of our Inquisitorial office, which would turn the mind of the reader to wonder if it were expedient to relate them. But since self praise is sordid and mean, it is better to pass them over in silence than to incur the stigma of boastfulness and conceit. But we must except those which have become so well known that they cannot be concealed" (90).

Despite their embarrassment and self-consciousness, if people have already heard a story, Sprenger and Kramer will trumpet it even further. Still, their reluctance to boast by publishing their experiences is repeated more than one hundred years later in King James's witchcraft treatise *Daemonologie* (1597) and again some eighty years after that in Mary Rowlandson's and in other captivity narratives. It is part of a pattern that demonstrates how writers considered prose storytelling a low form. Those with lofty ambitions eased their consciences when they did tell stories by claiming they were forced to do it, that they wrote out of pure motives or only to clear their names. After proving their lack of base motives, their testimony about the presence of God, the devil, familiar spirits, and witches could be more readily accepted.

Sprenger and Kramer anticipate the apologetic voice that becomes an integral part of this form one hundred years later. They also begin to develop a rationale for preferring storytelling over theory that in itself becomes an important trope running through English providence tales of the mid–seventeenth century. These devices help to overcome authors' "storytelling" guilt. Again at the beginning of part 2, while outlining the subjects they will investigate, Sprenger and Kramer attempt a brief justification for relying on examples, rather than theory, to make their case: "And because we are now dealing with matters relating to morals and behaviour, and there is no need for a variety of arguments and disquisitions, since those matters which now follow under their headings are sufficiently discussed in the foregoing Questions, therefore we pray God that the reader will not look for proofs in every case, since it is enough to adduce examples that have been personally seen or heard, or are accepted at the word of credible witnesses" (89).

Their storytelling is excused, in part, because theory has already been included in their treatise.[2] In later works, authors advance storytelling as necessary to convince unreasonable atheists of the existence of a supernatural world. Whatever the specific explanation, however, *Malleus Maleficarum* establishes an important paradigm, the need for a rationale for storytelling. Writers' guilt highlights the irony behind the development of these narratives, which were being created, especially by the mid-1600s, despite their authors' "better" intentions. The apologetic tone seems natural when we consider that these writers were advancing a form associated with materialism and the senses, with the passions of people who read sensational stories in pamphlet literature, even as they, the providence tale writers, believed themselves to be championing the cause of God and the spirit world.

Having an entire section of *Malleus Maleficarum* devoted primarily to relations signals the movement toward more storytelling. Though Glanvill and More still include sections of theory, they fill later editions of their collections with even more relations. Another type of witchcraft literature, the trial pamphlet, which started to develop around 1570, did away with explicit theory completely. These pamphlet writers, like later providence tale writers, found ways to embed theory in the narratives themselves. One example of this theory in the captivity narratives is when the captives quote Scripture, which comes to them at especially dramatic moments and helps them overcome spiritual doubts. Another closely related form of theorizing within narratives appears in some of Glanvill and Sinclair's most famous stories, and in John Williams's captivity narrative. This form emerged earlier in works by Anglicans such as Archbishop William Laud, William Chillingsworth, and Samuel Harsnett. The trope depicts characters from opposing faiths who cite Scripture to debate important theological points; often the state of someone's eternal soul rests in the balance.

The stories in the *Malleus Maleficarum* also share with later English witchcraft tales a sensationalistic, low realism filled with violent, gothic, and supernatural events. The following is a witch's confession before Peter the Judge in Boltingen, in the state of Berne, which Sprenger and Kramer took from one of their favorite sources, the *Formicarius* of the doctor and judge Jon Nider. The confession relates to the "manner [in which] they [the witches] ate children" (infanticide is also a very popular trope in both witchcraft and Indian captivity narratives):

> We set our snares chiefly for unbaptized children, and even for those that have been baptized, especially when they have not been protected by the sign of the Cross and prayers, and with our spells we kill them in their cradles or even when they are sleeping by their parents' side, in such a way that they afterwards are thought to have been overlain or to have died some other natural death. Then we secretly take

them from their graves, and cook them in a cauldron, until the whole flesh comes away from the bones to make soup which may easily be drunk. Of the more solid matter we make an unguent which is of virtue to help us in our arts and pleasures and our transportations; and with the liquid we fill a flask or skin, whoever drinks from which, with the addition of a few other ceremonies, immediately acquires much knowledge and becomes a leader in our sect. (100–101)

Some of Sprenger and Kramer's stories concerning bodily transportation through the air illustrate the supernatural and fantastic qualities of the tales. One story, from a priest in Oberdorf, tells of a group of scholars gathered for a night's beer drinking. A scholar volunteers to fetch the beer in exchange for not paying for his portion. When he sees, "upon opening the door . . . a thick cloud before the grunsel," he refuses to go. A companion of his says angrily, "Even if the devil were there, I shall fetch the drink." And, "going out, he was carried through the air in sight of all the others . . . borne on high with arms stretched out, shouting but not whimpering" (105). Another anecdote on this transvection theme tells of "a woman in the town of Breisach whom we asked whether they [witches] could be transported only in imagination, or actually in the body; and she answered that it was possible both ways. For if they do not wish to be bodily transferred, but want to know all that is being done in a meeting of their companions, then . . . in the name of all the devils they lie down to sleep on their left side, and then a sort of bluish vapour comes from their mouth, through which they can clearly see what is happening" (108). All these ghoulish, lurid, disgusting, and occult elements, sharply delineated, play significant roles in the stories of divine providence.

The Witchcraft Mania in England and the Scientific Witchcraft Tale

Similar literary elements: "low realism," gothic violence and fantasy, and self-conscious narrators to name three, are evident in late-sixteenth and early-seventeenth-century English witchcraft relations as well as in other forms of providence tales. These later relations are quite different, however, from those in *Malleus Maleficarum*. What is added to Sprenger and Kramer, especially during Queen Elizabeth's witchcraft mania, is a layer of legalistic testimony in which the writer strives to prove the veracity of all the facts depicted. No longer can a witness's credibility be merely asserted as in *Malleus Maleficarum*, or theoretically "proved" as in Caesarius. Writers have to reproduce the testimony of at least several reliable eyewitnesses. Witchcraft skeptics were one cause of these new standards. The physician Johan Wier's 1563 *Pseudomarchia Daemonum*, which denied that many so-called instances of witchcraft were in fact anything but cases of melancholia or madness, and Reginald Scot's 1584 *The Discoverie of Witchcraft* both opposed the severity of the witchcraft trials.

Francis Bacon's earliest work appeared in 1597. His skepticism rested on a belief he expresses in *Novum Organum* that "all the received systems are but so many stage plays, representing worlds of their own creation after an unreal and scenic fashion" (470). To counter these false "received systems" of knowledge, he proposes a more complete collection of data. Scientists have, he says, "to collect a store of particular observations sufficient in number, or in kind, or in certainty, to in form the understanding. . . . [In the current state of philosophy there is] nothing verified, nothing counted, weighed or measured" (515).

Bacon called for a more comprehensive examination of the facts of nature, an examination similar to the then contemporary legal examinations of those accused of witchcraft. Sprenger and Kramer's work foreshadows these scientific trends in the systematic way it classifies its information; but *Malleus Maleficarum* reproduces traditional ideas, and does not, in Baconian fashion, seek out new facts that might overturn or change accepted views. "Philosophy," Bacon writes, "is based on too narrow a foundation of experiment and natural history, and decides on the authority of too few cases" (481). He would "sink the foundations of the sciences deeper and firmer" (443). He states, "One method of delivery alone remains to us: which is simply this; we must lead men to the particulars themselves, and their series and order, while men on their side must force themselves for a while to lay their notions by and begin to familiarise themselves with facts" (468).[3]

Michael Winship notes the influence of Bacon's methodology on Matthew Poole's design for illustrious providences, which was in turn followed by William Turner and the Mathers.[4] Bacon's methodology clearly had a widespread impact on providence tale writers. Along with the age's increasing skepticism and the ministers' sensationalistic attempts to convert atheists, Bacon's ideas contributed to the vivid but credible accounts of witchcraft and other unusual phenomena that occurred in the seventeenth century.

Witchcraft made a useful subject for Baconian analysis. Proofs of the existence of invisible creatures required more than the usual amount of convincing evidence. In addition, witchcraft was an especially popular subject for writers influenced by Bacon's call for an examination of prodigies, of the unusual and the bizarre, of facts which did not fit with preconceived axioms and theories. Lorraine Daston explains regarding Bacon that, "with Aristotle, Examples do not float free of an argumentative context . . . whereas Natural Philosophy must also collect [Bacon says] 'Deviating instances, such as the errors of nature, or strange and monstrous objects'" (110/111).

Bacon's focus on prodigies promoted the sensationalism that pervades providence tales, while his concern with convincing evidence made those sensational tales works of natural history as well. These characteristics became evident in English witchcraft tales beginning around 1570, before the publication of Bacon's work, when the first trials were held under the new Elizabethan witchcraft statutes. According to William Lecky's 1867 *History of the Rise and Influence of the Spirit of Rationalism*, the first "regular enactment against sorcery" (119) in England occurred in 1541. Before this law there had been isolated persecutions and rare executions.[5] The spreading influence of the central state, the increasing fear of Spanish and Catholic power, and the religious disorder of the period combined to produce this attack on witchcraft. The return of thousands from the Continent who had fled during the Marian persecutions augmented it. That these returnees while in Europe had developed their own ideas about witchcraft and been influenced by literature printed on the new presses of Switzerland and Germany on herbal medicine and other folk practices made witchcraft seem more prevalent and dangerous.

Elizabeth's law, Lecky says, stipulated that "for the first conviction [of] witches not shown to have destroyed others by their incantations . . . [they should be] punished by the pillory and imprisonment, while those who were condemned to death perished by the gallows instead of the stake" (121). (Lecky adds the last regulation as an example of English leniency compared to the Inquisition.) Elizabeth's 1563 statute marked for death those who "shall use, practise, or exercise any Witchcrafte, Enchantment, Charme, or Sorcerie, whereby any person shall happen to be killed or destroyed. . . . [They and] their Concillors and Aidours . . . shall suffer paynes of Death as a felon or felons" (qtd. in Notestein, 14).

According to Wallace Notestein, this was the beginning of the prosecution of witchcraft in England as a secular crime. In 1581, Elizabeth passed another law, which was aimed against those who sought to "know, and shall set forth by express words, deeds or writings, how long her Majesty shall live, or who shall reign as king or queen of this realm of England, after her highness' decease." The proscribed methods of prognostication included "setting or erecting any figure, casting of nativities or by calculations. . . . Any prophesying, witchecraft . . . [or] conjurations . . . [and such offenses] shall be felony, and every offender therein, and also all his aiders (etc.), shall be judged as felons and shall suffer pain of death" (Kramer and Sprenger xxi).

But when James came to power, the severity of the penalties increased for a wider variety of acts; the law now said that anyone who "shall practise or exercise any Invocation or Conjuration of any evil and wicked Spirit, or shall consult, covenant with, entertaine, employ, feede, or rewarde any evil and wicked Spirit to or for any intent or purpose; or take up any dead man, woman, or child, to be imployed or used in any manner of Witchcrafte" should suffer death as a felon. In addition, anyone who should "take it upon him or them by Witchcrafte to tell or declare in what place . . . [to] find gold or Silver or lost or stolen goods [or] provoke any person to unlawfull love, or sicken, waste or impaire Goods or Cattell" (Notestein 103) would, for a first offense, spend a year in prison and make four appearances in the pillory. The punishment for the second offense was death. In addition, by James's time, torture as a method of extracting confessions had become widely accepted.

James developed his fear of witchcraft while presiding over the 1590 trial of Francis Stewart, the Earl of Bothwell, and of John Fian, Agnes Simpson, and some one hundred other so-called witches and sorcerers accused of conspiring to kill the king and his new wife, Princess Anne of Denmark, on their return to England. These witches confessed that while sailing across the Channel in sieves ("cives") or "riddles" they threw a baptized cat, to which they had appended some joints and other body parts of a corpse, into the sea to roil it up. During the testimony, Agnes Simpson was said to have told James the words he first spoke to Anne immediately after their wedding. Her knowledge of those words made him a believer in witchcraft.

At least two works were inspired by this trial, and though they were published twelve years apart, I would like to examine them as a pair. These two works, like Beard's providence tale collection mentioned in chapter 2, look simultaneously backwards, in this case to *Malleus Maleficarum*, and forward, to the witch and apparition stories of the 1650s and beyond. Characteristics of *Malleus Maleficarum* that persist in these works include narrative self-consciousness, the combination of storytelling and theory, and low realism. Interest in punishing witches also remains, but the self-assurance of Sprenger and Kramer dissolves. King James's attack on witches in his treatise on witchcraft, *Daemonologie* (1597) now becomes attached to a guilt-ridden suspicion that collecting evidence about witchcraft can turn the accuser into one of the devil's disciples himself. Both James's text and *Newes from Scotland*, an anonymously written narrative of the witchcraft trial James judged, display more factual, corroborated evidence of witchcraft, more vivid language to describe the prodigious events, and more emphasis on drama and narration than earlier witchcraft discourse does.

Newes from Scotland (1591) was one of a group of witchcraft trial pamphlets that had first begun to be published around 1570. Its concern with punishment appears immediately in the title: *Newes from Scotland . . . Declaring the Damn-able Life and Death of Dr. Fian, a notable sorcerer.* The title then relates that Fian was "burned at Edenbrough in January last." Fian's punishment is the most prominent piece of news in this pamphlet. In James's preface to *Daemonologie*, he also introduces those images of demonic chaos, that concern with punishment, and that embarrassment over storytelling which all were found in Sprenger and Kramer:

> The fearfull aboundinge at this time in this countrie, of these detestable slaves of the Devill, the Witches, or enchaunters, hath moved me (beloved reader) to dispatch in part, this following treatise of mine, not in any wise (as I protest) to serve for a shew of my learning and ingine, but onely (mooved of conscience) to preasse thereby, so farre as I can, to resolve the doubting harts of many; both that such assaults of Sathan are most certainly practized, and that the instruments thereof, merits most severely to be punished. (xi)

James raises new doubts, though, about prosecuting witches, and begins a trend which culminates in William Turner's 1697 encyclopedic providence tale collection, *A Compleat History of Remarkable Providences.* Turner describes his project as "mustering up the Legions of Devils to attack the infidel bravadoes" (29). James does not go as far as Turner, but he is aware of the possibility of an alliance of the faithful with the devil in the war against the Hobbesians and Cartesians. He structures his treatise as a Platonic dialogue, a form he could have borrowed from Caesarius. James's teacher character, Epistemon, advises his student, Philomathes, that the knowledge he is imparting could be dangerous. Any contact with the devil, including learning about his ways, could draw one into sin. Despite assurances that knowledge and practice differ, and that one can know about witchcraft ("of the circles and art of Magic," for example) "without committing an horrible defection" against God, Epistemon (as he is informing Philomathes of the devil's ways) claims, "Yet to speak truly for my owne parte (I speake but for myselfe), I desire not to make so neere riding: for in my opinion our enemie is over craftie, and we over weake (except the greater grace of God) to assay such hazards, wherein he preases to trap us" (15).

James fears that damnation itself could result from learning the devil's ways. Different types of partnerships with the devil do indeed occur in Glanvill's works and works by other mid-century writers, and then in several Indian captivity narratives, in which punishment of demonic elements becomes a secondary concern. To James, magical acts are "the devilles rudiments . . . baites, casten out by him, for trapping such as God will permit to fall in his hands" (15). And yet, "since the Devill is the verie contrairie opposite to God, there can be no better way to know God, then by the contrairie; as by the ones power (though a creature) to admire the power of the great Creator: by the falsehood of the one to considder the truth of the other . . . and so fourth in all the rest of the essence of God, and qualities of the Devill" (55).

James looks to the past in using a scholastic device, arguing by contraries, while simultaneously adding a "modern" note, the breakdown of the boundary between accuser and accused. The tension between accusation and alliance persists throughout *Daemonologie*. James keeps insisting that he doesn't want to reveal too much about the devil's ways, while he informs his readers that those who do want to know more details can consult writers such as Agrippa and Wier.[6] James's rationale for publishing explanations of the devil's activities becomes the model for all future providence tales. He says, "But I feare in deede, there be over many Sadduces in this worlde, that denies all kindes of spirites: for convicting of whose errours, there is cause enough if this were no more, that God should permit at sometimes spirits visiblie to kyith" (55).

Newes from Scotland and *Daemonologie* both promote the increasing popularity of narrative over theory. The former is a narrative of the 1590 trial. It contains no theory or commentary. Like other witchcraft trial narratives from the 1570s onward, it embeds contemporary scientific theories of knowledge into the narrative by telling the same story over from the perspective of different witnesses. James's use of characters to expound his theories is an attempt to dramatize his ideas. Viewed as a pair, however, *Newes from Scotland* and *Daemonologie* suggest that authors still believed that stories needed validating theoretical commentary.

Newes from Scotland introduces a heightened concern with the reliability of testimony. Sprenger and Kramer sometimes mention the credibility of their witnesses, but they make no sustained efforts to present corroborating evidence. In the story of the sexually cursed count, Sprenger and Kramer go as far as they ever do toward expressing concern with the truth of their evidence: "If I were to collect all the similar instances which here occurred in one town of that diocese it would take a whole book; but they are written and preserved at the house of the Bishop of Brixen's, who still lives to testify to their truth, astounding and unheard of though they be" (98).

In *Newes from Scotland* several witnesses give testimony. The story uses the trial structure of a variety of witnesses and deponents as its narrative framework. The pamphlet is also extremely interested in proving that the plot against James was discovered through judicial means, particularly the legal torture of one witch, Agnes Simpson, and not through stories about supernatural transvection told by a poor peddlar, the main source of a competing version. James seeks to "resolve the doubting hearts of many" about witchcraft in general. In his prefatory remarks, he echoes these concerns when he assures his readers that his motives in writing about the devil are purely objective, mixed neither with vanity nor self-interest.

Another outcome of this overriding concern with truth is that pamphlet literature such as *Newes from Scotland* becomes much more vivid and detailed than anything in previous witchcraft literature. Of torturing witches, the *Malleus* says, "if neither threats nor such promises will induce her to confess . . . she must be examined . . . often and frequently exposed to torture, beginning with the more gentle of them; for the judge should not be hasty to proceed to the graver kind" (226). *Newes from Scotland* offers a more horrific description of the torture of the so-called leader of the witches. John Fian's nails were pulled off, one of the witches confesses, and pins inserted up to their heads into the flesh underneath. Even the torture known as "the bootes" didn't make him confess; only when the other witches found two charmed pins under his tongue and removed them did he make his confession. The pamphlet treats the reader to a lusty description of how the bootes worked on Fian: "Wherein he continued a long time, and did abide so many blowes in them, that his legges were crushte and beaten togeather as small as might bee, and the bones and flesh so brused, that the bloud and marrowe spouted forth in great abundance, whereby they were made unserviceable for ever" (27–28).

The Fian pamphlet also features "low realism," again a quality which continues throughout the century, and which, in less detailed form, had been evident for centuries. Agnes Simpson, the witch who knew the king's intimate words to his new queen, confessed only after the devil's mark was found on her "privities," where the devil had first shaved and then licked her (12). Her cohort, Agnes Tompson, testified that the devil, angry that many witches came late to his meeting, had made them all kiss his buttocks, "which being put over the Pulpit bare, everyone did as he had enjoyned them" (14). Desiring a "gentlewoman" whom another "Gentleman" also loved, Fian first caused this man to fall into "lunacie and madness" for one out of every twenty-four hours. His plan did not work, so he tried to get the woman's brother, a former pupil of his, to bring him "three haires of his sister's privities," since the boy "did lye with his sister." He promised the boy, if he got the hair, he would "teach him without stripes" (21). Fian gave him a piece of "conjured paper" to deliver the hairs upon. The boy "practised night after night to obtaine his master's purpose, especially when his sister was a sleepe," to no avail.

The young woman cried out to her mother that her brother would not "suffer her to sleep," and her mother, a witch herself, recognized the hand of Dr. Fian in her son's actions. She cut off three hairs from the udder of a "young Heyfer which never had borne Calfe nor gone to the Bull," and had her son deliver them on the conjured paper to Fian. The doctor then "wrought his arte upon them." Then the "cow . . . came into the doore of the Church wherein the Schoolmaster was . . . and made towards the schoolmaster, leaping and dancing upon him, and following him forth of the Church and to what place so ever he went, to the great admiration of all the townes men of Saltpans . . . Thereupon . . . the said Doctor . . . was secretly nominated for a notable conjurer" (23–24). Such a blend of folk humor with legal testimony exemplifies another juxtaposition of scientific and sensationalistic elements in seventeenth-century witchcraft texts.

THE "NEW REALISM," 1646–1697

Joseph Glanvill's relation of the Fian/Simpson conspiracy first appeared in the posthumous 1681 *Saducismus Triumphatus; or, Full and Plain Evidence Concerning Witches and Apparitions. In Two Parts. The First Treating of Their Possibility, The Second of Their Real Existence*, edited by Henry More, the new and greatly enlarged edition of Glanvill's 1666 *A Philosophical Endeavour towards the Defense of the Being of Witches and Apparitions*. That work used a combination of Neoplatonic and scriptural arguments to prove that witches exist. The 1681 edition was primarily intended to provide a new, more convincing version of "Tedworth," originally added in a 1668 edition. More also added a great deal of supporting information about the demon and those who had observed it. He aimed to silence critics who were saying that Glanvill and J. Mompesson himself, the man whose house and family were afflicted by the demon, had admitted the story was not true. More also included Glanvill's "Proofs of Apparitions, Spirits and Witches from Holy Scripture" and portions from "a Choice Collection of Modern Relations," which he gathered from Glanvill's papers. The latter relations constitute over forty narratives, of which the story of Agnes Simpson and John Fian/Fiene is among the last. Tales in this 1681 edition of *Saducismus Triumphatus* and in another edition from 1682 seek to conform to the standards of the new science, especially to the demand for believable, physical evidence and stylistic simplicity.

These scientific criteria operate alongside more sensationalistic elements in Glanvill and More's work. Like the earlier version of the story, and like the description of demonic chaos in Pope Innocent's 1484 bull, Glanvill's Fian/Simpson tale also depicts a scene of disorder caused by witchcraft. Fian is "transported [over] many Mountains" to a conventicle of witches where everyone "kissed the Devil's Breech." He and the witches raise winds over the sea as the king sails to Norway, and then raise a mist at his return, "whereby the king's

Majesty might be cast upon the Coast of England." Glanvill describes similar misrule in the Tedworth tale, as does Henry More in "The Devil of Mascon," from his 1653 *Antidote to Atheism*. Samuel Clarke's tale of Mrs. Teate, from his 1646 *A Mirrour or Looking Glass Both for Saints and Sinners*, and Indian captivity narratives by Mary Rowlandson, Hannah Duston, and John Williams also begin with an unleashing of devils.

Invariably, the release of the demons occurs in the absence of a male authority figure, usually the husband who is often a minister. The Simpson/Fian narrative varies this motif; the story concerns an unsuccessful attempt to keep King James from getting home with his new wife, whereas these later tales focus on the troubles of the family the husband has temporarily left. The separation of the husband from his family is echoed in many captivity narratives, including Rowlandson's and Dustan's. In Hannah Swarton's captivity tale (first published in Increase Mather's 1684 *Essay*), a move by the entire family into the wilderness, which results in the family's separation from their close-knit church, has occurred prior to the onslaught of the demons. James's trip to Denmark and Norway (away from "Mother" England and his "children" there), resembles these other separations. The return of the husband or eventual reuniting of husband and wife is an emblem for the reinscription of God the Father on the wilderness or demonized space, or on the woman who had gone into the wilderness without her man. Many critics have noted that Indian captivity narratives were written to reassert Puritan authority against both inner and outer stresses of the late 1600s, but clearly this "return of the father" trope was also a motif borrowed from these providence tale precursors. What we see in the Indian captivity narratives' missing and then returning husbands has a broader meaning than the reassertion of Puritan authority in New England. This motif also serves as a mechanism of God's regaining control over an assortment of "devils," including Indians, Papists, and sinful Puritans,[7] who represent the denial of God's existence threatened by the onset of the Enlightenment.

Authority in the anonymous *Newes From Scotland* asserts itself most forcibly by punishing witches. The pamphlet's penultimate paragraph concerns the death by strangulation and fire of Doctor Fian, and the imprisonment of the other witches. King James judges the case himself, and his judgment gains divine sanction in the last paragraph, which states that over him preside God and his providence: "Truly, the whole scope of this treatise dooth so plainely laie open the wonderful providence of the Almightie, that if he [King James] had not been defended by his omnipotence and power, His Highness had never returned alive in his voiage from Denmarke" (29).

Glanvill's version of the story says nothing about the fate of Fian, Simpson, or any of the other witches. On occasion he seems to praise Simpson outright, and usually presents her in a mixed light. He tells of her "taking the sicke par-ties pains and sicknesse upon her self for a time, and then translating it to a third person" and of her use of "long scriptural Prayers and Rhymes, contain-ing the main points of Christianity, so that she may seem to have been not so much a white witch as an holy Woman" (471). Glanvill and More do not bother to describe Simpson's fate. Instead they assert that her story, along with all the other relations, has successfully revealed the "weak, sorry and sophistical" (474) quality of the arguments of Glanvill's critics, "Webster, Wagstaffe, and the Au-thor of the *Doctrine of the Devils.*" The witches, then, have become the allies of Glanvill and More in their attempt to undermine the skeptics and atheists. More makes this quite clear in another section of the theoretical apparatus he adds near the beginning of the 1681 edition of *Saducismus Triumphatus*, entitled *Dr. H. M. his Letter With the Postscript to Mr. J. G. Minding him of the great Expe-dience and Usefulness of his new intended Edition of the Daemon of Tedworth, and briefly representing to him the marvelous weakness and gullery of Mr. Webster's "Display of Witchcraft"* (16), where More says,

> And forasmuch as such course-grain'd Philosophers as those Hobbians and Spino-zoans, and the rest of that Rabble, slight Religion and the Scriptures, because there is such express mention of Spirits and Angels in them, things that their dull Souls are so inclinable to conceit to be impossible; I look upon it as a special piece of Providence that there are ever and anon such fresh Examples of Apparitions and Witchcrafts as may rub up and awaken their benummed and lethargick Minds into a suspicion at least, if not assurance, that there are other intelligent Beings besides those that are clad in heavy Earth or Clay. In this, I say, methinks the Divine Provi-dence does plainly outwit the Powers of the dark Kingdom, in permitting wicked men and women, and vagrant Spirits of the Kingdom, to make Leagues or Cove-nants one with another, the Confession of Witches against their own Lives being so palpable an Evidence (besides the miraculous feats they play) that there are bad spirits, which will necessarily open a Door to the belief that there are good ones, and lastly, that there is a God. (26)

That witches exist, then, pleases More because they trouble atheists who are "very horribly afraid there should be any Spirit, lest there should be a Devil, and an account after this life; and therefore they are impatient of any thing that im-plies it that they may with a more full swing, and withall security from an after-reckoning, indulge their own lusts and Humours in this" (23).

Questions about punishing the drummer or demon of Tedworth occur only briefly in that first and most famous of Glanvill's tales. In this story, M. John Mompesson, visiting the neighboring village of Ludgarshal, hears the beating of a drum and asks the bailiff what it means. The bailiff tells Mompesson that the sound is coming from an "idle" drummer who has been troubling them for "some days" by demanding money "of the constable by vertue of a pretend pass, which he thought was counterfeit" (321). Mompesson checks the signatures on the pass, and knowing the signatories, sees they are forgeries. He has the drummer's drum confiscated and declares the bailiff should bring him before a judge. The drummer asks for his drum, but Mompesson says he'll get it back only if he finds out he really was employed by the man he claimed had signed his pass. Mompesson leaves; the constable soon lets the drummer go.

One month later, as Mompesson prepares to journey to London, the drum arrives at his home in Tedworth, sent by the bailiff. While he is away, invisible spirits afflict his wife, children, servants, dogs, and possessions. These afflictions are accompanied by much "thumping and drumming" from unknown sources. After Mompesson returns, these varied afflictions, described in careful detail, continue for two years. Finally the drummer is tried and imprisoned for stealing, and after some remarks he makes in jail, he is "try'd for a Witch at Sarum" (333). He is then "condemned to Transportation, and accordingly sent away [to the colonies]: but I know not how ('tis said by raising storms, and affrighting the Seamen) he made a shift to come back again" (333). In a seventeen-page story, Glanvill writes three paragraphs about this wizard's sentences, from which he always escapes. Glanvill uses none of the melodramatic language to describe the drummer's punishments that characterizes the descriptions of punishments in *Newes from Scotland, Malleus Maleficarum*, and *Daemonologie*. This alliance with the demons must have further facilitated Glanvill's ability to write about them clearly and to shed such inhibitions about "disclosing" their workings as James evinced in *Daemonologie*.

More devotes this 1681 and the subsequent 1682 edition of *Saducismus Triumphatus* to the battle against the Sadducees. He attaches an extensive theoretical apparatus to the "Tedworth" tale, in order to confirm the irreproachable probity, moral worth, and innocence of his witnesses. In his "Account of the Second Edition," at the beginning of the 1682 version, he confesses to several errors in the 1681 *Saducismus Triumphatus*, and then shows how these errors (not made by him but by an untrustworthy witness) in no way alter the truth of the case. Glanvill himself already had written similar confessions in the Tedworth tale itself. After relating in close detail what he learned about the case from Mompesson and his neighbors, Glanvill digresses to describe the results of his own investigation of the house and its demon. "About this time," he relates of a time more than a year after the beginning of the incident, "I went to the House on purpose to inquire the truth of those passages of which there was so loud report" (328). On the first night he stays in the house he hears and sees effects produced by what he believes must be a demon in the bedroom of two of Mompesson's children. Glanvill describes the sounds and motions made by the demon and his attempts to discover their origin. After two pages devoted to the scene, he says that he did not include it in earlier versions of the story "because it depended upon my single Testimony [even though Mompesson and another gentleman were in the room with him], and might be subject to more Evasions than the others I related; but having told it to divers learned and inquisitive Men, who thought it not altogether inconsiderable, I have now added it here. . . . There were other passages at my being at Tedworth, which I published not because they were not such plain and unexceptionable Proofs. I shall now briefly mention them" (330). Just as More finds a way to minimize some previously published false testimony, Glanvill introduces some questionable testimony by first acknowledging its weakness.

More finds other ways to support the tale's and his own credibility. To discredit John Webster, he retells the story from Webster's *Displaying of Supposed Witchcraft* about the apparition of the murdered Anne Walker, which even the skeptical Webster believed. In this retelling of Webster's story, More inserts a letter he received from one of the witnesses, and then adds a commentary in which he highlights specific points where the eyewitness's account and Webster's differ, always showing how the former makes far more sense (and thus that Webster couldn't make sense even when he told the "truth"). Regarding "Tedworth" itself, More inserts a letter from Mompesson to Glanvill into the preface of part 2 of the 1681 *Saducismus Triumphatus*, in which Mompesson denies having confessed to lying about the case. He adds another letter by Mompesson to a Mr. James Collins, "Concerning the Attestation of [Mr. M] and others upon Oath at the Assizes" (263). Then, after the "Proofs from Scripture," which follow this preface in part 2, More also extends the actual retelling of the Tedworth tale with one of his "Advertisements."

More writes of these "Advertisements" that their purpose is to discover "whatever flaw might seem to occur in any of the Narratives" and offer "satisfaction touching the same" (11). In other words, they are used to discuss issues of credibility. Since they appear directly after each narrative, they become integral parts of the tales they comment on. More's apparatus makes current scientific theory, particularly the need for thoroughly corroborated evidence, part of the narratives themselves. This apparatus, with its repetitive assertions of the truth of the tales, constitutes a "modern" version of the older theological theory about the existence of spirits. It also attaches itself more seamlessly to the narratives than the abstract and philosophical Neoplatonic theory of More and Cudworth and the other Cambridge Platonists.

This does not mean, however, that More abandoned the theory he had formerly used. He did add to *Saducismus Triumphatus* the section from *Enchiridion Metaphysicum* called "The Easie, True, and Genuine Notion and Consistent Explication of the Nature of a Spirit"—a Neoplatonic description and defense of the spirit world and its operations on earth against "Nullibists" and "Holenmerians," or Cartesians and Hobbesians. He also included the "Proof of Witches by Holy Scripture," in which he attempts to prove that the witchcraft stories in the Bible, especially that concerning the Witch of Endor, are true. Once again, he juxtaposes commentaries with narratives to emphasize the truth of his sensational evidence. For the same reasons, after his letter to Glanvill at the beginning of the 1681 edition, he directly debates Webster's attack on the reality of the ghost in the "Witch of Endor" tale in his own "Postscript" to the 1681 edition's letter. In a 1682 edition he added another theoretical section, "An Answer to a Letter of a Learned Psychopyrist," along with "A Continuation of the Collection" (six relations). Other relations from other writers had also been added in 1681. More employed all the weapons he could in his attempt to convince: arguments from the church fathers and Neoplatonism, as well as storytelling, but he recognized that the latter worked best for his purposes.

In his 1682 "Account of the Second Edition of *Saducismus Triumphatus*," More says this about his theoretical insertions: "The style of this Answer [to the psychopyrist's letter mentioned above] I must confess, may haply make it to some Readers the less grateful, but the letter it self being in such a Scholastick Style, it was natural for me to follow it in my Answer" (9).

This comment regarding style evokes Glanvill's stylistic changes in his later editions of *Vanity of Dogmatizing*.[8] More too concluded that his theoretical discourse sounded awkward and had a limited audience. He adds in his opening "Account" that he has included "six remarkable true stories, all of them fresh enough, but some of them of things happening within these two or three years, so that they that are diffident and curious may satisfie themselves upon the spot, of the truth of relations of Fact, by sufficient witnesses." He also has been sure to "retain the Scotch Dialect . . . for the more Authentickness of the matter" (473). In this search for a simple and concise style, he is following Bacon, who wrote in *The Great Instauration*, "It is a part of my design to set everything forth, as far as may be, plainly and perspicuously (for nakedness of the mind is still, as nakedness of the body once was, the companion of innocence and simplicity)" (439). In his letter to Glanvill, More further illustrates his recognition of the power of storytelling:

> And I knew by long experience, that nothing rouzes them so out of that dull Lethargy of Atheism and Saducism as Narrations of this kind. For they being of a thick and gross spirit, the most subtile and solid deductions of reason does little

execution upon them; but this sort of sensible Experiments cuts them and stings them very sore, and so startles them, that by a less considerable story by far than that of the Drummer of Tedworth or of Anne Walker, a Doctor of Physick cry'd out presently, "If this be true, I have been in a wrong Box all this time, and must begin my account anew." (23)

Stylistic simplicity helped create leaner, more powerful, and more believable narratives. Glanvill found other ways to dramatize theory in "Tedworth." Describing some prodigies, he writes

And after this, the old Gentlewoman's Bible was found in the Ashes, the Paper side being downwards. Mr. Mompesson took it up, and observed, that it lay open at the third Chapter of St. Mark, where there is mention of the unclean Spirits falling down before our Saviour, and of his giving power to the Twelve to cast out Devils, and of the Scribes Opinion, that he cast them out through Beelzebub. The next night they strewed Ashes over the Chamber, to see what impressions it would leave. In the morning they found in one place the resemblance of a Great Claw, in another of a lesser, some letters in another, which they could make nothing of, besides many Circles and Scratches in the Ashes. (328)

This miraculous and portentous appearance echoes other miraculous appearances of such things as food and scriptural passages in sea deliverance tales and in Indian captivity narratives. It also resembles scriptural debate, that method of dramatizing theory already mentioned found in texts by Laud, Harsnett, and John Williams and in George Sinclair's signature piece "The Devil of Glenluce." Sinclair's 1685 collection of witchcraft tales was an attempt at a briefer, simpler, more readable version of *Saducismus Triumphatus*, which Sinclair greatly admired. Sinclair had first published "Glenluce" in a 1672 scientific work on mathematics and engineering, *Hydrostatix*. Glanvill and More had in turn included a version of the story in *Saducismus Triumphatus*.

Briefly, "Glenluce" is another story of a haunted house and family, like "Tedworth"; here, though, the curse comes from a beggar who had been refused alms by Gilbert Campbell, a weaver. Campbell's trade and family are then upset by an invisible goblin. This demon throws stones at them, keeps them from sleeping, and turns their house and their possessions topsy-turvy. The demon's tricks with their food and Campbell's tools nearly bring the family to starvation. The family is broken apart because Campbell, thinking that the demon might be after just one of his children, sends them away to stay elsewhere. Things only get worse. The house is set on fire, and the family suffers other crises, such as "the throwing of Piets, the pulling down of Turff and Feal from the Roof, and Walls of the house, and the stealing of the Clothes, and the Pricking of their Flesh, and Skin with Pins" (80).

Eventually the observers hear a voice and speak with the demon. The devil announces that he and his father will "come and fetch you [the observers] to Hell, with Warlock Thieves." He then says he will only speak with the minister in charge: "And so the Devil discharged the Gentleman to speak any thing, saying, let him speak that hath a Commission . . . for he is the servant of God. The Gentleman returning back with the Minister, sat down near the place, whence the voice seemed to come, and he opening his mouth spake to them, after this manner":

> "The Lord will rebuke this Spirit in his own time and cast it out." The Devil answering said, "It is written in the 9th of Mark, the Disciples could not cast him out." The Minister replyed, "What the Disciples could not do, yet the Lord having hightened the Parents Faith, for his own glory did cast him out, and shall he thee." The Devil replyed, "It is written in the 4th of Luke, and he departed and left him for a season." The Minister said "the Lord in the dayes of his Humiliation, not only got the victory over Satan, in that assault in the wilderness, but when he came again, his success was no better, for it is written, John 14, Behold the Prince of the World Cometh, and hath nothing in me, and being now in glory, he will fulfill his promise, and God shall bruise Satan under your feet shortly, Rom. 16." (84–85)

The demon then relates the parable of the twelve virgins, and after a few more volleys says

> "Sir, you should have cited for that place of Scripture, the 13 chapter of Zech.," and so he began at the first verse, and repeated several verses, and concluded with these words, "In that day I will cause the Prophet, and the unclean Spirit, pass out of the land, but afterwards it is written, I will smite the Shepherd, and the Sheep shal be scattered." The Minister answered and said, "Well are we that our blessed Shepherd was smitten, and thereby hath bruised thy head, and albeit in the hour of his suffering his Disciples forsook him Matth. 26, Yet now having ascended on high he sits in glory, and is preserving, gathering in, and turning his head upon his little ones, and will save his poor ones in this Family from thy malice." (86)

A readership immersed in Scripture would probably have been thoroughly entertained by this interchange in which theology and narrative drama are so woven together into the advancing plot.

Glanvill and More demonstrate a more pronounced self-consciousness about storytelling than either King James or Mary Rowlandson. In both the preface to part 1 of *Saducismus Triumphatus*, written in 1668, and the preface to part 2, published in 1681, Glanvill illustrates his embarrassment when he explains his reasons for writing and publishing his tales. In part 1 he explains,

> I have no humour nor delight in telling stories, and do not publish these for the gratification of those that have; but I record them as Arguments for the Confirmation of a Truth which hath indeed been attested by multitudes of the like Evidence in all places and times. But things remote, or long past, are either not believed, or forgotten: whereas these being fresh and near, and attended with all circumstance of credibility, it may be expected they should have the more success upon the obstinacy of unbelievers. (63–64)

Then in part 2 he explains,

> I know it is a matter of very little Credit to be a Relator of Stories, and I of all men living, have the least reason to be fond of the Imployment. For I never had any facility in telling of a story, and have always had a particular indisposition and backwardness to the writing any such. But of all Relations of Fact, there are none like to give a Man such trouble and disreputation, as those that relate to Witchcraft and Apparitions, which so great a part of Men (in this age especially) do so railly and laugh at, and without more ado, are resolved to explode and despise, as meer Winters Tales and Old Wives Fables. (257)

Glanvill's membership in the Royal Society and his position as an Anglican minister would of themselves have accounted for his reluctance to tell sensational witchcraft stories, but his embarrassment also had a more literary side. It invokes the convention, going back to *Malleus Maleficarum*, of the self-conscious, trustworthy, and objective narrator, and it thus identifies Glanvill structurally with that conventional figure. In a more immediate, psychological way, his embarrassment also induced readers to trust him, to see him as someone without self-interested biases.

Narrative self-consciousness, then, was another stylistic device that signaled Baconian simplicity. It served a scientific purpose, and Glanvill and More were especially dedicated adepts at employing it. The different ways in which More, in 1681, and Sinclair, in 1685, treated the ending of Sinclair's "Devil of Glenluce" also illustrate Glanvill's and More's emphasis on this stylistic simplicity. More included a version of "Glenluce" in the 1682 *Saducismus Triumphatus* because of its simplicity, especially its abrupt ending. Sinclair, seeking a wider audience in 1685, explicitly notes that he added a neat conclusion to the ending. He reintroduced the story in his 1685 work, in part because in his new version it "ends not so abruptly, as the other did" (76). For More, the same story's value lay in the fact that its "narration is so simple and plain, and without design . . . not to add that the very abruptness of its ending shews it to be fresh writ, while the thing was doing, and that meer Matter of Fact was the measure of the Writer's Pen" (497). More also praises the tale for its moral ambiguity. That neither the forces of good nor those of evil emerge as clear winners is a sign of the tale's frankness for More.

Glanvill employed Baconian methodology in other ways to advance the credibility of his tales. The Agnes Simpson tale in some ways did not suit these methods and was therefore put last, for two specific reasons. The first was because it was a Scottish relation and therefore could not be readily corroborated by an English readership. The second reason was that it was an old story among primarily contemporary stories, which were more easily proven. More used the story, because it involved a former king and because it was "a true Copy of Record so Authentick, [which describes] effects, kinds or Circumstances of Witchcraft [that had not occurred] in the foregoing series."

Glanvill's version of the Simpson story does make his adherence to Bacon's ideas apparent, despite the tale's age and locale. Unlike the author of *Newes from Scotland*, Glanvill does not attempt to construct an emotional, melodramatic narrative. He selects "small shreds out of this ancient record" and adds a concluding paragraph drawn from the actual confessions of Simpson to King James. The information about Simpson reads more like an inventory of curious facts than like an exposé of sins. Glanvill informs us that the devil appeared to John Fiene (Fian) in *white* rayment, rather than black, and that, when the devil preached "in a kirk in the Pulpit in the night by candle light, the Candle [was] burning *blue* [my italics]." These details, following Bacon's regimens, seem disconnected and almost irrelevant. This too was in keeping with Bacon's belief that to discover truth one had to record every detail concerning one's subject, even those that didn't directly support one's own ideas. The resulting axioms and laws would be deeper and more truthful than laws with which people had become familiar. In his selection of pertinent details, Glanvill follows Bacon's anti-Aristotelian method, refusing to choose only facts that fit his own theorems. He thereby joins with Bacon's complaint about the scholastics that "though there be many things in nature which are singular and unmatched, yet it [this faulty reasoning] devise for them parallels and conjugates and relatives which do not exist" (470).

We can trace Bacon's influence in Glanvill's own theorizing in his first published work, *The Vanity of Dogmatizing*, where he writes, "It was the duty of every man to suspend his full and resolved assent to the doctrines he had been taught till he had impartially considered and examined them for himself" (qtd.

in Lecky, 133). Glanvill follows Bacon's admonitions in the *Great Instauration* sixty years earlier, where Bacon calls for "collecting and perfecting of a Natural and Experimental History, so philosophy and science may rest on the solid foundation of experiences of every kind (not on air) and the same well examined and weighed" (427). Bacon complains that "there is none who has dwelt upon experience and the facts of nature as long as is necessary." Glanvill's and More's continual piling up of detail is clearly an attempt to use scientific methods to prove the existence of spirits.

Glanvill enriches his mix of supernatural occurrences and physical details with legalistic facts. He tells the reader that "in a Conventicle of Witches, whose Names are specified in the Record, he [Fiene] with the rest, at parting, kissed the devil's Breech; the Record speaks more broadly" (470). He inserts the record and the names in question two pages later, unlike in *Newes from Scotland* or Sinclair's version of the tale. Glanvill collects all the facts, not just that the participants kissed the devil's rear end, but their names as well. Unlike the earlier pamphlet, he omits physical descriptions of the breech kissing by referring interested readers to another source. Glanvill wanted to engage the senses too, but he had more of the scientist in him than the entertainer.

Glanvill's Baconian fact collecting in the occult world corresponds with accounts of prodigies in the New World from natural historians such as Thomas Hariot and writers of Indian captivity narratives such as John Gyles.[9] Glanvill calls the psychic world a "New Frontier, a kinde of America"; in two non-witchcraft providence tales by other authors which both take place in the New World, the scientific and the sensational aspects of this vivid, detailed new gothic realism can also be seen.

Samuel Clarke, in *A Mirrour or Looking Glass for Saints and Sinners*, describes in great detail the story of eight men accidentally left behind one winter in Greenland by an English fleet on a whaling and discovery voyage in 1630. The story, Clarke says, was first written by one of the stranded men, the gunner's mate, Edward Pelham. Clarke vividly portrays the bleak hopelessness of their situation, and then describes their attempts to survive:

> They resolved to build another smaller tent within that (a larger one where previous Coopers worked and lodged while making Casks for putting up Traine-Oyle) for their habitation; and accordingly taking down a lesser Tent that stood near to it, wherein the land men lay whilst they made their Oyl, they fetched their materials from thence, both boards, Posts, and rafters, and from the Chimnies of the Furnaces they took a thousand Bricks; they found also four Hogsheads of lime, which mingled with sand from the shoar, made good mortar. (2:513)

In the following passage, he tells another story of being stranded. Clarke found this tale in Johann Mandelsloe's *Voyages and Travels* and added to it information from someone who knew the man the story is about. Clarke tells how the stranded man stayed alive in the freezing cold: "He put out a little stick at the crevice of his hut, and backing it with a little Sea Dogs' Fat, by that means he got some Sea Mews, which he took with his hand from under the snow, and so kept himself from Starving" (2:620).

The closely detailed, plain prose here is what Marjorie Nicolsen might have meant when she describes More's "homely details" as introducing a "new realism." These details are further examples of an application of Baconian methodology. Clarke's sea mews illustrate the timely food trope found in so many captivity narratives and sea deliverances. This trope also appears in other remarkable deliverances, such as Clarke's story of Mrs. Teate's escape from Irish "savages." Miraculous appearances of scriptural passages also resemble the providential arrival of food. In many captivity narratives and other providence tales, such as "The Tedworth Demon," the Bible opens to relevant passages of Scripture in time to calm the doubts of sorely afflicted protagonists. Scenes of the discovery of food and Scripture, both of which help save afflicted people, combine scientific and religious motifs in their closely detailed prose, the intrusion of supernatural prodigies into those carefully delineated worlds, and their allusions to biblical types.

The Edward Gibbon story, another popular scientific tale of horror, appears in many collections, including Janeway's 1674 *Legacy to his Friends, Containing Twenty Seven Famous Instances of God's Providence in and about Sea Dangers and Deliverances* and Increase Mather's *Essay for the Recording of Illustrious Providences.* Janeway, much more than Increase Mather, adds scriptural passages to his narrative and locates it within a theological context. A preface to Janeway's book, written by John Ryther, maintains that Janeway "stooped lower" in relating these stories than he had in his previous works. Thus we see the self-conscious narrator again, in a providence tale of disaster and deliverance at sea. Credibility is insisted upon at the beginning of the story when Janeway assures us that Gibbon was "well-known in New England, . . . a Gentleman of good education, good parts, and of good conversation." Gibbon's ship, on a trading voyage off the New England coast, sinks, and only twelve of the crew manage to get aboard the lifeboat. Soon food runs out. Facing starvation, they cast lots to determine whom they will eat first. Three times on the verge of murdering the first victim, they are saved; once a giant fish jumps into their boat, "which no question made them quick Cooks"; a second time they catch a bird with their bare hands; and finally they are saved by a French pirate whom Gibbon had once helped in Boston Harbor. The crew's remarkable deliverance from death and the overhanging threat of cannibalism are gothic elements which were so often set in matrixes of empirical truth in these providence tales.

Different versions of the Gibbon tale also illustrate how writers became more oriented toward straightforward narration. Increase Mather rewrote Janeway's tale by deleting his melodramatic language and most of his biblical citations and digressions. In varying proportions, melodrama and empirical analysis did combine in the new realism of these scientific providence tales. The joining of such disparate discourses put enough pressure on the structure created in *Malleus Maleficarum* to produce significant transformations in key elements and figures in these providence tales.

THE CONFIDENCE MAN AS PROTAGONIST

Stories of discovery, of the new or of the occult world, made good providence tales because they combined sensational with scientific elements. Both forms dealt in prodigies, with new facts that went beyond the known limits of natural philosophy and natural history. Occult tales required scientifically sound, well-corroborated evidence to be credible. Discovery tales could not have been written without such technological advances as the astrolabe and magnetic needle, gunpowder, and the printing press. Explorers and their sponsors also needed convincing reports of their discoveries to finance future voyages and colonization efforts.

George Sinclair's *Satan's Invisible World Discovered* joins sensationalism to science in other ways. Sinclair was a "Master, Regent, and Professor of Philosophy in the College of Glasgow from 1654 to 1666." He lost that post, "for refusing to take an oath of allegiance or to accept the legally established Episcopalian form of church government" (Sinclair vii). He also "held a mathematical position, in the University of Edinburgh." Coleman Parsons, in his introduction to Sinclair's work, says that "during his uprooted life, he was a freelance expert on mining and mineral deposits, a scientific experimenter, and a deviser of projects. He superintended the laying of the water pipes in Edinburgh and was apparently employed by the owners of coal and salt mines in the Lothians and elsewhere" (vii). Sinclair also sought to prove the existence of God against denials from various Sadducean elements. As he rewrote many of Glanvill's stories, he eliminated Glanvill's more scientific, less sensationalistic details. Some of his relations lack strong narrative structures, but he succeeded in writing a book with widespread appeal.

Sinclair's synthesis of sensationalism with science shows in his dedication to George, Earl of Winton, Lord Seton and Tranent, a member of the king's privy council. After outlining the Winton family's many great exploits, he writes of the current earl that,

> By Your transcendent Skill, you have discovered an Invisible World . . . I mean your Subterranean World. . . . What running of Mines and Levels? What piercing of Gaes? What cutting of impregnable Rocks, with more difficultie than Hannibal cutted the Alps. . . . What Deep-Pits, and Air holes are digged! What diligence to prevent Damps. . . . What floods of Water run thorow the Labyrinths, for several miles, by a free Level, as if they were conducted by a Guide! . . . What curious Mechanical Engines has your Lordship, like another Archimedes, contrived for your Coal works, and for draining of Coal sinks. . . . Your Experimental Skill in improving your Coal, for making of Salt, is praise worthie. . . . Your renting of Rocks for clearing of Passages into your Harbours . . . is stupendious. (xii, xiii)

A concern with science, exploration, and the prodigious come together in Sinclair's paean. These remarks also share with apparition, discovery, and Indian captivity narratives a fascination with the hidden, the unknown, or the invisible. The always present focus on credibility, added to this interest in mystery and invisibility, creates an apt context for the important and at times central role played in these tales by con artists, magicians, and a variety of other masters of the occult. By definition, these characters did their jobs in hidden, invisible ways. Such masters of persuasion were obvious figures of fascination in discourses featuring the debate about versions of the "Truth" that had raged inconclusively for decades. A sense that Enlightenment culture was gaining ascendancy in seventeenth-century England made figures able to persuade people to believe in the supernatural seem unusually gifted.[10] The figure of the impostor or of the con artist also becomes important in Indian captivity narratives such as Quentin Stockwell's and John Williams's. It lurks suggestively in the background of Mary Rowlandson's and Hannah Dustan's tales. Cotton Mather seems at times like a carnival barker or impresario as he presents his providence tales in *Magnalia Christi Americana*. Although I can only briefly mention these later connections here, the confidence man also occupies important places in the work of such writers as Charles Brockden Brown, James Fenimore Cooper, Edgar Allan Poe, Nathaniel Hawthorne, and Herman Melville.[11]

The story of the notorious Magdalena Crucia, included in many providence tale collections, concerns an abbess considered an ideal of purity for over thirty years in Cordoba, Spain. She finally confesses to having carried on a sexual relationship with the devil, "in the shape of an Aethiopian," throughout that period. Much of her story involves descriptions of how she and the devil tricked people into imagining her to be in one place performing her religious duties when she was in fact consorting with her lover, the devil. According to both Richard Baxter and Henry More, the very year the devil first seduced her, she had gone as a twelve-year-old penitent to see Pope Paul III. She was considered a saint, yet Baxter compares her to "Mrs. Hutchinson and Mrs. Dyer in New England during the time of Henry Vane's government" (102), calling her a "concubitis of the Devil's." She had extraordinary powers, knew of things happening far away from her, had wafers transported to her through the air, and could make her hair grow to cover and hide her completely. Another servant to the devil, Baxter says, took her place while she was with him. After being imprisoned, she still managed to appear in chapel at prayers. The repetition of her story, in Baxter, Wier, Bodin, Casaubon, More, Turner, and others, demonstrates the fascination people had with the devil's and his consorts' powers to deceive. Baxter says Bodin writes that her story was famous throughout the world. There are warnings about the devil's temptations implicit in such tales, of course, but also a distinct sense of awe and admiration for such powers and skills as those Crucia developed.

Other relations show the same high esteem for powers which in *Malleus Maleficarum* would have been seen as diabolical. Even in *Malleus Maleficarum*, though, Sprenger and Kramer's story of the cursed count praises the count's ability to deceive the witch into revealing the hiding place of her diabolical posset. Francis Bacon seems to have had a large influence in encouraging increased respect for deceptive powers. In his *New Atlantis*, one of the chief roles of the wise men in the House of Solomon is to judge the veracity of alleged miracles. These wise men practice feats of magic and jugglery to learn how such creators of false miracles work. Surely some of these wise men, seeking even more knowledge, would have attempted actual feats of magic on human subjects; sound scientific method would have required it. As early as Bacon's time, the demonic arts had become another tool useful in the search for new scientific truths.

Such detailed interest in the devil and his tricks went back at least as far as the treatise on witchcraft by one of Wier's influences, Henry Cornelius Agrippa. This interest expressed itself in seventeenth-century narratives in many ways. Glanvill's relation of the witchcraft and trial of Julian Cox compares the devil's powers of deception to those of a painter. Birds fly into canvases because of some artists' abilities to create realistic representations of reality, Glanvill notes. In the Cox story, a huntsman and his dogs chase Cox, thinking she is a hare. When they finally corner this "hare," they find instead old Julian Cox, groveling naked, "globes upward" on the ground (388). More and Glanvill's commentary explains the huntsman and the dogs' mistake as having been caused by the devil, who interposed, they say, a scene of the hare running, a painting in effect, between Cox and the huntsman. Cox was on trial for having cursed and then stuck full of pins a young maid who refused her alms. She herself has the ability to create illusions. She makes toads appear suddenly between her own legs and the legs of people she curses. When these toads are thrown into fires, these persistent emblems of lust prove impervious to the flames. Glanvill and More compare Cox's deceptive talents to the skills of fire eaters.

I have already mentioned the ability of the drummer in "The Drummer of Tedworth" to escape twice from the law, as well as his attempts at forgery. Another feat of deception with demonical overtones that continually appears and fascinates witnesses is ventriloquism. Demons constantly speak, but the source of their words can never be found, as is the case in Sinclair's "Glenluce" story. Some other interesting narrative uses of the con man / magician trope come at the end of both "Glenluce" and "Tedworth." Both these tales end ambiguously, without anything like a victory for the forces of good. The only relief for the victims of witchcraft comes through the efforts and charms of other conjurers. The weaver Campbell, in the "Glenluce" tale, does get back his "peaceable habitation," but only through "some conjurations or other." Sinclair closes by adding, "The Weaver has been a very Odd man, that endured so long these marvelous disturbances" (92–94), as if Campbell himself were somehow involved with the infernal world. This suggestion is enhanced by the appellation "odd." Glanvill also uses it at the end of "Tedworth" about one "like a Wizard," an "odd fellow." This odd fellow convinces one of Glanvill's most trustworthy sources of information, Robert Hill, that he was able to conjure the image of Hill's wife in a looking glass. This wizard, a physician named Compton, had told Hill that the whole problem at Mompesson's had been caused by but a "Rendezvous of Witches," which he could get rid of for a mere one hundred pounds. Glanvill never says whether anyone ever employed him, but he does say Hill believed he had seen his wife in Compton's glass, and that Compton did successfully discover another witch, Elizabeth Styles, whose story comprises the third relation in *Saducismus Triumphatus*. This wizard is also compared to another "odd" person, another wizard who Glanvill says had taught the drummer in the "Tedworth" tale all he knew about the infernal arts.

These examples show the fascination the conjuring arts had for those either using or investigating them. Though the *OED* lists no definition of *odd* which refers specifically to the infernal or demonic, the word does have both negative and positive definitions which, in contexts such as those above, could be construed as applying to the occult. These include, on the positive side, "singular in value, worth, merit or eminence; unique, remarkable"; while, more negatively, "not even . . . uneven; . . . extraordinary, strange . . . [and] strange in behaviour or appearance, peculiar; eccentric." The word itself, like the person it referred to, could mean both one thing and its opposite.

Another tale told both by Glanvill and Sinclair also illustrates this use of the confidence man in seventeenth-century providence tales. Glanvill's Relation 28 describes the "Confessions of certain Scotch Witches, taken out of an Authentick Copy of their Trial at the Assize held at Paisely in Scotland, February 15, 1678" (463), touching the bewitching of Sir George Maxwell. This case of murder by wax and clay effigy was motivated by a variety of arguments involving class differences, sexual harassment and jealousy, land disputes, and family rivalries. The testimony relies on the confession of the fourteen-year-old daughter of Jannet Mathie, one of the principal witches. Sinclair's Relation 1, also of this case, opens with a letter to Sinclair from a son of the victim, John Maxwell, which adds new information from an informant, who was not one of the accused witches. George Maxwell falls sick, and his physician is unable to cure him. Then Sinclair writes that "there had come to Pollock town a young dumb Girle, but from whence was not known." This is Jennet Dowglass, who soon befriends Maxwell's daughters and then "signified unto them, that there was a woman, whose son had broke his fruit yeard, that did prick him in the sides" (3). Dowglass accuses Jennet Mathie, "relict of John Stewart, under Miller in Schaw-Mill."

"At first they hardly understood her," Sinclair writes, shrouding Dowglass deeper in mystery. She finally acts out her meaning with beeswax. Accompanied by two servants of Maxwell's, she goes to Mathie's house to reveal the effigy. This little girl, the servants on either side of her, "putteth her hand in the boll behind the fire, and then flings into Andrew Martine, beneath his cloak the Waxen effigy" (18). The description of finding the effigy happens so quickly and is described so sketchily as to constitute a kind of narrative sleight-of-hand in itself.

The next day Mathie is arrested. She claims Dowglass had planted the effigy there herself (the ambiguous construction of the description of Dowglass's "discovery" does little to disprove this claim). Maxwell improves slightly, but then relapses. Dowglass then reveals the existence of another effigy, at the house of Jennet Mathie's son, John Stewart. From this point on a variety of confessions are extracted, and eventually Sinclair tells us several witches are burned to death, "and their effigies with them." But Dowglass remains a curiously enigmatic figure throughout, somehow supernatural and tinged with evil: "It is to be noted, the dumb Girle, whose name was Jennet Dowglass, doth now speak, not very distinctly, yet so as she may be understood, and is a Person that most wonderfully discovers things past, and doth also understand the Latin Tongue, which she never learned" (18).

In this story, signs of complicity with Satan in earlier works such as *Malleus Maleficarum* and *Daemonologie* become notable skills of a young, mysterious girl whose role in the narrative has decidedly been that of an agent of God. Her silences and ambiguous moral state are echoed in Indian captivity narrative figures such as Mary Rowlandson, Hannah Dustan, and Eunice Williams. Where earlier witchcraft literature had placed anything associated with the demonic, supernatural world clearly against the good, and where conjuration by itself could be a capital offense, Sinclair's Jennet Dowglass / George Maxwell tale places the supernatural world on the side of God, against those skeptics and materialists, Cartesians, Sadducees, and Hobbesians (Holenmerians) who would deny any but natural, mechanistic, or deceitful causes for all these phenomena.[12]

The con man figures prominently in the trial pamphlets about the witchcraft cases of the late–sixteenth and early–seventeenth centuries as well. These also share many providence tale traits, though they were not written as parts of providence tale collections. Thomas Potts wrote his *Wonderfull Discoverie of Witches in the Countie of Lancaster* to show, "how to judge witches . . . to implore us to punish them vigorously . . . [and to show how] God through his witches shows his power in saving us from them" (156). Like so many narrators of these stories, Potts wrote his reluctantly, only at the command of the judge whose clerk he was. Of himself he said, "It is no part of my profession to publish any thing in print, neither can I paint in extraordinarie termes" (154). This case involved nineteen alleged witches, ten of whom were executed. Twenty years later the testimony against them was proved to have been fabricated by another con man, a poor miller named Edmund Robinson, with the help of his son. The original tale with its updated denouement was rewritten by Webster in his 1677 *Displaying of Supposed Witchcraft*, as one among his large gallery of impostors. These involved figures from several other renowned cases involving con artists who had already been exposed by the time Potts related the case of the Lancashire witches.

Potts's narrative presents a vivid look at English provincial life in Shakespeare's day. It is filled with gothic touches (one character declares, "I will procure them to bee laid where they shall be glad to bite lice in turn with their teeth"), but here I want to point out only two of its features which later appear in the Indian captivity narratives. Part of the testimony against the witch nicknamed "Dembdike" from her son James was that he found scalps, teeth, and clay images in the ground at her home. These scalps and teeth had come from corpses which had been dug up for use in magical possets. A second feature is that Potts's work was not only called for, but it was also edited by the judge, Edward Bromley, who here seems to have taken on a role later occupied by the

Mathers in their editing of the Indian captivity narratives, and taken on earlier by inquisitors such as Kramer and Sprenger.

Two works about a famous trial from 1597 involving alleged dispossessions by the famous exorcist John Darrell illustrate how the theatrical skills of con artists came to fascinate those bent on exposing their shenanigans. Darrell, a minister, became famous as an exorcist at the age of twenty-four, but then had gone without such lucrative work for ten years. After 1596 his fortunes improved. He became renowned for dispossessing Thomas Darling, the Boy of Burton, the seven Starchey children in Lancashire, and William Somers of Nottingham. The Somers case was the most notorious of Darrell's dispossessions. Between a variety of dispossessions and repossessions, confessions of dissembling, and then recantations of those confessions, Somers produced a state of panic, of demonic chaos, in the towns around Nottingham. Eventually he and Darrell were tried and convicted before the high commission at Lambeth. In 1599, the Bishop of London's chief clerk, Samuel Harsnett, narrated the case in *A Discovery of the Fraudulent Practices of John Darrel, Bachelor of Artes, in his Proceedings Concerning the Pretended Possession and dispossession of Wm. Somers at Nottingham [and of several others]* . . . , *detecting in some sort the deceitful trade in these latter Dayes of casting out Devils.* Darrell responded with his own version of the case, *A True Narration of the Strange and Grevous Vexation by the Devil of Seven Persons in Lancashire, and William Somers of Nottingham. Wherein the Doctrine of Possession and Dispossession of Demoniaks out of the Word of God is particularly applyed unto Somers, and the rest of the Persons Controverted* . . . *Together with the use we are to make of these Workes of God.*

Darrell's work displays many of the same literary tropes that appear in all the other providence tales discussed in this chapter. He claims to have been reluctant to publish his stories, but had to because so many had witnessed them. He also describes, echoing this narrative self-consciousness, how he had even been reluctant to take on the dispossession cases for the aggrieved parties' families. Nevertheless, the spiritual call to write providence tales overcame his reluctance. "We are commanded to publish the work of God, whereof any of us be witness," he writes, as if he too had been included in one of Matthew Poole's future providence tale collecting projects.

He also reasserts the positive value of affliction. Somers became repossessed after he had supposedly dispossessed him, Darrell writes, because Satan especially afflicts "they who have been delivered out of the power and possession of Satan" (244). He adds that "he who is the devil's child, and captive unto Satan to day, may be to morrowe the sonne of God, and delivered out of that spirituall bondage" (245). He echoes the idea, so prevalent in captivity narratives, that God likes to test his children's faith and spiritual mettle, so that they will become even stronger adherents.

Darrell's work also alternates sections of narrative with sections of commentary. He applies biblical precedents to the narrative sections of his tale to justify his and Somers's actions. Gothic details and low realism fill his account. One of the Starchey children "did eat greedily, slossinge up [her] meal like a greedy dog or hogge" (175). Somers's foaming at the mouth, blasphemous utterances, swelling up to twice his size, and becoming hard as iron over parts of his body, along with other grotesque and occult activities, receive full and vivid treatment.

What is most striking about Darrell's account is his tremendous interest in and admiration for his and Somers's storytelling and acting abilities. He defends the truth of his stories more than he asserts that God was present in his and Somers's actions, or that Somers actually was possessed by a spirit. Darrell says that if one does not believe him, finally, because so many witnesses had seen what he saw, you "may as well deny or doubt, whether any thing be true that is written in other stories" (188). Insisting on the unfeigned and unpremeditated nature of Somers's acts, Darrell himself displays admiration for what he very much seems to be calling, even as he denies it vehemently elsewhere, Somers's acting ability: "In a word these things [the "sins" of Nottingham Somers acted out including "brawling, quarreling, fighting, swaring, robbing by the high ways, picking and cutting of purses . . . abortions"] were in such lively and orient coloure painted out . . . unto us that were present, being to the number of 60, that I for my part . . . do verily thinke it is not in the skile and power of man to do the like" (188).

On another occasion Somers described his relationship with Darrell in terms of an actor's with his director: "The next morning being Sunday . . . before Church time, M. Darrell came unto me, and told me wherein I had done well over night (for the night before he had plaied his feates very artifically) and wherein I had failed, wishing me to acte my fits more boldly and lively" (Harsnett 17). It is not clear in the first passage whether Darrell is saying Somers had the help of the devil or that he himself was an extraordinary actor; in either case, his talent is certainly being applauded.

Not only does Darrell, God's agent and defender, extol Somers's acting ability; Harsnett too, denouncing the impostor's deception, at times seems to laud it as well. He describes the great panic induced by Darrell and Somers, making the people of Nottingham be "afraid to stir in the night," while the pulpits rang with "spectres of devils and witches." Nevertheless, he seems to grudgingly praise Darrell for being his "crafts maister." Comparing him to a variety of other impostors noted in Reginald Scot's work, he admits that Darrell did produce reverence and fear in the "simpler and loose sort." Harsnett compares Darrell's work to "the Day of Judgement acted on a stage," and likens his skill to those good at "painting . . . Almighty God like an ancient Philosopher, with a grave long beard, and a booke in his hand, that the boyes might have a reverend impression of his father like wisdome" (A3, recto). Finally, in a kind of back-handed compliment, he accuses Darrell of storytelling, and compares him to Homer. Cotton Mather also denounces Homer in *Magnalia Christi Americana* for writing fictions, which are so unlike the truth Mather claims to relate. Harsnett even calls Darrell a better storyteller than those master liars themselves, the Papists. His "jugling mistery of casting out devils [is as] blanched over with as fair a face of good intent to the glorie of God [as] the blessed Budget of all the pope his pedlary and trash . . . [and leads to having] religion like a Homer's Ilias, a fardle of fiction, and a bundle of lies" (A3, recto).

Harsnett, then, also seems quite struck with Darrell's and Somers's play-acting or storytelling powers. In exposing them, which he does quite thoroughly, he not only writes his own manual of vice, as Agrippa was said to have done in the fifteenth century and Wier in the sixteenth in their treatises on witchcraft; he also probes psychologically like a modern novelist in attempting to unmask both Darrell and the so-called possessed Somers. He notes that Darrell claimed to have renounced everything to follow Christ, but in fact he was living off the income from the sale of his father's farm. Harsnett classifies Somers among young scholars seeking openings at seminaries, sick youths seeking to avoid noxious medicines, such as mixtures of "rue, sack, oyl and brimstone," boys trying to get out of school, and "wenches" seeking "to be made much of, to be dandled, and to be idle." Harsnett writes in the manner of a mystery writer, piecing together evidence to create a convincing portrait of collusion between Somers and Darrell over a six-year period prior to 1597.

This sleuthing also results in some of the same Baconian prodigy and evidence collecting, as well as in some of the same bawdy realism evident in so many other works under consideration here. One example, which features Harsnett seeking the source of some strange, supposedly supernatural movements seen beneath Somers's clothing as he lay in bed, illustrates these qualities and also recalls writers such as Baxter sticking their hands into maids' mouths to see if any pins were hidden there: "Catching on a time at that which I saw move the cloathes, I got holde of it, and offering to cast uppe the cloathes, to see what I had in my hand, it slipped from me, and I did then suspect, and do now believe it to be true, that the thing I had holde of was the boyes privie members, and that I offering to pull up the cloathes, he shrinking in his bed, pulled them out of my hand, I not holding fast, because I then suspected so much" (239).

Even those unmasking the impostors, then, seem to have been taken by those impostors' deceptive powers. A junction appears here where science, religion, and the art of make believe come together.

I have attempted in this chapter to portray the development of a new narrative literature, combining scientific precision with dramatic sensationalism. Influenced by reason and the new science, the ministers who wrote these providence tales discovered a variety of techniques for embedding religious ideas into prose narratives convincing enough for an increasingly skeptical and materialistic age. They created, particularly in their apparition stories, a prose form which secularized God and the devil, the former disguised as an innocent, the latter as a deceptive actor or con artist. In the next chapter, I will turn to the New England witchcraft relation, where these apparition tale tropes were transplanted in colonial soil, before returning to the New England Indian captivity narratives, where this disguised God and devil were further reassembled and transformed.

4

Providence Tales in the New World
New England Witchcraft Narratives, 1684–1702

New England witchcraft discourse paralleled its English forebears. And just as critics of the Cambridge Platonists have derided those writers' witchcraft relations and other types of providence tales, so critics of early New England culture have viewed the witchcraft mania and its attendant discourse in very negative lights. John Demos, in his historical study of early New England witchcraft, *Entertaining Satan: Witchcraft and the Culture of Early New England*, illustrates this by quoting Perry Miller's *New England Mind: From Colony to Province*: "The intellectual history of New England can be written as though no such thing [as the witchcraft mania] ever happened. It had no effect on the ecclesiastical or political situation, it does not figure in the institutional or ideological development" (Demos 412n).

Whereas Perry Miller found witchcraft discourse insignificant and anomalous, writers such as Nathaniel Hawthorne and Arthur Miller have expressed the more common negative views of the New England witchcraft trials. In their outlook, the Salem trials and all discourse from them represent the sexist, repressive, and oppressive soul of New England Puritanism.

Current critical discourse continues these traditions. Marc Sargent's "The Witches of Salem, the Angel of Hadley, and the Friends of Philadelphia" (1993) credits a group of Romantic novelists prior to Hawthorne with firmly establishing Salem as this supreme monument to America's evil tendencies. These Romantic writers include Sir Walter Scott (*Peveril of the Peak*, 1847), James Fenimore Cooper (*Wept of the Wish Ton Ton*, 1829), James McHenry (*The Spectre of the Forest*), and James Nelson Baker (*Superstition*). For Sargent, they all use Salem and the trials as a scapegoat, an emblem of immoral, pre-American attributes which persist and periodically erupt in American culture. Their scapegoating, Sargent says, was intended to purge this old-world bigotry from the New England soul. Sargent sees this attitude continuing today; specifically, he writes of the 1992/93 tercentennial of the trials as a "turning [of] the spotlight on the Salem crisis . . . [to] represent the trials as atypical, as a hideous throwback to a pre-American illiberalism and irrationality" (106), something, that is, purely horrible and evil which we've escaped from but still must always guard against since it continues to reemerge.

Though Sargent describes the Salem trials, seen through the work of these Romantics, as atypical of America rather than as a product of essential and formative American cultural traits, he still sees them foremost as an American creation, as, that is, another example of American exceptionalism. He believes Salem remains today the "symbolic capital of witchcraft on the map of European and American history," which has been continuously used by writers and critics as a symbol of Puritan medievalism and European autocracy and superstition, while being rejected over and over as un-American. In pointing out this tradition, Sargent does not explicitly oppose it; yet he does find in Salem a good deal more than examples of European autocracy when he writes that "the darkness of the American woods—the province of witches, regicides and savages—was a rich source for American fiction, a realm of the mysterious and the 'sublime.' American authors could find their national voice by giving the devil his due" (118). Sargent's analysis brings together Indians and witches in the cultural process of finding a national identity, even as he relegates the events at Salem to an abhorrent and aberrational role in that unending national drama. Finding a national voice and proving God existed, then, could be accomplished by writing witchcraft relations. Sargent moves toward such a view, but only paradoxically, and while contradicting himself.

Whereas Sargent's Romantics, and Sargent too, see Salem as an anomaly, a demonic other outside mainstream American culture, yet still highly significant to that culture's identity, other negative views see Salem as more permanently fixed within American culture. Salem and its attendant and ensuing discourse as emblematic of American sexism is the story told in Gabriele Schwab's "Seduced by Witches: Nathaniel Hawthorne's *The Scarlet Letter* in the Context of New England Witchcraft Fictions." For Schwab, the trials "allowed . . . fantasies [of women seduced by the devil] to be acted out collectively. . . . [The] 'witch stereotype' [is] a cultural pattern of interpretation used by New England Puritans against deviant women in general" (171). As for later works, including those by Hawthorne and Arthur Miller ("The Crucible"), rather than undermining this stereotype, they "reinvent it under a fictional guise" and see the witch "as a feared but seductive object of desire." Schwab goes on to explain that "even if the romanticized [or, as in Miller, "hystericized"] witches function, in one way, as a demystification of the historical witches, their aesthetic effect is drawn from the phantasm of this desirable but also threatening witch who, because of her seductive powers, retains an aura of the supernatural, even in a disenchanted world" (179).

For Schwab, the trials and all subsequent discourse about it have served as a deviant and voyeuristic attack on women. She reads in witchcraft texts a form of public pornography legitimized and authorized insofar as finding and exposing signs of witchcraft was a step toward redemption. Even when an Arthur Miller brought what was "unconscious" to the surface, instead of what was merely and quaintly "invisible," for Schwab he was still repeating old repressive and sexist patterns. Schwab does see the immense significance of the concrete, of empirical evidence in these tales. She does recognize the importance in these texts of making the invisible real and visible, of "exposing the invisible to the gaze" (172); she notes that "the gaze as medium of interpretation became a guarantor, albeit an ambivalent one, of a reality that was actually invisible" And she adds that the pattern served "to publicly reaffirm the reality of witchcraft, which had long since become precarious" (173). However, in the end, for her such evidence serves a purely misogynistic, autocratic, and pornographic purpose:

> The public sphere was organized according to an overall cultural attempt to expose the invisible to the gaze. . . . [The accused] performed their symptoms of affliction under the community's gaze, and their ecstatic convulsions, betraying an erotic semantics of the body carried to the brink of insanity, visibly demonstrated the act of witchcraft through encoded gestures of demonic possession. . . . The body became the medium of an interaction enacting a spectacle of seduction. . . . Whatever the alleged witches would say, the community would interpret through a reading of their bodies. (173)

Sargent's and Schwab's articles, though focusing on post-Salem discourse about the trials, reflect a common critical obsession with Salem as a manifestation of negativity, either of America's dark side or its pre-Revolutionary, medieval side. Neither of these critics, as is true with most other critics, views the witchcraft texts as literature, and therefore they make no attempt to analyze in depth the literary characteristics of the Salem texts. Such an analysis, as this chapter will clarify, demonstrates other provocative and significant intentions and concerns of the Puritans who were caught up in those wild and divisive events of 1692.

Ann Kibby also recognizes how the witchcraft stories demonstrated God's active role and power in the everyday life of New England Puritans, but this ostensible purpose, in her view, only camouflaged the real thrust of the trials and of the discourse about them. Kibby's 1982 article "Mutations of the Supernatural: Witchcraft, Remarkable Providences, and the Power of Puritan Men" essentially argues, through several subtle stages employing psychological, religious, historical, and literary perspectives, that the trials and the ministers' accounts of them were mainly about defending patriarchal authority against women, while simultaneously dramatizing a shift in that patriarchal power from a traditional household father figure to more figurative "fathers," the accusing judges at Salem and, more significantly, the power of the state behind them. She notices that many remarkable providences are, in fact, malicious and vengeful acts on God's part, rather than merciful and benevolent ones. At first she explains this, to her, surprising fact by saying the Puritan deity had taken over from demons and witches the traditional power of committing maleficia, or harm doing by occult means or vengeful supernatural acts of damage to material possessions, and that such maleficia were sent as testaments to God's continued concern for his chosen people. These heavenly curses were jeremiads, she argues, warnings meant to restore the chosen to their correct path. At this point, though, Kibby pushes further, and claims that in fact Puritan men were the real inheritors of the power of maleficia, and that this power was used to gain revenge on women and children who had been challenging the men's authority for years.

Kibby's article is by turns insightful, dazzling, and provocative, but, as seems to be the case with so many critics who look at these Puritans, in her eagerness to explain and criticize their actions she sometimes fails to look squarely at the evidence before her. Bewildered by the apparent haphazardness of Increase Mather's *Essay for the Recording of Illustrious Providences*, by the way he "included every form of supernatural power he knew of, good or evil, and inexplicably offered them all, under one cover, as the 'illustrious providences' of the Puritan deity" (127), she calls his editing "just as fickle" as the testimony of Mary Warren, the accused witch who kept changing her story. To explain his editing she returns to the notion of God afflicting his chosen to improve them, to Bercovitch's ideas about jeremiads, those calls for moral reform amid laments of pending moral and physical destruction. Then, to illustrate how men became the agents of this power, she uses sea deliverance tales in which it can be shown that the moral lapses of Puritan men could literally kill their own wives and children. However, she also says that, in using this ancient tradition, Puritans "felt no need to prove to themselves or to others, that these events were preternatural, or even that they were expressions of a personally directed anger: maleficia bore the sanction of centuries of custom declaring them to be just that" (137). Unfortunately, this statement belies the unmistakable effort in every providence tale collection to do just what Kibby says the writers couldn't be bothered with, that is, to prove to their readers that the events they described were both real and preternatural. Again, a focus on negativity and final causes blinds a critic to essential literary characteristics of the tales.

Historians, more than literary critics, have, over the past twenty years, recognized the important narratological characteristics of providence tales. John Demos's *Entertaining Satan: Witchcraft and the Culture of Early New England* makes no attempt to dispute the tragic and unjust results of witchcraft persecutions in New England. Demos does, however, assert that such persecution was neither unique to New England nor insignificant in its overall impact on New England culture of the seventeenth and later centuries. Instead, Demos introduces his study by saying that "witchcraft cast a long arc through the cosmology of the pre-modern world" (4). One way he makes this argument is by revealing how some accused had already been involved in disputes before the witchcraft trials occurred. This perspective comes through in this conclusion to his reconstruction of the witchcraft case of John Godfrey of Boston, whose children were afflicted by witchcraft in the summer of 1688:

> These pathways of identification suggest how fully John Godfrey and his neighbors served and used—one might even say, needed—each other. They afford, moreover, a new point of approach to questions which otherwise seem particularly baffling.
>
> Recall that John Godfrey was suspected of practicing witchcraft during a span of at least fifteen years. Two or three times he was prosecuted on charges that might have brought the death penalty. After each trial, no matter how narrow his escape, he returned to the same locales and was re-incorporated into the same network of ongoing relationships. The problem of John Godfrey simply would not go away. Perhaps now we can begin to understand why. For this was a problem deeply rooted in the collective life of the community, and in the individual lives of its various members. It is not too much to say in conclusion, that there was a little of Godfrey in many of the Essex County settlers; so his fate and theirs remained deeply intertwined. (56)

Demos continually refers to the deeply pervading impact of witchcraft on New England culture. He writes that "the Goodwin children will be leading characters in a local best seller." Here he refers to the most famous account of the case, Cotton Mather's *Memorable Providences, Relating to Witchcrafts and Possession* (1689). Demos tells us that "witchcraft was a capital crime in every one of the New England colonies, as it had been in Old England from long before" (10), and he notes that Plymouth's 1636 statute against witchcraft was the earliest such law established in the British colonies (413n). He shows, in his careful reconstruction of the social contexts of the accused and of their accusers, how complex these situations could be, and how the problem of witch-craft was deeply embedded in Puritan culture, and not just a sudden aberration. Even more important for my purposes is Demos's recognition about the literary power of the witchcraft discourse:

> Whatever their contribution to the cause for which they were intended, these writings are a godsend to historians. For evident human interest, for richness of detail, for all they reveal about the intersection of character and culture, they are unsurpassed among extant materials from the seventeenth century. They present a picture that is almost clinical in substance and tone; comparison with psychiatric case reports in our own time does not seem far-fetched. There is, in short, no better window on the inner world of mental and emotional structures that supported the belief in witchcraft in colonial New England. (99)

Such ideas are seconded in Richard Godbeer's *The Devil's Dominion: Magic and Religion in Early New England* (1992). Godbeer generally concurs with Carol Karlsen's negative view that "New Englanders used witch accusations to attack women who challenged the expectations placed on them by gender norms, neighbors, and acquaintances with whom accusers had quarreled, and the members of rival factions" (19n). However, Godbeer also agrees with Hall's ideas about the texts' narratological significance, and concludes by saying, "The time has surely come for a full scale study of narratology in the culture of early New England." Interestingly, Godbeer also states, "Nor do I address the hazy relationship between magic and science in early modern thought," suggesting that such a relationship would be an apt subject of inquiry.

Finally, I would mention the work of Paul Boyer and Stephen Nissenbaum, both their *Salem Possessed* (1974) and their *Salem Witchcraft Papers* (1977). The transcripts themselves serve a useful narratological purpose and make an implicit statement about the relevance of these early American narratives in general. Boyer and Nissenbaum also argue that, contrary to most assertions, the trials were not directed totally against women, the poor, and less privileged, nor against the deviant and outcast. They claim that one-third of the accused were men in the period 1640–1699. "Whatever else they may have been, the Salem witchcraft trials cannot be written off as a communal effort to purge the poor, the deviant, or the outcast." Often they find the witch accusers were less wealthy and powerful than the accused. They say, "It was, after all, a series of historians from George Bancroft to Marion Starkey who first treated the event as a dramatic set piece, unconnected with the major issues of American colonial history. When Arthur Miller published *The Crucible* in the early 1950's, he simply outdid the historians at their own game" (22). What Boyer and Nissenbaum really think is that "what emerges most strongly from the records is the sense of a society, confronted with a tenacious outbreak of a particularly baffling crime at a time of severe political and legal disruption, nevertheless striving in an equitable way, to administer justice and to restore order" (19).

Given such divergences of views, we are once again confronted with the mystery of Salem in 1692. What did happen there? This chapter makes no claim to answering that, but it does try to take a closer and fresher look at what the people who lived through it actually wrote about it and why they did so.

Before turning to some of the main witchcraft texts, a brief summary of the statistical record built up about witchcraft in New England over the last twenty years by writers such as Demos and Boyer and Nissenbaum is in order. Demos presents quantitative figures to illustrate the extent of witchcraft persecutions in seventeenth-century New England, which demonstrate how fully witchcraft permeated the culture. Outside of the Salem trials of 1692, he calculates that from 1630 to 1700, between 93 and 114 people were brought to trial, of which some sixteen were eventually executed. When the Salem cases are considered, his figures rise to approximately 250 individual cases and thirty-six executions. He contrasts these figures with records from England for the years 1542–1736, during which time he estimates some two thousand indictments and three hundred to one thousand executions. On a comparative basis, per 100,000 population, New England had at least as high an incidence of witchcraft cases as England did. Moreover, Demos believes these figures considerably underestimated the actual numbers. He believes his figures could be merely the tip of the iceberg. If he is correct, then there is a strong basis for suggesting a relative similarity between incidences of witchcraft persecution and Indian captivity during this period of New England history, and I have already argued how such a frequency, in terms of Indian captivity and New England's overall population, would certainly have made these cases matters of, at the very least, considerable importance. Demos's figures are, in part, meant to prove his contention of witchcraft's all-pervading influence throughout New England culture, an influence he also shows qualitatively in his narratives of individual cases, reconstructed from various archival sources.

INCREASE AND COTTON MATHER AND THE
CONSTRUCTION OF SALEM WITCHCRAFT LITERATURE

The first important publication of witchcraft tales in New England appeared in a providence tale collection, Increase Mather's *Essay for the Recording of Illustrious Providences*, published in 1684. Another major collection of witch-craft tales occurs in book 6 of Cotton Mather's *Magnalia Christi Americana* (1702), where Mather recycles material from his father's witchcraft relations and from earlier witchcraft texts he wrote, the 1689 *Memorable Providences Relating to Witchcrafts and Possessions* (published in England in 1691 as *Late Memorable Providences*) and *Wonders of the Invisible World* (1693). Increase Mather's work includes narratives of witchcraft cases from the 1660s, 70s, and 80s. Cotton Mather's *Memorable Providences* focuses on other noted cases leading up to the Salem trials of 1692, especially that of the Goodwin family of Boston. *Wonders of the Invisible World* was adapted from court records of the 1692 Salem trials which Mather received from Samuel Sewall's brother Stephen, the court clerk, and is Cotton Mather's account and apology for the judgments made and exe-cutions pronounced at the Salem witchcraft trials.

Increase Mather's providence tale collection includes all the different types of the form, and his witchcraft stories comprise a significant portion of his col-lection. Mather demonstrates the English sources of these tales by first dis-cussing theoretical points about witchcraft and how to detect it, ideas he has garnered from the English writers John Gaule (*Select Cases of Conscience Touch-ing Witches and Witchcrafts*, 1646), Richard Bernard (*Guide to Jury Men*), and William Perkins (*Discourse on the Damnable Art of Witchcraft*, 1609). He then retells several English apparition tales to illustrate these theories. Throughout the narratives, he cites English authorities to further prove his points, thus duplicating the standard English providence tale mix of theory and narrative. He tells, for example, a story from Joseph Glanvill about the apparition of a pious woman who orders her former maid to tell the apparition's brother to return land their father had stolen from the poor. The husband of this woman "gave a large narrative of his Wive's Apparition to several, and amongst others to Dr. Whichcote [the noted Cambridge Platonist associate of Henry More and Glanvill]. . . . And this Narrative was attested unto by Mr. Edward Fowler, Feb. 16, 1680" (223). Once again, truth, credibility, and verifiability are paramount, and the standards for these virtues have been set by the British.

For Increase Mather, authorities cited by Glanvill are his authorities too. He tells another Glanvill story of a man named Taverner, who is asked by an appari-tion to intervene for him with his former wife and her new husband because they have been denying his son his due inheritance. After trying to ignore it, Taverner sees this specter again when he spends a night at the country home of Lady Anne Conway, the doyenne of England's premier occult circle at that time. There at Ragley, Henry More, Ralph Cudworth (author of the Neoplatonist tome *The True Intellectual System of the Universe*), Joseph Glanvill, and the rest of the Cambridge Platonists gathered to discuss the occult and verify its manifestations, and to meet with such eminent healers as Valentine Greatrakes, the "Irish stroker," who, with the stroke of his hand and the word "Abadacara," could cure the king's scrofula, the ague, and other diseases (Increase Mather, *Essay*, 258). The certification of the apparition by the Ragley circle "proves" Taverner's vision and Mather's story. Even when Mather tells New England stories, he finds English parallels to prove them, as when he compares the 1679 case of William Morse's haunted house in Newbury, Massachusetts, to Joseph Glanvill's "Drummer of Tedworth." The truth of a supernatural presence results from that presence's adherence to preestablished generic narrative forms.

Other essential providence tale markers appear in this English prologue section of Mather's witchcraft relations. He emphasizes the importance of eyewitness accounts by citing how even a famous witchcraft skeptic, John Webster, believed one story of a supernatural appearance because he was an "ear Witness of their Confession, and eye witness of the Execution [of the murderers]". Moreover, in this case the murderer is found on the basis of an overheard account when, after the apparition of the murdered man appears, the murderer's sister hears her distracted brother confess while talking to himself, and then informs on him. Webster's story points up the importance of physical details, as well as of eyewitness testimony. It wasn't until he actually saw the victim, named Fletcher, buried in his clothes, that he fully believed the murderer's and his sister's testimony. Webster and Mather do not spare the reader a detailed account of these clothes, which consist of "'a green Fustian Doublet pinckt upon white, and his walking Boots and brass Spurs, without Rowels.' Thus Mr. Webster" (230–32).

Providence tale markers are evident also throughout the New England tales Mather collects and narrates. A concern with empirical truth appears everywhere. As with English tales, the reliability of narrators, witnesses, and direct participants in these events is asserted by various means. Mather holds out the reputation of Ann Cole, a girl afflicted by witchcraft in 1662, as proof of her reliability, in that she is known as a teenage girl of "real piety and integrity," living with an equally pious father. Then, in the case of William Morse's haunted house, Mather tells his readers that he took the tale from Morse's own letters and that these letters are now in his own possession. They are firsthand accounts, and therefore believable. They are empirical facts, physical presences.

These tales have clearly evolved out of English models, which Mather adapted to fit New England circumstances. He employed all the gothic horror, salaciousness, melodrama, and sentimentality his English models and his other New England tales used. Prodigies abound in these tales. Ann Cole, an afflicted girl, could "express things which she herself knew no thing of," Mather writes, referring to her speaking of weighty theological matters in High Dutch, neither of which subjects she had been taught or should have known anything about, according to Mather. The old woman executed for bewitching Ann confesses to having seen the devil in the shape of a deer and a crow, and to having had sex with him for years. Of Elizabeth Knapp, afflicted in October of 1671 in Groton, Connecticut, Mather writes that "her tongue was drawn out of her mouth to an extraordinary length; and now a Demon began manifestly to speak in her" (140). Mather writes ten pages filled with supernatural prodigies in the relation of William Morse's haunted house, largely about objects flying around uncontrollably through no visible or natural means. He describes stones, clods of earth, and corn cobs falling on Nicholas Desborough of Hartford in 1682; candlesticks, stones, and fence gates flying around at George Walton's Portsmouth home; and a 1689 vision in Salmon Falls by Mary Hortado of a white, bald-headed man with a cat's tail and no body visible in between, swimming across a river.

Mather clearly frames the whole set of relations within the overarching providence tale theme of combating atheism. His contemporary instances of witchcraft were, he says, ordered by Divine Providence and "make it manifest beyond all contradiction that there are devils infesting the lower world" (168–69). Later he tells us why: "Sometime the Great and Holy God hath permitted, and by his Providence ordered such Apparitions, to the end that Atheists might therefore be astonished" (241). His use of the story from Webster was another implicit attack on atheists, since Webster's book was among the foremost attacks on witchcraft belief in England. That an eminent skeptic and atheist could be used to prove witchcraft's presence shows how contentious and chaotic the entire issue had become; people's opinions and feelings were flying in every direction, just like the objects many people claimed to be seeing zooming through the air.

The younger Mather's *Memorable Providences* are also plotted according to this basic providence tale formula. Four ministers, including Samuel Willard, the noted pastor at Groton and at Old South Church in Boston, introduce Cotton Mather's work in their "To the Reader":

> The old Heresy of the sensual Sadducees, denying the Being of Angels either good or evil, died not with them; nor will it, whiles men (abandoning both Faith and Reason) count it their wisdom to credit nothing but what they see and feel. How much this fond opinion has gotten ground in the debauched Age is awfully observable; and what a dangerous stroak it gives to settle men in Atheism, is not hard to discern. God is therefore pleased (besides the witness born to this Truth in Sacred Writ) to suffer Devils sometimes to do such things in the world as shall stop the mouths of gainsayers, and extort a Confession from them.

It has also been made a doubt by some, whether there are any such things as Witches, i.e., Such as by Contract or Explicit Covenant with the Devil, improve or rather are improved by him to the doing of things strange in themselves, and besides their Natural Course. But (besides that the Word of God assures us that there has been such, and gives order about them) no Age passes without some apparent Demonstration of it. For though it be Folly to impute every dubious Accident, or unwonted Effect of Providence, to Witchcraft; yet there are some things which cannot be excepted against, but must be ascribed hither. (Burr 95)

Right at the outset of the work, then, Mather's four certifying ministers state that the following providential narratives will, in effect, prove that God exists. Toward the end of the narrative itself, Mather himself says, "I am resolv'd after this, never to use but just one grain of patience with any man that shall go to impose upon me a Deniall of Devils or of Witches. I shall count that man ignorant who shall suspect, but I shall count him down right impudent if he Assert the Non Existence of things which we have had such palpable Convictions of" (Burr 123).

Cotton Mather takes the oldest Goodwin girl home, "to confute the Sadducism of this debauched Age" (110), he writes during the narrative; in an appended sermon, "A Discourse on Witchcraft" (that is, in a more theoretical part of the metanarrative), he says that in the Goodwin story he has seen "a Providence, wherein the power of God, the Success of Prayer, and the Existence with the operation of Devils, has been demonstrated in a manner truly extraordinary" (*Memorable Providences*, "A Discourse on Witchcraft," 1). At the end of this sermon he repeats this message, but in a more melodramatic, Melvillian flourish: "I am now to tell you, that these eyes of mine have beheld all these things. . . . Christians, there are Devils, and so many of them too, that sometimes a legion of them are spar'd for the vexation of one man. The Air in which we breathe is full of them. . . . There are Troops of Tempters on every side of thee. . . . Those Philistines of Hell are upon you." (*Memorable Providences*, "A Discourse of Witchcraft," 15–16).

Cotton Mather refers to his English sources and inspirations when he writes in the introduction that "the examples of Baxter, Glanvill and More" induced him to "publish Histories of Witchcrafts and Possessions" (Burr 98). Baxter himself, in the 1691 London edition of the text, extends his English seal of approval in his "Preface" to the work, in which he also delineates the basic purpose of these stories: "I have therefore long taken it for a great mercy of God, to cause Devil's themselves by witches, Apparitions, Possessions and temptations to be made even to sense, convincers of the Sadducees; And therefore in my *Unreasonableness of Infidelity* and in the Second Part of the *Saints Everlast-*

ing, I recited many Histories to that use." Specifically of Mather's work he says, "My scope is to tell the Reader, that in this Age where so many are brutised, and live by Sense, and Sadducees says, If they could but see the Devil, or a Departed Soul in a true Apparition, they would Believe; it is of great use to Publish such instances, as will convince them or leave them without excuse (*Late Memorable Providences*, A5 verso; A recto).

These various forewords, prefaces, sermons, recommendations, dedications, and other surrounding material comprising *Memorable Providences*'s meta-narrative contain all the various attestations of narrative innocence, truth, credibility, and reliability which are found in all providence tales. Mather opens, in his dedication to Wait Winthrop, the grandson of Governor John Winthrop of Massachusetts Bay, in a very humble tone: "It must be the Subject, and not the Manner or the Author of this writing, that has made any people desire its Publication; for there are such obvious Defects in Both, as would render me very unreasonable, if I should wish about this or Any Composure of mine, that it were printed in a book" (Burr 94).

He says, near the end of his introduction, in another instance of this narrative humility (which served to further prove his innocence and reliability), "Go then, my little Book, as a Lackey to the more elaborate Essays of those Learned men" (Burr 98–99), referring to Baxter, More, Glanvill, and other "Great Names." (This text was, according to Burr, "among his earliest published works" [92], but that alone does not explain the persistent use of this trope.)

Claims to truth and reliability were so hotly contested in providence tales that frequently the innocence of a narrator or protagonist in the tale had to be continuously asserted or defended. One instance of this comes in the text near the end of Mather's relation of the Goodwin family's afflictions and deliverances, which story is the core of the entire text. Ministers involved in witchcraft cases frequently faced the dilemma that even though various charms such as horseshoes on doors or bottling urine and nails in certain ways had proven effective against witchcraft, the only lasting and correct form of defense was prayer, from a Puritan standpoint. Otherwise, one was using witchcraft oneself, employing a "devil's shield" against a "devil's sword." Mather, on several occasions, advises readers not to use popish or pagan rituals and charms; but simply the knowledge he gains about the devil's ways casts suspicions on him, making it necessary to defend himself against the idea that he is dabbling in witchcraft. Section 31 of the Goodwin tale contains a fascinating scientific experiment to test the hypothesis that the devil knows our thoughts (which experiment I describe below). It opens with the following apologetic, which attempts to maintain Mather's spiritual innocence and legal credibility while simultaneously attesting to his scientific, firsthand knowledge of the subject:

I was not unsensible, that it might be an easie thing to be too bold, and go too far, in making of experiments: Nor was I so unphilosophical as not to discern many opportunities of Giving and Solving many Problems which the pneumatic Discipline [the science of spirits, pneumatology, i.e., the science of angels and demons, according to Burr, 122n] is concerned in. I confess that I have Learn't much more than I sought, and I have bin informed of some things relating to the invisible World, which as I did not think it Lawful to ask, so I do not think it proper to tell; yet I will give a Touch upon one problem commonly Discours'd of; that is, Whether the Devils know our Thoughts, or no? (Burr 122)

The metanarrative constantly asserts the truthfulness of its sensational, inexplicable content. Mather stakes his reputation on this truth, brandishes the piety and innocence of his subjects, tells us over and over that he and the witnesses saw everything with their own eyes. He writes all this, he tells us, in the appropriately plain and simple style which truthfulness and the scientific method generally require. Again in the last section about the Goodwins, he crows:

> This is the story of the Goodwins children, a story all made up of Wonders! I have related nothing but what I judge to be true. I was my self an Eye Witness to a large part of what I tell; and I hope my neighbors have long thought that I have otherwise learned Christ, then to ly unto the World. Yea, there is, I believe, scarce any one particular in this Narrative, which more than one credible Witness will not be ready to make Oath unto. The things of most Concernment in it were before many Critical observers; and the Whole happened in the Metropolis of the English America, unto a religious and industrious Family which was visited by all sorts of Persons, that had a mind to satisfy themselves. I do now likewise publish the History, while the thing is yet fresh and New; and I challenge all men to detect so much as one designed falsehood, yea, or so much as one important Mistake, from the Egg to the Apple of it. I have writ as plainly as becomes an Historian, as truly as becomes a Christian. (Burr 123)

A plain style had been an important element of scientific discourse since Bacon's various admonitions in *Novum Organum*, and providence tale writers also wrote in such a manner. At another point in the dedication, Mather reemphasizes his commitment to this plain style and states his aim to move away from theoretical speculations. He equates these moves with his idea of what constitutes "America." He says he aims at "Edification of plain folks," and thus refrains from "Platonic Notions of daemons . . . [and] Speculations about magical mysteries. . . . [Instead] I have therefore here but briefly touch't every thing with an American pen" (94). Interestingly, here he even tries to separate himself from his Cambridge Platonist influences.

To Winthrop, he emphasizes the eyewitness nature of this evidence, and asserts he is writing up "astonishing Witchcrafts and Possessions, which partly my own Ocular Observations, and Partly my undoubted Information, hath enabled me to offer unto the Publick Notice of my Neighbors" (Burr 94).

Baxter's "Recommendation" reemphasizes this need for contemporary, current tales with living witnesses. No longer would providence tale collections rely on the authority of past accounts, on stories out of Kramer and Sprenger, Bodin and Remy, or even stories certified by the Royal Society's Robert Boyle, such as the "Devil of Mascon" (from events of 1612, first published in 1653), as these will not convince the atheists of the 1690s. However, references or connections to science, to natural philosophy and the Royal Society, fill Cotton Mather's tales and introductions, and they also illustrate the witchcraft tales' "truthful" and "factual" nature. I have already quoted his reports on the "Pneumatic Discipline." The experiment he publishes in this field, on the question of "Whether the Devils know our thoughts or no," is an interesting example of how empiricism could be applied to instances of witchcraft, and how a scientific report could also be a fairly sensationalistic narrative:

> I will not give the Reader my Opinion of it, but only my Experiment that they do not, was conjectured from this: We could cheat them when we spoke one thing, and mean't another. This was found when the children were to be undressed. The Devils would still in wayes beyond the force of any Imposture, wonderfully twist the part that was to be undress't, so that there was no coming at it. But, if we said, untye his neckcloth, and the parties bidden, at the same time, understood our intent to be, only his Shooe! The Neckcloth, and not the shooe, has been made strangely inaccessible. But on the other side, That they do, may be conjectured from This. I called the young Woman at my House by her Name, intending to mention unto her some Religious Expedient whereby she might, as I thought, much relieve her self; presently her Neck was broke, and I continued watching my Opportunity to say what I designed. I could not get her to come out of her Fit, until I had laid aside my purpose of speaking what I thought, and then she reviv'd immediately. Moreover, a young Gentleman visiting of me at my Study to ask my advise about curing the Atheism and Blasphemy which he complained his Thoughts were more than ordinarily then infested with; after some Discourse I carried him down to see this Girl who was then molested with her unseen Fiends; but when he came, she treated him very coursly and rudely, asking him What he came to the house for? and seemed very angry at his being there, urging him to be gone with a very impetuous Importunity. Perhaps all Devils are not alike sagacious. (Burr 122)

Mather uses the language of Royal Society, seventeenth-century natural philosophy in his introduction when he says of his stories, "They are only one Head of Collections which in my little time of Observations I have made of Memorable Providences, with reflections thereupon, to be reserved among other effects of my Diversion from my more stated and more weary studies" (Burr 98). Calling these witchcraft tales one *head* of his total collection recalls Robert Boyle's prescriptions for writing natural philosophy accounts of foreign lands, which he had done for seamen and explorers under the title "General Heads . . . For the natural History of a Country, Great and Small."

Another truth-certifying, scientific aspect of these witchcraft tales is that physicians are often brought into court or cited as expert witnesses. An old woman accused of bewitching the Goodwins, Goody Glover, is checked by physicians who find she's not "crazed in her intellectuals" (Burr 104–105). Again in the Goodwin case, Mather reports that local doctors could not cure them, and that even they concluded that "nothing but an hellish Witchcraft could be the original of these maladies" (Burr 100). Later, when John Goodwin returns home, he feels a bone in his stomach. A "chirurgeon" removes from him a brass pin which "could not possibly have come to ly there as it did, without the Prestigious Conveyance of a Misterious Witchcraft." And once again, in his appended sermon on the Goodwins, "A Discourse on Witchcraft," Mather says that the confessions of the afflicted and of the witches were "often made by them that are owners of as much reason as the People that laugh at all Conceit of Witchcraft. The exactist Scrutiny of skillful Physicians cannot find any Distractions in their minds" (*Memorable Providences*,"A Discourse," 8).

Facts and truth in providence tales were always combined with sensational events and mysterious prodigies. Mather's title, like those of most such collections, testifies to this mixture of factuality and sensationalism: *Memorable Providences relating to Witchcrafts and Possessions. A Faithful Account of many Wonderful and Surprising Things . . . Particularly a Narrative of the Marvelous troubles and Relief experienced by a pious family in Boston . . . ."*

In the narratives proper we see many of the above-mentioned tropes, emphasizing various aspects of the tales' credibility, as well as other providence tale markers, particularly examples of preternatural, gothic occurrences and of domestic, everyday details of New England Puritan life, depicted concretely and often in a sentimental or melodramatic way. Serving as a bridge between the metanarrative's methods and this style of the narrative is a "Mantissa" Mather places directly after his relation of the Goodwin story. This Mantissa is a letter from the father of the afflicted children which, Mather says, is an "attestation" to the truth of Mather's own account. Of the author of the Mantissa, Mather adds that "a Pen hath not commonly been managed with more cleanly discourse by a Hand used only to the trowel" (126). In this remark alone we can see in the trowel both an example of simplicity and of the everyday details just mentioned.

After Mather's opening remarks about his honesty, Goodwin presents a melodramatic, sentimental picture of a father tormented by the sight of his suffering children and trying to remain calm and pious in the face of it. Mr. Goodwin starts out calmly enough, quite reasonably in terms of standard religious practice:

> In the year 1688, about Midsummer, it pleased the Lord to visit one of my children with a sore Visitation; and she was not only tormented in her Body, but she was in great distress of mind, Crying out, that she was in the dark concerning her soul's estate, and that she had misspent her precious time; She and we thinking her time was at an end. Hearing those Shrieks and Groans which did not only pierce the ears, but the Hearts of her poor Parents, now was a time for me to Consider with my self, and to look into my own heart and life, and see how matters did there stand, between God and my own soul, and see Wherefore the Lord was thus contending with me. (Burr 127)

But then other children of his are similarly smitten, so that he cries out even louder: "Oh! The Cries, the Shrieks, the Tortures of these poor Children! Doctors cannot help, Parents weep and lament over them, but cannot ease them. Now I considering my affliction to be more than ordinary, it did certainly call for more than ordinary Prayer" (Burr 127). He asks local ministers for help, and they, of course, agree; still, he says, "but as for my part, my heart was ready to sink to hear and see these doleful Sights." Such language is reminiscent of Mary Rowlandson's voiced despair when she watched the Indians in the wilderness after her capture.

In the thirty-three sections that make up the core of the Goodwin tale and of *Memorable Providences*, Mather reiterates all the tropes already discussed. The tale begins with a typically concise relation of the social circumstances that instigated the entire case. In fact, many of these witchcraft cases and their ensuing narratives start with such everyday, domestic arguments. Here, the oldest Goodwin daughter brings on the curse of a washerwoman's mother, after the Goodwin girl asks the Irish washerwoman if she's taken their linen. These stories reveal, in a few, swift strokes, the social circumstances of those involved, as is typically the case with witchcraft trial relations.

Certified, truthful testimony and domesticity are evident in the way the Goodwin children are described as good and godly children, whose fits could not have been faked. That the ensuing afflictions are also beyond natural law and prodigious is attested to by Mather's scientific, medical assertion that the girl is "visited with strange fits beyond those that attend an Epilepsy, or a Catalepsy, or those they call the Diseases of Astonishment" (Burr 101). On the subject of their innocence he adds that the four afflicted children (aged from four to nineteen) had "enjoyed a Religious Education, and answered it with a very towardly Ingenuity . . . such is the whole Temper and Carriage of the Children, that there cannot easily be anything more unreasonable, than to imagine that a Design to Dissemble could cause them to fall into any of their old fits." And then, for the necessary corroboration from eyewitnesses, he adds, "though there should not have happened, as there did, a Thousand Things, wherein it was perfectly impossible for any Dissimulation of theirs to produce what scores of spectators were amazed at" (100).

Truth and sensationalistic prodigies are interwoven throughout this narrative. The accused witch, Goody Glover, can suddenly and inexplicably only speak Irish at the trial, and her words are translated by two "honest and faithful men" (104). Like all so-called witches, Glover can't say the Lord's Prayer. When she wets her finger in court and strokes a poppit (an image of a babe stuffed with goat's hair), one of the children has a fit. Mather asserts these occurrences cannot be scientifically explained: "The fits of the children yet more arriv'd unto such Motions as were beyond the Efficacy of any natural Distemper in the world" (107). He continues to present the evidence in this simple, straightforward manner, telling how the children barked like dogs, purred like cats, complained of being in a red hot oven, rolled over, groaning as if on an invisible roasting spit, had their heads seemingly nailed to the floor so that a strong man could barely pull them up, seemed as loose jointed as puppets on strings, and then went suddenly rigid and stiff, and seemed to "fly like geese, and be carried with an incredible Swiftness thro the air, having but just their Toes now and then upon the ground, and their Arms waved like the Wings of a Bird. One of them, in the House of a kind Neighbor and Gentleman (Mr. Willis) flew the length of the Room, about 20 foot, and flew just into an Infants high armed chair; (as 'tis affirmed) none seeing her feet all the way touch the floor" (Burr 108).

Through all this, witnesses and examiners do not forget to gather scientific evidence: "A Blow at the place where the Boy beheld the Spectre was alwaies felt by the Boy himself in the part of his Body that answered what might be stricken at; and this tho his Back were turn'd; which was once and again so exactly tried, that there could be no Collusion in this Business" (Burr 107).

Mather even further deepens this mysterious and inexplicable, gothic element of the tale by shrouding it in mystery. He won't reveal all that occurred because "non est Religio ubi omnia patent [where there is no mystery, there is no religion]" (Burr 125).

The narrative piles on still more details of strange and grotesque physical contortions, all these carrying the implication of having been supernaturally caused. The children's tongues were "drawn down their throats" or "pull'd out upon their chins, to a prodigious length" (101). Their jaws were pulled open invisibly so they "went out of joint, and anon, they would be clapt together again with force like that of a Strong Spring Lock" (101–102). Their heads were twisted around, their bodies cut with invisible knives, their neck bones dissolved, then stiffened; their bodies were simply and continually tortured in ways or by means no one understood. They would be "stretched out, yea drawn Backwards, to such a degree that it was Fear'd the very skin of their Bellies would have cracked" (Burr 102). Such freakish physical deformities also occurred to afflicted children when they heard certain prayers or specific words in prayers. The afflicted often had fits around people praying, and in the case of Goodwin's oldest daughter, Mather describes how,

> before Prayer was out, she would be laid for Dead, wholy senseless and (unless to a severe trial) Breathless; with her Body swelled like a Drum, and sometimes with croaking Noises in it; thus would she ly, most exactly with the stiffness and posture of one that had been two Days laid out for Dead. Once lying thus, as he that was praying was alluding to the words of the Canaanites, and saying, "Lord have mercy on a Daughter vexed with a Devil"; there came a big, but low voice from her, saying, "There's two or three of them" (or us!) and the standers-by were under that Apprehension, as that they cannot relate whether her mouth mov'd in speaking of it. (Burr 120–21)

These stories were very popular. A list of books published by the London publisher of the 1691 *Late Memorable Providences* includes Increase Mather's *Essay* and Mary Rowlandson's captivity narrative. Their usefulness is illustrated in the fact that, as one attempt to cure the Goodwins, Cotton Mather reads his father's story of Ann Cole's possession to them (they can't listen to it). This close relationship to Indian captivities is evident in other ways, as in the following melodramatic passage from Mather's introduction:

> Go tell Mankind (little book) that there are Devils and Witches; and that tho those night-birds least appear where the Day light of the Gospel comes, yet New-England has had Exemples of their Existence and operation; and that not only the wigwams of Indians, where the pagan Powaws often raise their masters, in the shape of bears and Snakes and Foxes, but the Houses of Christians where our God has had his constant Worship, have undergone the annoyance of Evil Spirits. (Burr 98–99)

In the end Mather regrets that he hasn't collected even more providence tales, and in his regrets he once again explicitly defines these witchcraft tales, as he will also scientifically classify his Indian captivity narratives and all the other types of providence tales he relates, as "memorable providences": "Had there been Diligence enough used by them that have heard and seen amazing Instances of witchcraft, our number of memorable Providences under this Head, had reached beyond the Perfect. However, before I have done Writing, I will insert an example or two, communicated unto me by a Gentleman of sufficient Fidelity, to make of a Story of his Relating Credible" (Burr 141).

It was in two works that came after *Memorable Providences* that Cotton Mather made good on this wish to present more material "under this Head," material which reflected his vision of a world filled with "untold Devils, in bondage and chains," wandering through the air strangely "trapped and free" to wreck havoc (*Memorable Providences,* "A Discourse on the Power and Malice of Devils," 5). These works were *A Brand Pluck't out of the Burning*, written in 1693 but only circulated privately until published in 1914 in Burr, and *Wonders of the Invisible World*, which was published in 1693 and was, among other things, Mather's version of the Salem witchcraft trials of 1692.

In *A Brand*, Mather tells of Mercy Short, a teenage girl from Salmon Falls, New Hampshire, who was captured by Indians in 1690, ransomed in 1692 by the English fleet at Quebec, and was supposed to have suffered from witchcraft committed by Sarah Good, who was executed at Salem in 1692. Mather gives the reader a vivid picture of 1692 Boston in his opening account of the origins of her case. Working as a maid after her return from Canada, after her parents and much of the rest of her family had been killed, Short had been sent on an errand to the prison in Boston. Passing by where several accused or condemned witches were being held, Short, after being asked for some tobacco by some of the women, threw wood shavings at the "hag [Sarah Good]" and replied, "That's tobacco good enough for you." Good then cursed Short, after which her afflictions began. Mather tells us of the preternatural nature of these events right away: "A world of misery did she endure, for diverse weeks together, and such as could not possibly bee inflicted upon her without the Immediate efficiency of some Agent, or Rational or Malicious; until God was pleased at length to hear the multiply'd prayers of His people for her Deliverance. There were many Remarkable Things in the molestations then given her; Whereof one was that they made her Fast for Twelve Days together" (Burr 260).

Mather uses this "preternatural" survival ability of Short's to certify the veracity of her tale by linking her story to one told by Robert Platt, later to become secretary of the Royal Society, in his 1676 *Natural History of Oxfordshire*, in which he relates a similar case of someone surviving without food, in this case for ten weeks. Mather also stresses Short's reliability in her vision of the devil as a "Short and Black Man" (Burr 261), because, he says, her story matched English tales: "It was remarkable that altho' shee had no sort of Acquaintance with Histories of what has happened elsewhere, to make any Impressions upon her Imagination, yett the Devil that visited her was just of the same Stature, feature, and complexion with what the Histories of the Witchcrafts beyond sea ascribe unto him" (Burr 261).

Throughout this relation, Mather continues to present eyewitness accounts of inexplicable events: "On the twenty fifth of December it was, that Mercy Short said they [the demons] were going to have a dance; and immediately those that were attending her most plainly Heard and Felt a Dance, as of Barefooted People, upon the Floor; whereof they are willing to make oath before any Lawful Authority" (Burr 274). These phenomena rose to an increasingly more melodramatic pitch: "And the dolours now Raised in her were inexpressible. She shriek'd, she Roar'd, she Cry'd out, 'this is worse than all the Rest! What? Must I be Banished from the Favour of God after all?'" (Burr 277).

Throughout Short's story, Mather presents eyewitness testimony of supernatural, inexplicable evidence. In the following incident he links his work with that of a much earlier, classical master of fiction, Virgil, even though in *Magnalia Christi Americana* he condescendingly calls Homer's *Iliad* a "fardle of fiction." Mather himself seems to be losing his certainty about the distinction between fact and fiction, just as earlier in his experiment about whether the devil knows our thoughts and can read our minds, the results were ambiguous. Here, Mather and other spectators could feel specters afflicting Mercy. These specters felt something like cats or dogs:

Yea, several Persons did sometimes actually lay their Hands upon these Fiends. The Wretches were Palpable, while yett they were not visible, and several of our People, tho' they saw nothing, yet felt a Substance that seem'd like a Cat, or Dog, and tho' they were not fanciful, they Dy'd away at the Fright! The thing was too Sensible and Repeated a thing to bee pure Imagination. . . . It was particularly remarkable, that some who were very Busy in this method of treating the Specters [striking them with swords], upon a presumption that they might be corporally present (tho' covered with such a Cloud of Invisibilites as Virgil, I remember, gave once unto his Aeneas), were terribly scared with Apparitions in their journeyes home. (Burr 275)

Once again, Mather now describes the scientific experiments he uses to test his hypotheses. Short tells Mather about a book of Catholic rituals he owns which the devils steal from his library and use in their ceremonies. Mather tests this idea by making sure none of the leaves of the book are folded, as the devils have told Mercy they have folded down leaves at certain pages when they've taken it before. When he returns the next morning, he "found three leaves unaccountably folded, and then visiting Mercy, he perceived the Specters bragging that tho' she had [said] she would warrant them, that Gentleman would keep his Book out of their Hands, yett they had Last Night stole the Book again unto one of their meetings, and folded sundry leaves in it" (Burr 283). So here, in the tale of Mercy Short, was another providence tale full of prodigies, gothic flourishes, testimonials of truthfulness, domestic melodrama, everyday details, and scientific certainties.

The full title of *Wonders of the Invisible World* immediately tells us it contains a synthesis of prodigies told in a factual, legalistic way that would be consistent with the requirements of natural philosophy set forth by Boyle and the Royal Society: "*The Wonders of the Invisible World. Observations As well Historical as Theological, upon the Nature, the Number, and the Operations of the Devils. Accompany'd with I. Some Accounts of the Grievous Molestations, by Daemons and Witchcrafts, which have lately annoy'd the Country; and the Trials of some eminent Malefactors Executed upon occasion thereof; with several Remarkable Curiosities therein occurring* . . . Published by the Special Command of His Excellency, the Governour of the Province of the Massachusetts Bay in New England" (Burr 209). The title reassures us too that Mather has written and published this at another's insistence, in this case for Acting Governor William Stoughton, acting on behalf of Governor William Phips. Mather calls himself "one of the least among the children of New England" (Burr 211) and "one of my darkness" (Burr 211). Besides this pressure from Phips, Mather says, "I Live by Neighbours that force me to produce these undeserved lines" (213), as additional rationales for this work. He clearly establishes his humility, innocence, and thus his credibility, at the outset. Like Mary Rowlandson, he publishes not to magnify himself, but because his superiors ask him to.

The many assertions of truth these narratives include highlight the contested nature of that truth which these tales dramatize. These narratives do not smugly believe in the righteousness and correctness of their position, and this dialectical argumentation is perhaps one of the main characteristics that add to their dramatic appeal. Mather even calls attention to the instability of his position, when he agrees that the accused could be victims of illusions manufactured by the devil: "The Daemons might Improve the Shapes of innocent Persons in their Spectral Exhibitions upon the Sufferers (which may perhaps prove no small part of the Witch Plot in the issue)" (Fowler 390). In other words, the Salem judges, whom he is writing to defend, might have been wrong! These tales, then, share in that morally ambiguous nature I described in the English witchcraft tales, and will further describe in the Indian captivity narratives below. Mather immediately tries to deny this possibility, and in doing so shows just how much is at stake in these narratives; essentially, he claims the accused's voluntary confessions must be true, there having been so many of them, or else there is no truth left in the world. Satan may have created some illusions, but "one would think all the Rules of Understanding Human Affairs are at an End, If after so many most Voluntary Harmonious Confessions, made by Intelligent Persons of all Ages in sundry Towns, at several times, we must not Believe the main strokes wherein those Confessions agree. . . . If these Confessions are false, it is a thing prodigious beyond the Wonders of the Former Ages, and it threatens no less than a sort of a Destruction upon the World" (Fowler 390–91).

So harrowing was the idea of such an immense deception that he couldn't even call its imminence a simple destruction of the world; the only term he could find to imagine it was a "sort" of destruction, something, that is, entirely out of the realm of the known universe.

Before turning to his relations of "the Chief Matters of Fact, which occur'd in the Tryals of some that were executed," which he will present in an "Abridgment Collected out of the Court Papers," Mather looks at "like things happening in Europe, [so] we may see the Witchcrafts here most exactly resemble the Witchcrafts there." Again, this shows the European providence tale background of these New England witchcraft stories, and also points up that what happened in Salem and throughout New England during this time was not some bizarre, purely New England Puritan anomaly but one of the last excrescences of a phenomenon that had been occurring in Europe for centuries, and had been written about in similar ways for nearly fifty years. Salem discourse was unique in its realistic trends, its moves away from theoretical arguments in its use of an "American" pen, and its gothic flavor may have been augmented by the events' proximity to both a western and an eastern frontier. Still, our transatlantic view allows us to see that, overall, the events at Salem were not solely the product of American exceptionalism as they are often made out to be, while discourse about those events was, in fact, literature, and not just the rantings of leftover medieval superstition.

Mather now summarizes some notorious English witchcraft cases, and in so doing lists a fairly common set of prodigies and realistic details found in providence tales of all kinds and from both sides of the Atlantic. One story begins when an old woman, baby-sitting a child, angers the mother by breast feeding the child. The mother objects, the old woman curses her, and some fairly typical results ensue. A boy catches a toad, throws it in the fire where it explodes, while simultaneously, without having been near the fire herself, the old baby-sitter is found to have been scorched herself, "proving" the toad was her familiar spirit, or that her specter used and transported her body, in the form of its familiar spirit, a toad. The cursed mother does fall lame and her child dies, events which had been mentioned in the old lady's curses. Crooked pins and nails are coughed up by other children in the family, another generic trope of witchcraft tales. Bees and flies fly at children's faces and force nails in their mouths (an event perhaps unique to this tale). Another witch is accused of getting into bed with another afflicted girl (Mather doesn't say what happens there), and this witch is subsequently found to have (also quite common) "teats on her privy parts and belly newly sucked and oozing milky matter" from where the devil was said to have fed off of her" (Fowler 424–26). Other English stories inserted here feature gigantic lice, cursed and subsequently dying cattle and horses, farm gates flying off their hinges, axles breaking off wagons, and trees falling down after these very mishaps had been threatened by witches, or after some insult involving a wagon or a fence or gate had occurred to a witch and the person she cursed.

A further connection between Indian captivity narratives and witchcraft tales emerges when Mather asks, before recounting his abridged Salem trial accounts, "when will the Devil be sent to everlasting fire," and he answers when "the Captives of the mighty shall be taken away and the prey of the terrible shall be delivered" (Drake, *The Witchcraft Delusion in New England*, 73). Possession, that is to say, is a form of captivity. His work will help bring this about, perhaps, by helping New Englanders make "a Right use of the Stupendous and prodigious things that are happening amoung us" (Burr 210), by helping "Engage the Minds of the People in such Holy, Pious, Fruitful Improvements, as God would have to be made of His Amazing Dispensations now upon us" (211). All this is well and good, quite orthodox and politically correct, but once again, it is the cross currents in these narratives which produce the tensions that raise them to a new level; in the "Author's Defense," we are next reminded that in addition to the above reasons for writing this work, in addition to trying to "Countermine the whole plot of the Devil against New England" (211), he also has "been driven a little to do something likewise for Myself; I mean, by taking off the false Reports and hard Censures about my Opinion in these matters" (212). Mather's own political and professional position is on the line in these tales, his position a microcosm of God's precarious position in these texts. His innocence will not be so easily maintained; nothing can be taken for granted, and he admittedly had his own bias in these reports.

Mather's relations about the Goodwins and Mercy Short are compact, unified, and complete examples of providence tales in the witchcraft genre; but for that specific combination of realistic and gothic details achieved in all these narratives, Mather's accounts of the Salem trials are the best examples. Essentially his narrative abridgements of court documents and his own observations seek to present the standard evidence used to commit each of the accused, and in some of these stories he does take us through the typical forms of trial evidence with precision and alacrity. Along the way, however, he manages to vividly immerse us in the life of 1690s Salem, as he does in this cameo from the trial of Bridget Bishop (alias Oliver): "John Ingersoll's negro saw the shape of Bridget Bishop on the Beam of a Barn with an egg in its Hand, and that while he looked for a Rake or a Pitchfork to strike it with, it vanished" (Drake 163).

In another Salem trial account, George Burroughs is accused partly on the basis of evidence about his performing "feats of strength, as could not be done without a Diabolical Assistance" (Burr 216). His teeth marks are found on witches who claim he'd bit them. Burroughs is seen picking up whole "barrells of Molasses or Cider, in very Disadvantageous Postures, and Carrying of Them Through the Difficultest Places out of a Canoo to the shore" (Burr 222).

Bishop's story delineates the traditional presentation and form of spectral evidence: in the courtroom, there was invariably a scene similar to the following, where the witches' powers were evinced: "If she [Bishop] did but cast her Eyes on them [the afflicted and possessed], they were presently struck down; and this in such a manner as there could be no Collusion in the Business. But upon the Touch of her Hand upon them, when they lay in their Swoons, they would immediately Revive; and not upon the Touch of any ones else. Moreover, upon some special Actions of her Body, as the shaking of her Head, or the Turning of her Eyes, they presently and painfully fell into the like postures" (Burr 223–24).

Another standard moment in the plot featured testimony about the attempted diabolical covenant. Here, a witness testified to having been accosted by "a Black Thing . . . the Body was like that of a Monkey, the feet like a Cock's, but the face much like a man's [all this after an argument with Bishop over her fowles]. He being so extremely affrighted, that he could not speak, this Monster spoke to him, and said, 'I am a Messenger sent unto you, for I understand that you are in some Trouble of Mind, and if you will be ruled by me, you shall want for nothing in the world'" (Burr 227).

Such events coincide with their English precursors, and this traditional element gives the stories and the evidence weight and solidity. Another episode from Bishop's trial brings us back to John Darrel's alleged exorcism of William Somers, and all of Somers's confessions, recantations, renewed confessions, and continued such turnabouts on numerous occasions. In this instance, Mather's section 4 in the Bishop relation, Deliverance Hobbs confessed to performing witchcraft with Bishop and then said that Bishop was tormenting her for confessing and tempting her to recant: "She affirmed, that it was the shape of the Prisoner, which whipped her with Iron Rods, to compel her [to recant] thereunto. And she affirmed, that this Bishop was at a General Meeting of the

Witches, in a field at Salem Village, and there partook of a Diabolical Sacrament in Bread and Wine then Administered" (Burr 224).

More local color infuses Mather's account in item 9 of the Bishop trial, which tells of a child of Samuel Shattock, afflicted with strange fits in 1680 after numerous visits by Bishop on "foolish and frivolous errands," including times she

> would bring him things to Dy, whereof he could not imagine any use; and when she paid him a piece of Money, the Purse and Money were unaccountably conveyed out of a Lock'd box, and never seen more. The child was immediately hereupon taken with terrible fits, whereof his friends thought he would have dyed; indeed he did almost nothing but cry and Sleep for several Months together; and at length his understanding was utterly taken away. Among other Symptoms of an Inchantment upon him, one was, that there was a Board in the Garden, wherein he would walk; and all invitations in the world could never fetch him off. (Burr 225–26)

It turns out Bishop and Shattock's wife had argued, and Bishop, calling her proud, vowed to bring her down by hurting her child. A stranger who told this to Shattock then suggested taking the "Bewitched Boy with him to Bishop's house, on pretense of buying a pot of Cyder [but really to "fetch blood of *her*"]; in fact, "the Woman Entertained him in a furious manner; and flew also upon the Boy, scratching his Face till the Blood came. . . . Ever after the Boy was follow'd with grievous Fits, which the Doctors themselves generally ascribed unto Witchcraft; and wherein he would be thrown still into the Fire or the water, if he were not constantly look'd after; and it was verily believed that Bishop was the cause of it" (Burr 226).

Details about getting clothes dyed and paying calls for pots of cider are what domesticate these supernatural tales. Similarly, section 10 of Mather's account of Bishop's trial centers upon that most typical and domestic of New England icons, the apple orchard, which in the following example becomes a symbol of community and tradition even as it is being contested and defined as an alien, unknown, preternatural space.

John Louder, after some "little controversy with Bishop about her fowles" (226), is oppressed by Bishop's likeness, then by a "Black Pig," and then a "Black Thing . . . like that of a Monkey, the feet like a Cocks, but the face much like a Man's" (227). The thing tries to rule him, but he strikes at it and it vanishes. He then

> went out at the Back Door, and spyed this Bishop, in her Orchard, going toward her House; but he had not power to set one foot forward unto her. Whereupon return-

ing into the House, he was immediately accosted by the Monster he had seen before; which Goblin was now going to Fly at him; whereat he cry'd out, "the whole Armour of God be between you and me!" So it sprang back, and flew over the Apple Tree, shaking many Apples off the Tree, in its flying over. At its leap, it flung Dirt with its Feet against the Stomach of the Man; whereon he was then struck Dumb, and so continued for three Days together. Upon the producing of this Testimony, Bishop deny'd that she knew the Deponent: yet their two Orchards joined, and they had often had their Little Quarrels for some years together. (Burr 227)

Bishop's tale mixes domestic and preternatural elements using a plain style, the precise recipe for synthesizing empiricism and prodigies that providence tales had been refining for half a century.

Mather's account of the trial of Susanna Martin (tried and executed in 1692) has three splendid anecdotes illustrating these tales' marvelous dialogues between the commonplace and the bizarre, between the realistic, the sentimental, and the sensational. John Allen of Salisbury argues with Martin over Allen's refusal to cart her staves. She curses him, and he then tries to throw her into a brook, but she flies away. One of his cursed oxen going lame, Allen unhitches them all

upon Salisbury Beach, where Cattle did use to get Flesh. . . . [The oxen] were found by their tracks, to have run into the mouth of Merrimack River, and not returned. . . . They that sought them [at Plum Island] used all imaginable gentleness, but they would still run away with a violence that seemed wholly Diabolical, till they came near the mouth of the Merrimack River; when they ran right into the sea, swimming as far as they could be seen. One of them swam back again, with a swiftness amazing to the beholders, who stood ready to receive him, and help up his Tired Carcass; But the Beast ran furiously up into the Island, and from thence, through the Marishes, up into Newbury Town, and so up into the Woods; and there after a while found near Amesbury. So that, of Fourteen good Oxen, there was only this saved; the rest were all cast up, some in one place, and some in another, Drowned. (Burr 230–31)

In another anecdote regarding Martin, apple orchards are replaced by the quintessence of the cute and domestic, puppies. One John Kembal wants to buy a puppy of Martin's, but she refuses him the one he wants. He then says he'll get one elsewhere, and she curses him: "Within a few Dayes after, this Kembal coming out of the Woods, there arose a little Black Cloud in the N.W. and Kembal immediately felt a Force upon him, which made him not able to avoid running upon the stumps of Trees, that were before him, albeit he had a broad, plain

Cart way, before him; but tho' he had his Ax on his Shoulder to endanger him in his falls, he could not forbear going out of his way to tumble over them" (Burr 232–34). Next a puppy appears and darts between his legs, but before he can hit it, it disappears into the ground. Then a second puppy comes, which nearly "tore his throat out," but he calls on God and it too departs. The next day, though Kembal told no one what had happened, a witness heard Martin say she'd heard Kembal had been "frighted last night . . . with Puppies" (Burr 234).

A third incident involving Martin achieves its depiction of impending terror by combining the domestic with the supernatural in ways suggestive of later stories by writers such as Charles Brockden Brown (especially in *Wieland*, where the afflicted man sees a supernatural light) and Edgar Allan Poe:

John Pressy testify'd, that being one Evening very unaccountably Bewildred, near a field of Martins, and several times, as one under an Enchantment, returning to the place he had left, at length he saw a marvelous light, about the Bigness of an Half-Bushel, near two rod out of the way. He went, and struck at it with a Stick, and laid it on with all his might. He gave it near forty blows; and felt it a palpable substance. But going from it, his Heels were struck up, and he was laid with his Back on the Ground, Sliding, as he thought, into a Pit; from whence he recover'd, by taking hold on a Bush; altho' afterwards he could find no such Pit in the place. Having, after his Recovery, gone five or six Rod, he saw Susanna Martin standing on his Left hand, as the Light had done before; but they changed no words with one another. He could scarce find his house on his Return; but at length he got home, extremely affrighted. The next day, it was upon Enquiry understood, that Martin was in a miserable condition by pains and hurts that were upon her. (Burr 235)

The piece ends with this bit of legalistic, domestic pathos: "It was further testify'd by this Deponent, that after he had given in some Evidence against Susanna Martin, many years ago, she gave him foul words about it, and said, He should never prosper more; particularly, that he should never have more than two Cows; that tho' he were never so likely to have more, yet he should never have them. And that from that very Day to this, namely for Twenty Years together, he could never exceed that Number, but some strange thing or other still prevented his having of any more" (Burr 235). In Martin's tale we again see that providence tale combination of the factual with the fanciful, of legalistic discourse woven together with gothic scenes.

Yet another Salem case concerned one Elizabeth How. Regarding her black arts we hear how she afflicted Nehemiah Abbot's cow: "She wished his Oxe Choaked, and within a Little while that Oxe was Choaked with a Turnip in his Throat" (Burr 239). This range, from the dark invisible depths of the spiritual, supernatural world to the a simple, everyday world of a turnip, is among the foremost characteristics of witchcraft tales and of providence tales in general, and echoes the grander dialectical synthesis of science and religion.

We can find all the essential providence tale tropes in a body of seventeenth-century discourse, in this case New England witchcraft texts. The argument between empiricism and the supernatural stands out, with all its attendant figures. In particular, an unusual blend of the gothic and the domestic emerges, especially in Cotton Mather's relations of the Salem trials. Perhaps this domesticity voices Cotton Mather's desire to write with a simple, nontheoretical, American pen. In the next and final chapter, we will see that American pen become even more pronounced, as it takes up the matter of Indian captivity.

5

The Birth of the Indian Captivity Narrative

The empiricism of the new science and the early Enlightenment and the religious counterattack of the late Reformation influenced Indian captivity narratives, as they did providence tales in general. Innocent, truthful narrators, credible witnesses, and precise details of unusual occurrences lent scientific validity to the narratives, as they had to other providence tales, and a variety of prefaces, introductions, dedications, appended sermons, advertisements, and cases of conscience further confirmed the truth of the tales. These metanarratives maintained the providence tale paradigm of joining theoretical to narrative discourse. "Miraculous" appearances of consoling or revelatory passages of Scripture, as well as debates predicated on biblical texts, dramatized theological concepts within the captivity narratives.

Exotic characters and settings in the Indian stories gave new life to the carefully documented, sensational renderings of the material world in previous providence tales. The captivities thus quickened the rate of secularization in providence narratives, even as their authors added layers of religious discourse to them. These writers needed to satisfy both their readers' reason and their senses to reaffirm God's existence and his direct participation in human affairs. The attempt to satisfy these contradictory requirements, to be both reasonable and sensational, produced a morally ambiguous literary world where con men, occult healers, magicians, conjurers, and other formerly diabolic figures became figures of wonder and fascination. Good characters became tainted with the same devilish features possessed by their deceitful adversaries. Those who sought to make readers or other characters believe in their version of the truth, whether they were the editors, the captives, or the devil's explicit agents (the witches, possessed people, healers, and Papists), became the central figures. Their stories generated a new type of narrative prose discourse which employed scientific methods to establish the validity of religious faith, thus constituting a literary bridge from the late Reformation to the Enlightenment. The outlooks and techniques that these writers refined in constructing melodramatic religious narratives from empirical observations of the material world facilitated the development of eighteenth-century fiction.[1]

MARY ROWLANDSON AND OTHER PIONEER SCIENTISTS

The first lengthy seventeenth-century New England Indian captivity narrative was Mary Rowlandson's *Sovereignty and Goodness of God*. This work was published in 1682 with an anonymous preface by "Per Amicum," generally considered to be Increase Mather.[2] He praises her narrative because it illustrates the principle that "not the general but the particular knowledge of things makes deepest impression upon the affections." In praising her vividly detailed prose, Mather links Rowlandson to the science of natural history and philosophy as set forth by Bacon and the Royal Society.[3] Of Weetamoo, one of King Philip's wives, Rowlandson writes, "A severe and proud dame she was, bestowing every day in dressing herself neat as much time as any gentry of the land, powdering her hair and painting her face, going with necklaces, with jewels in her ears, and bracelets upon her hands. When she had dresed herself, her work was to make girdles of wampum and beads" (Clark and Vaughan 61). Another passage describes the Indians' pre-battle ceremonies:

Before they went to that fight, they got a company together to powow; the manner was as followeth. There was one that kneeled upon a deerskin with the company round him in a ring, who kneeled, and striking upon the ground with their hands and with sticks, and muttering or humming with their mouths; besides him who kneeled in the ring, there also stood one with a gun in his hand. Then he on the deerskin made a speech, and all manifested assent to it, and so they did many times together. Then they bade him with the gun go out of the ring, which he did, but when he was out, they called him in again. But he seemed to make a stand; then they called the more earnestly till he returned again. Then they all sang. Then they gave him two guns, in either hand one. And so he on the deerskin began again, and at the end of every sentence in his speaking, they all assented, humming or muttering with their mouths and striking upon the ground with their hands. Then they bade him with the two guns go out of the ring again, which he did a little way. Then they called him in again, but he made a stand; so they called him with greater earnestness, but he stood reeling and wavering as if he knew not whether he should stand or fall or which way to go. Then they called him with exceeding great vehemency, all of them, one and another. After a little while he turned in, staggering as he went, with his arms stretched out, in either hand a gun. As soon as he came in, they all sang and rejoiced exceedingly awhile. And then he upon the deerskin made another speech unto which they all assented in a rejoicing manner, and so they ended their business and forthwith went to Sudbury fight. (Clark and Vaughan 63)

In this passage the Indians are presented without editorial comment. Rowlandson seems to have taken notes, or in some way recorded this ceremony as any "Baconian" scientist would have, carefully gathering facts without yet reflecting on their meaning. The following passage describes a more lighthearted Indian dance:

Mr. Hoar [who had come leading a group to redeem the captives] called them [various Indian dignitaries] betime to dinner, but they ate very little, they being so busy in dressing themselves and getting ready for their dance, which was carried on by eight of them—four men and four squaws, my master and mistress being two. He was dressed in his Holland shirt with great laces sewed at the tail of it; he had his silver buttons, his white stockings, his garters were hung round with shillings, and he had girdles of wampum upon his head and shoulders. She had a kersey coat and [was] covered with girdles of wampum from the loins upward; her arms from her elbows to her hands were covered with bracelets; there were handfuls of necklaces about her neck and several sorts of jewels in her ears. She had fine red stockings and white shoes, her hair powdered and face painted red that was always before black. And all the dancers were after the same manner. There were two others singing and knocking on a kettle for their music. They kept hopping up and down one after another with a kettle of water in the midst, standing warm upon some embers, to drink of when they were dry. They held on till it was almost night, throwing out wampum to the standersby. (Clark and Vaughan 66–67)

Rowlandson seems to be casting the Indians as parodies of Cavalier courtiers, but she draws her satire with precision. Her editor, Mather, does not feel that her observations alone will convince readers of her honesty. He reminds us that Rowlandson's is a firsthand account of her experience (the tale was, he says, "written by her own Hand"). Mather also employs the providence tale trope of certifying witnesses' reliability in his 1684 *Essay for the Illustration of Remarkable Providences*, which includes the captivity narrative of the Massachusetts war veteran Quentin Stockwell. This collection begins with several occult tales of judgments and deliverances involving apparitions and the devil. It follows with a chapter of "remarkable" sea deliverances, and then places Stockwell within a more varied assortment of "remarkable preservations." Each of these tales contains testimony establishing the credibility of its author or of the person who collected the story. The first tells of a Dr. Frith, who sees apparitions of his entire family in coffins; shortly thereafter, they all die. "The Relator of this story . . . a Person of great integrity," Mather writes, "had it from Dr. Frith's son, who also added, 'My Father's Vision is already executed upon all the family but myself. My time is next and near at hand'" (A4). Such a witness would hardly have been one to lie, as near as he was to eternity.

Mather also tells of a contract between a wayward scholar and the devil. The devil takes the document away, but after much prayer among several ministers, the deed for the scholar's soul descends from a cloud and is torn up. Mather writes that "the Relator had this from the mouth of Mr. Beaumond, a Minister of Note at Caon in Normandy, who assured him that he had it from one of the Ministers that did assist in carrying on the day of prayer when this memorable providence hapned. Nor is the relation impossible to be true, for Luther speaks of a providence not unlike unto this, which hapned in his Congregation" (A5). Such attestations attend practically every tale. Of Stockwell's tale, Mather says, "A Worthy Person hath sent me the Account which one lately belonging to Deerfield (viz. Quintin Stockwell) hath drawn up respecting his own captivity and Redemption, with the more notable Occurrences of divine Providence attending him in his distress, which I shall therefore here insert in the Words by himself expressed" (39).

Mather further certifies Rowlandson's credibility by emphasizing her moral innocence and her self-consciousness about her role as a writer. On the title page he writes that she published her story only because of her friends' "earnest desire" that God's powers be displayed. He immediately refutes any suspicion of vanity or self-advancement. She is an innocent, publishing only under outside pressure, just as Thomas Potts wrote of the Somers trial only at Judge Bromley's request, and John Williams wrote his captivity narrative at the insistence of Cotton Mather.[4]

"Per Amicum" injects gender considerations into his claims for Rowlandson's innocence and credibility. He explains that she "wouldn't thrust it [her narrative] into the Press," except she was forced to by her dear friends convincing her to do so "that God might have his due glory . . . [because of the] many passages of working providence discovered therein." He uses her feminine modesty as further proof of her innocence and reliability. In the narrative itself, Rowlandson synthesizes reason, expressed in terms of her authorial self-consciousness and her sexual innocence, with more sensational aspects of the role of explorer she also plays. She represents herself in the following passage paradoxically, as an innocent humbly renouncing her role of heroine, as a worldly explorer, and as a near savage: "O the wonderful power of God that I have seen, and the experience that I have had! I have been in the midst of those roaring lions, and Salvage Bears, that feared neither God, nor Man, nor the Devil, by night and day, alone, and in company, sleeping all sorts together; and yet not one of them ever offered the least abuse of unchastity to me, in word or action. . . . Though some are ready to say I speak it for my own credit, but I speak it in the presence of God, and to his Glory" (Clark and Vaughan 70).

The passage proclaims her sexual innocence by casting her as another Daniel in the lions' den, a lamb unharmed and undefiled amidst wolves and other wild beasts. She also sounds like some new-world discoverer exulting in her adventures. In this paean to the spirit of discovery, she joins her innocence to the scientific and sensationalistic spirit of seventeenth-century voyages dedicated to uncovering and exploring the world's prodigies. She also evokes such sensationalistic elements as her near rape and "remarkable" deliverance from it. She edges closer to an affinity with the Indians, finally, both by these exultations over her wilderness experiences and also by simply reporting the Indians' civilized behavior in not having "offered the least abuse of unchastity in word or action." The passage's syntax foregrounds her adventures in the wilderness over the exhibitions of God's mercy and power she also saw there. The second sentence of this excerpt reverses the order of the ideas she expresses in her opening line where she first spoke of God's power. The passage then ignores God until the end, and thus subordinates God's power to her experiences. Rowlandson the truthful and meek becomes Rowlandson the savage and bold.

Savage Mather: The Further Union of Science and Sensation

Cotton Mather also employs a variety of means to establish his tales' credibility in *Magnalia Christi Americana*. He insists on the generic superiority of his histories over such "poets' papers" as Homer's *Iliad*. This argument appears in the dedicatory preface to the appendix to book 7 of the *Magnalia* (book 7 is called *Ecclesiarum Praelia, or A Book of the Wars of the Lord*—meaning the Indian wars between 1688 and 1698). All of his captivity narratives, except Hannah Swarton's (which appears in book 6), appear in this appendix,[5] which is titled *Decennium Luctuosum* and reproduces an earlier version of this history of the wars published separately in 1698. Of this work, in its "Dedication Prefaced unto the First Edition" in *The Magnalia*, Mather insists that "the Fault of an Untruth can't be found in it. . . . The famous History of the Trojan War itself comes behind our little History of the Indian War; for the best Antiquaries have now confuted Homer; the Walls of Troy were, it seems, all made of Poets' Paper;

and the Siege of the Town, with the Tragedie of the Wooden Horse, were all but a piece of Poetry" (bk. 7, p. 58).

Its historical truth, then, comprises one cornerstone of his magnum opus. Later Mather adds that his aims in *Decennium Luctuosum* are "the doing of Good, as well as the telling of Truth" (59). But this announcement doesn't suffice to establish his credibility. He next copies Glanvill, More, and his father in confessing to minor sins to appear more honest:[6]

> I shall now with all Faithfulness Endeavor it [telling of the Indian wars]. With all faithfulness, I say, because tho there should happen any Circumstantial Mistake in our Story (for 'tis a rare thing for any Two Men concern'd in the same Action, to give the story of it without some Circumstantial Difference) yet even this also I shall be willing to Retract and Correct, if there be found any just Occasion. But for any one Material Error in the whole Composure, I challenge the most Sagacious Malice upon earth to detect it, while matters are yet so fresh as to allow the Detection of it [here Mather further invokes Glanvill's and Sinclair's credo of relating only current tales because they were more readily provable]. . . . No, I will write with an Irreproachable and Incontestable Veracity; and I will write not one thing but what I am furnished with so good Authority for, that any Reasonable Man, who will please to Examine it, shall say, I do well to insert it as I do. (bk.7, p. 60)

In another section of the dedication, Mather depreciates his work in order to appear more humble and credible. However, at the end of this section he savagely attacks those who contradict his claims. He modestly says, "If a War between Us and an Handful of Indians do appear no more than a Batrachomyomachie[7] to the World abroad, yet unto us at home it hath been considerable enough to make an History" (58). He does not want his name attached to it, because "but a little boil'd Indian Corn in a Tray, is as much as our Best History of an Indian War, compos'd perhaps in fewer Days than there were Years in the War, may presume to be compar'd unto" (58). He asserts both his scientific and ministerial designs by saying, "But whatever this History be, it aims at the doing of Good, as well as the telling of Truth; and if its Aim shall be attained, that will be sufficient Reward for all the Troubles of Writing it" (59). After his admission of the possibility of having made a "circumstantial mistake" but not a "Material Error," he ends his opening certification of reliability by changing his tone considerably: "And I will hope that my Reader hath not been studying of Godefridas de Valle's Book, *De Arte Nihil Credendt: About the Art of Believing Nothing*. Wherefore having at the very Beginning thus given such a Knock upon thy Head, O Malice, that thou canst never with Reason Hiss at our History, we will proceed unto the several Articles of it" (60–61).

Mather uses scientific notions of empirical truth to further religion against the spirit of skepticism and atheism which so pervaded Enlightenment thought. In the above passage, he chooses a uniquely New England figure as another weapon against skeptics such as De Valle. The phrase "knock upon thy head" is used repeatedly in the work of William Bradford, William Hubbard, John Winthrop, and both Increase and Cotton Mather, to describe what Indians do in battling and killing the English. In establishing his credibility, Mather puts on the linguistic garb of an Indian. He does the same less spectacularly when he equates his work with a "little Indian boiled corn." Mather becomes, in effect, a savage himself, as does Rowlandson temporarily when she exults over her adventures. This "savage" battling his critics ironically invokes the simple, moderate Baconian style implicit in the figure of "a little boil'd Indian Corn in a Tray." Again the unique conflation appears in an Indian captivity narrative of the scientific method and sensationalism, of rationality with a gothic sensibility, of "civilization" and "savagery." Mather takes on skeptics on their own terms, using reason and evidence, but he also takes them on with figurative tomahawks and scalping knives. The resulting literary hybrid is an ambiguous amalgam of scientific and savage attributes. The writer of a work designed to justify and further support the English settlers' colonization of Indian territory becomes a figurative Indian himself. Similarly, this same writer, defending his faith against the godless materialists of his day, writes like a scientist and materialist.

The same kind of ambiguous metamorphoses occur in Cotton Mather's short captivity narrative of Sarah Gerish. In a preface to this story and to four other short captivities he relates in article 7 of *Decennium Luctuosum*, he notes that he "obtained [them] from credible witnesses" (69). During an Indian raid conducted by some one to five hundred Penacock and Saco Indians, the seven-year-old Gerish hides herself in bed with an even younger child. She wears "no more than one Stockin upon her" (66) as she's kidnaped; both images create an impression of great vulnerability. This vulnerability serves as a token of her reliability as a witness; innocence here is equated with truth. That one of her Indian captors is characterized as "a harsh and mad sort of a Dragon" (66) augments the figure of childish innocence by casting Gerish's narrative into the language of a fairy tale. In another sense, the dragon image makes the tale resemble an imaginary story, filled with metaphors and fanciful rhetoric. Thus, it is almost a work of fiction, as unreliable as Homer's "fardle of fiction," the opposite of a humble, straightforward, historical account. An emblem of objective truth, Gerish's innocence clashes with a form of sensational fantasy, the fairy tale, with all its attendant savagery, its monsters, dragons, half-naked young girls, and the like.

Another ambiguous linkage emerges in a scene in which this vulnerable child, finding herself lost in the snowy woods, makes her way back to her captors by tracking their footprints. On one hand, this segment represents her help-lessness and God's providential mercy, and thus empirically demonstrates God's direct involvement in human affairs. The event further confirms her reliability as a witness, since she's been found worthy of deliverance.[8] Another reading suggests that Gerish, in finding her way out of the woods, displayed practical skills more in line with George Sinclair's Baconian engineering skills or with the forest ways of the savages themselves. Gerish's feat makes her another example of a frontierswoman and natural philosopher. It also aligns her with the Indians.

Two other examples vividly illustrate ways in which captivity narratives keep shifting between empiricism and melodrama. Cotton Mather's gothic relation of the decapitation of a friend of the captive Mary Ferguson[9] ends on this melodramatic and sentimental note: "I know not, reader, whether you will then read this record with dry or tearful eyes; I only know I could not write it without tears in mine" (71). Mather then describes, like any world traveler and natural historian purveying his scientific prodigies, a petrified man on display at the Villa Ludovico in Italy; then he tells those who have read this story of Ferguson's friend without crying, that they are "so petrified" (71). Mather uses a scientific figure of an inexplicable curio or natural wonder to reinforce a sensational, sentimental element, the woman's pathetic death.

The most spectacular example of the synthesis of science and sensationalism appears in the narrative of Hannah Dustan. This young woman was captured in 1697 from Haverhill, Massachusetts, while lying in with her new born child and her elderly friend Mary Neff. The scene of her capture and of the murder of her child is vividly portrayed. After a brief journey with her captors, Dustan, with the help of Neff and a teenage boy, Sam Leonardson, kills ten of the twelve Indians who are leading them toward the French. These ten include two women and six children. The scene is a bloody one of revenge and horror, but despite their imminent danger, Dustan and her cohorts collect the scalps as evidence of what they had done. She may have been motivated by a desire to collect scalp money, and she did indeed receive a reward from the General Assembly of the Provinces and from the governor of Maryland. We know, however, that captives such as Rowlandson also received money without bringing home scalps. Even if money or revenge were their sole motivations, their gathering of the scalps, in the context of so many other captivity narrative references to evidentiary concerns, qualifies as an exercise in natural history, albeit a particularly ghoulish one.

Suffering as Creation:
The Captivity Narrative as Sacred Text

Rationalism and gothic sensationalism combine in these tales in other intriguing ways. Rowlandson describes in great detail her unsuccessful attempt to keep her six-year-old daughter, Sarah, alive on the trail. She relates finally how she sat with her dead child and talked to her, even though she had previously avoided the dead. Her account is pathetic and sentimental in the extreme. Rowlandson says she would have lost her reason at this point if not for God's mercy. Looking into the abyss of gothic horror, Rowlandson, with God's help, escapes that abyss and retains her reason. She makes reason dependent on supernatural aid, while the near loss of reason reinforces the existence of God.

Reason overcomes sensational horror insofar as captives' afflictions ultimately proclaim God's existence. Nothing was more reasonable to the Puritan mind than the notion that God created and rules the universe. As Rowlandson says, her purpose in writing was "to declare the works of the Lord, and his wonderful power in carrying us along, preserving us in the wilderness, while under the enemies' hand, and returning of us in safety again" (Clark and Vaughan 46). Her afflictions and her redemption give God an opportunity to reveal himself, both in his judgments and in his mercies. The plot follows a similar arc in the story of Hannah Swarton. Taken from Casco, Maine, in 1690, Swarton's husband and one of her children are killed and two of her four other children never return from captivity. She still can ask "What shall I render to the Lord for his Goodness and for his Wonderful Works to me . . . What shall I render to the Lord for all his benefits?" God's providential plan rationalizes her losses. Swarton clarifies this belief when she says, "So, tho' I had deserved all this, yet I knew not but one reason of God's bringing all these Afflictions and Miseries upon me and then ennabling me to bear them was that the work of God might be made manifest" (Cotton Mather, *Magnalia*, bk. 6, p. 13).

Despite the severity of their sins and the extent of their ensuing afflictions, despite the hopelessness of those afflictions, God does save some of them. These deliverances constitute happier versions of the story of Abraham, Lot, and Sodom and Gomorrah, where God agrees to save the cities if ten righteous people can be found. Ten aren't found and God destroys Sodom and Gomorrah. That anyone is saved in New England can only be explained by God's mercy, and thus each deliverance serves as empirical evidence of God's existence.

The miseries of the afflicted in providence tales help to "make manifest" God's work, both his scourges and his mercies, and thus, indirectly, to reveal God himself. Bearing afflictions resembles the creation itself, when God poured light over the darkness. Glanvill's, More's, and Sinclair's tales shine light on the invisible world. Sinclair's patron Tranent unearths buried materials, while sixteenth- and seventeenth-century explorers uncover new races and natural phenomena in previously "dark" corners of the world. Suffering, empirical observation, and engineering projects become religious acts in these providence tales. But more than the experience of suffering, the writing of that experience becomes the fulfillment of the biblical type of creation, for it is to *proclaim* and make manifest, rather than to merely experience, God's providential acts that is the Puritan's duty. These narratives, therefore, become new forms of sacred texts, which provide empirical proof of the existence of the supernatural world, of God's light.

Rowlandson's and Swarton's reactions to their afflictions demonstrate the widely used captivity narrative trope of ascetic suffering. Stoic fortitude balances the inherent sentimentality in accounts of severe tortures. This firm, outwardly unemotional bearing under torture inscribes another form of scientific objectivity in the stories. Stoicism upholds reason and faith in God over fear and emotional terror. Rowlandson's mini-martyrology of the suffering and death of Goodwife Joslin, a fellow captive on her march, illustrates this exemplary ascetic behavior.

The Indians burn Joslin, her two-year-old, and a child in her womb, forcing her other children to watch under the threat of being burned themselves. According to Joslin's children, Rowlandson says, Joslin "did not shed one tear, but prayed all the while" (Clark and Vaughan 42). Such asceticism and faith find parallels in John Williams's account of the death of his wife along the captivity trail. Mrs. Williams, Cotton Mather's niece, cannot keep up with the pace of their forced march, but she "never spake any discontented word as to what had befallen us . . . [and] with suitable expressions justified God" (175). Shortly after this report, she stumbles, falls into a river, and is killed by an impatient Indian, still without a loss of self-control. Reason and faith triumph over the fear of death; ironically, asceticism such as Joslin's and Williams's mirrors Indian braves who do not display fear or pain while being tortured by their captors. Ambiguity enters these narratives once again, as exemplary Puritans exhibit Indian virtues.

THE RETURN OF THE MISSING FATHER AS SACRED NARRATIVE

The captivity narrative operates as creation and resurrection myth, in which light is brought to the surrounding darkness. The common plot structure of the return of a missing father or husband also makes these stories into sacred narratives, myths of creation—of separation and return, in which order and reason emerge from chaos.

The absent patriarch foreshadows demonic chaos; the patriarch's return signals the restoration of God's order. The patriarchal figure is two-faced, provoking sensational disorder and reestablishing peace. Providence tales, such as the Tedworth relation, Mrs. Teate's story involving Irish "savages," as well as many Indian captivity narratives, begin with a missing or dead husband or father. Rowlandson's husband has gone to Boston. Sarah Gerish's and Remembrance Sheldon's fathers are out of town. Dustan's husband, absent at the time of the Indian attack, chooses to save his fleeing children rather than his wife and infant. These stories dramatically portray the separation between husband and wife as a space where devilry and savagery can enter. In Remembrance Sheldon's story of the Deerfield raid of 1704 when John Williams and his family were captured, this figurative breach becomes literally an open door. Sheldon, a friend of Stephen Williams, one of John's sons taken captive in 1704, relates that his own father was out of town, buying medicines, during the Indian raid. Sheldon and the rest of the people in his family's garrison house feel secure behind the thick wooden palisades they had been erecting for some weeks after being warned of an impending attack. But Deerfield is betrayed when someone leaves the back door of the garrison house open and Indians enter through it. This unknown deserter can be read as an emblem of Sheldon's missing father. Later, Sheldon's father becomes instrumental in redeeming captives. With the return of the father, reason and God are tenuously restored.

C. Alice Baker presents a variation on this trope in her account of Sarah Gerish's capture.[10] Gerish was captured in a raid on Quochecho (Dover, New Hampshire) in 1689. At the time of the raid she was staying with her grandfather, Major Waldron. Cotton Mather characterizes him as Gerish's "affectionate grandfather" (66), but Baker writes that Waldron's savagery and deceitfulness in his dealings with the Indians had motivated the raid. An immoral grandfather and an absent father permit gothic horror to enter the settlement.

John Williams's 1707 narrative presents another variation on this theme. Because the influence of captive adults had made it difficult for Jesuits to convert the youthful prisoners, the Jesuits tell the Maqua Indians holding the captives to sell some adult English so the Jesuits will have an uninterrupted opportunity to convince the children to pray at Mass. Yet another turn on this idea is how during captivity women obviously make do without men, and at times even surpass them. Swarton suffers in a more "manly" fashion than John York, a fellow captive. At another point during her ordeal, left alone by the men, she and her Indian mistress struggle to find food. They finally succeed after Swarton climbs a hill, makes a fire, and attracts a party of squaws in canoes bearing roasted eels. Fearing Indian treachery, Rowlandson refuses to ask her husband to redeem her. She also demeans his suffering, as well as her son's concern for him. She finds their pain insignificant compared to her own ordeals. Dustan leads Neff and Leonardson on a war party in which the ten Indian scalps, including some belonging to women and children, are taken.

Despite all these threats to the patriarchy, authority reasserts itself, sometimes quite sensationally. Swarton is "ravished" by God's Scripture; Dustan, back at home, receives her "humiliation" in church during Mather's sermon, while Rowlandson extols God's supernatural and "wonderful power and might in carrying of us through so many difficulties in returning us in safety and suffering none to hurt us" (Clark and Vaughan 74). In the first London edition of her narrative, a sermon by her husband Joseph is attached to the beginning of her text, and while Mary describes her alienation upon her return, Joseph, we learn, has been rewarded "manifold for preaching on the Sabbath at Newbury" (Clark and Vaughan 72). The men reap the rewards of their women's captivity, and their texts invade those women's texts. Women's captivities do involve an element of escape from societal norms. When taken captive Swarton experiences a near idyll with other Indian women. Dustan kills with Indian savagery. Rowlandson imagines an orgy with Indian men. But eventually all these women bow, with varying degrees of deference, to male authority.

THE WILLIAMS FAMILY SAGA:
THE SCIENCE OF SCRIPTURAL MELODRAMA

During John Williams's captivity, the French authorities keep him physically separated from the other Deerfield prisoners. John's son Samuel converts to Catholicism, making his separation from his father spiritual as well as physical. The elder Williams finally succeeds, through the course of a dramatic correspondence he has with Samuel, in winning Samuel back to Puritanism. In one of his letters, John Williams points directly to the issue of the missing father by asking his son to "let a father's advice be asked for the future in all things of weight and moment" (Clark and Vaughan 209). As in the other examples of this trope, the restoration of the father's authority ends the sensational flirtation with the forbidden other—Indian, Papist, or both. Such dramatic restorations reunite children with parents in literary marriages of sentimentality and reason.

This tale of a restoration of patriarchal authority evokes the pathos of the breach between a loving parent and his child, while it also features the sharp theological reasoning John uses to undermine Samuel's conversion. Countering the arguments of his Jesuitical adversaries, John Williams continues the tradition of the scriptural debate found in Caesarius, King James, Harsnett and Darrell, Sinclair's "Devil of Glenluce," and Glanvill's "Tedworth Demon."

After learning of Samuel's conversion, John Williams sends a letter filled with the sentimentality and raw emotion of his outrage and pain. In reply, Samuel explains his change of faith by recounting the deathbed confessions of two English captive maids, Abigail Turbet and Esther Jones. They had resisted the French priests for some time, and thus their alleged final turn affected Samuel deeply. John Williams feels certain that Samuel's letter has been dictated by Merial, the most prominent Jesuit priest. In his second and longer letter, Williams convinces Samuel to reconvert when he augments the emotion of the first letter with firm scriptural logic and common sense.

Williams's main tactic in this second letter is to counter the arguments of Merial, whose own arguments had been so influential in Samuel's conversion. Williams attempts to expose Merial as a liar, and he tells Samuel he wishes to "relate the just grounds we have to think these things [regarding Turbet and Jones's conversion] were falsehoods" (Clark and Vaughan 202). Williams goes after Merial in an epistolary war, where the winner is he who can make Samuel believe.

In the following selection, Williams discusses the Romanist concept of purgatory. He employs common sense rather than metaphysical abstraction in interpreting Scripture to bring his son back to him: "Besides, 'tis not consistent with reason to suppose that Enoch and Elijah, instead of having a peculiar privilege vouchsafed to them for their eminence in holiness, should be less happy for so long a time than the rest of the saints deceased who are glorified in heaven, which must be if they are yet kept, and must be till the Day of Judgement, out of heaven and the beatifical vision in an earthly paradise" (Clark and Vaughan 213). The subject of purgatory arises in Williams's attempt to prove that Christ alone can intercede before God on man's behalf. The Jesuits have been trying to persuade Samuel to pray to the Virgin Mary. He tells his son that "they [the apostles] never preached that we should pray to the Virgin Mary or other saints." Jesus Christ is the only true mediator we have before God, he says, reinforcing these notions with specific scriptural citations. In the following quotation he uses all the weapons he commands, both his scholarly knowledge and common sense. The Roman Catholics, he says,

> are not able to prove that the saints in heaven have a knowledge of what prayers are directed to them. . . . That which they have fixed upon as most probable to them, is, that they know of them from their beholding the face of God; seeing God, they know these prayers. But this is a great mistake. Though the saints see and know God

in a glorious manner, yet they have not an infinite knowledge . . . and it does no ways follow, that because they see God, they know all prayers directed to them upon the earth. And God has nowhere in his word told us, that the saints have such a knowledge. Besides, were it possible for them to have a knowledge of what prayers are directed to them, it does not follow that they are to be prayed to, or have religious honor conferred upon them. The Romanists can neither give one Scripture precept or Example for praying to them. . . . Further, it cannot be proved that it is consistent with the saints being creatures, as well as with their happiness, to have a knowledge of prayers from all parts of the world at the same time, for many millions together, about things so vastly different one from another. (Clark and Vaughan 211–12)

Williams's speculations here constitute a kind of fiction in themselves, a giving of literary body to invisible, imaginary conceptions and characters. In a sense, all religious discourse can be seen in this way; the providence tale writers of the seventeenth century greatly enhanced the dramatic and the narrative aspects of such "fictions" by surrounding them with their insistence on credibility and vivid particulars. A shorter example illustrates more forcibly the sensational, melodramatic and vividly detailed side of these scriptural debates. Williams's Indian master threatens to knock him over the head with his hatchet, or to bite off his nails if he will not cross himself. Simultaneously, an Indian "savagess" named Ruth tells him he is rejecting Scripture by not listening to his master. Williams replies to Ruth that God is his master. Shadowing this assertion of theological reason, Williams's Indian master has put one of Williams's fingernails into his mouth and threatens to bite it off (Clark and Vaughan 186). Williams uses similar sensationalistic devices when he scares Samuel with stories of the tortures used by Papists on unbending Protestants.[11]

OTHER PRETERNATURAL MANIFESTATIONS OF REASON AND SCIENCE

Hannah Swarton's narrative contains another conversion melodrama. She believes her afflictions are retribution for leaving her church in Beverly, Massachusetts, to gain more land in Casco Bay, Maine. Passages of Scripture come, chapter and verse, to comfort her and resolve her doubts while she is held in captivity. Like Williams, Swarton also uses Scripture in debates she has with French captors seeking her conversion. Swarton cites only the chapter and verse of the passages she and her adversaries deploy. Williams, however, makes his letter to Samuel and the debates they contain the longest element of his narrative, and develops in detail the specific points of each question.

Swarton's fears about her tepid relationship to God ("I have had many conflicts in my own spirit, fearing that I was not truly converted unto God in Christ and that I had no saving interest in Christ" [Clark and Vaughan 155]) find relief in scriptural passages she stumbles upon. During one moment of severe religious doubt brought on by French attempts to convert her, Swarton says she was "brought once to the very brink of despair about what would become of my soul. In this time I had gotten an English Bible. . . . I looked over the scripture and settled on the prayer of Jonah and at those words, 'I said I am cast out of thy sight, yet will I look again towards thy holy temple,' I resolved I would do as Jonah did. And in the meditation upon the Scripture the Lord was pleased by His Spirit to come into my soul and so fill me with ravishing comfort that I cannot express it" (155). The timely appearance of this "miraculous" Scripture dramatically restores God's authority. Swarton herself plays both Indian and atheist, savage and skeptic until she is ravished and returns to God, making the sacred narrative arc complete.

Mary Rowlandson also happens upon Scripture which guides and comforts her. Rowlandson had sinned in not observing the Sabbath, and she believes she deserves her afflictions. The Scripture which comforts and strengthens her reestablishes the patriarchal authority she had resisted. Ironically, and by now quite typically in these narratives, that authority is restored through the agency of the Indians, who present her with a captured Bible. In Rowlandson's text the return to order and reason climaxes on a broader stage when she cites, speaking of King Philip's War, a "strange providence of God in turning things about when the Indians [were] at the highest, and the English at the lowest" (Clark and Vaughan 69). Her text also illustrates authority imposed as metanarrative with the attachment of her husband Joseph's sermon to her account.

Dramatic discoveries of food by starving captives resemble these scriptural visitations. The Teate tale in Samuel Clarke's *Mirrour* contains one classic precursor of this figure which becomes paramount in many sea deliverances, and then, in a less dramatic form, appears in the Indian captivity narratives. Quentin Stockwell and his captors almost starve several times. Hannah Swarton and her Indian mistress are left alone with nothing but a maggot-filled moose bladder to eat, but they are saved by a group of other squaws bearing roasted eels. Food as miraculous salvation evokes the sudden appearance of the ram which replaces Isaac on Mt. Moriah. The trope mixes reason, in its reassertion of God's power,[12] with the savagery of an impending murder or human sacrifice. The sea deliverance tales feature frequent scenes of near cannibalism. Deliverances from these perils echo the manna in the wilderness sent to the Jews and Christ's loaves and fishes. Like the passages of Scripture which are inexplicably called to mind, they provide proof of supernatural intervention in the material world.

Ironically, when the food comes and reason prevails, captives begin to act like Indians. Swarton seems to sing of wortle berries and moose liver. Rowlandson says that at first it was "hard to get down their filthy trash. But the third week they were sweet and savory to my taste" (Clark and Vaughan 44). While waiting for some liver to be roasted, she says "I was fain to take the rest and eat it as it was with the blood about my mouth, and yet a savory bit it was to me" (45). Of a pancake of parched wheat fried in bear's grease she exclaims "I never tasted pleasanter meat in my life" (47). Eating bear, she admits that "now that was savory to me that one would think was enough to turn the stomach of a brute creature" (49).

Such descriptions of bizarre and savage foods constitute narrative forms of Baconian natural history, keen observations of the uncommon. Discoveries of unusual cures and remarkable recoveries from horrible injuries are another subject from natural history found in these providence tales. The war veteran Robert Pepper tells Rowlandson that oak leaves cure wounds. His medical discovery illustrates another conflation of the occult—in this case of knowledge gained from Indian powaws—with science, here the discovery of healing medicines. Many mid-seventeenth-century providence tales also unite "scientific" descriptions of surgical methods with sensationalistic, detailed accounts of ghoulish wounds. These wounds can only be "cured" through God's merciful intervention, rather than by bloodletting or surgical techniques like trepanning. The foods and cures function as elements in works of natural history, while they also exemplify the gothic sensationalism articulated and promoted by Glanvill, More, Sinclair, Baxter, and the Mathers.

Rowlandson's and Pepper's oak leaf cure typifies the folk medicine that had often been associated with witch/midwives. Many midwives returned from Europe at the end of the Marian persecutions with new knowledge of traditional folk medicine they had gleaned from pamphlets printed in Switzerland and northern Germany. Those women, however, unlike Rowlandson, were denounced and sometimes even executed for their involvement in occult practices. The change in attitudes toward folk medicine illustrates the shift in late-seventeenth-century providence tales away from the punishment of occult practices. This change further suggests the blurring of good and evil in providence tales, which focused increasingly on details of the secular, physical world.

Another earlier parallel to Rowlandson's discovery of the benefits of oak leaves were the cures of the notorious mid-seventeenth-century occult healer Valentine Greatrakes. Greatrakes "cured" hundreds, with his bare hands basted with his own spittle and the urine of the afflicted. His patients suffered from a wide variety of diseases including the king's evil. Lady Anne Conway, Henry More, and Glanvill's circle of occultists which met at Ragley, Conway's estate,

extolled the powers of Greatrakes and of the equally famous Francis Mercuri-
ous Van Helmont, the model for Arnold's "Scholar Gypsy." Greatrakes's and Van
Helmont's fame illustrate how arts that had been considered evil were accepted
by the late–seventeenth century. Greatrakes's mysterious healing abilities corre-
spond to Jennet Dowglass's inexplicable skill in detecting witches in Glanvill's
account of the murder of George Maxwell. Pepper's and Rowlandson's oak leaf
cures also belong in this category of sensational and scientific discoveries. Rowlandson's healing with oak leaves and Greatrakes's hands treated with urine
and spittle would once have made them prime candidates for the Inquisition,
rather than the hero and heroine of some of their country's leading ministers.
In these examples, science and sensational magic merge completely; reason and
the supernatural become one.

GOTHIC HORROR

The atmosphere of demonic chaos traceable to *Malleus Maleficarum* startles the reader of Indian captivity narratives. At the start of Rowlandson's narrative, children are separated from their mothers, "knock't on the head" (Clark
and Vaughan 33), their bowels ripped open, and then shot. "There was one [a
man in this case] who was chopped into the Head with a Hatchet, and stripp'd
naked, and yet was crawling up and down" (35), she relates. Cotton Mather out-
does Rowlandson in his account of the torture and murder of Robert Rogers,
who "through his corpulency [was] nicknamed Robin Pork" (*Magnalia Christi
Americana*, bk. 7, p. 69). Mather details, in a vein similar to the writer's in *Newes
from Scotland* describing John Fian's torture, the burning of Rogers after he has
been stripped, pricked, and tied to a tree while surrounded by singing, dancing,
and feasting Indians. I quote this lengthy passage as it illustrates the combination of close details and sensational, poetic rhetoric Mather so often brought
together in his ghoulish tales:

> They . . . cut a parcel of Wood, and bringing it into a plain place, they cut off the
> top of a small red oak tree, leaving the trunk for a stake whereto they bound their
> sacrifice. They first made a great fire near this tree of death, and bringing him unto
> it, they bid him take his leave of his friends, which he did in a doleful manner; no
> pen, though made of an harpy's quill, were able to describe the dolour of it! They
> then allowed him a little time to make his prayers unto heaven, which he did
> with an extream fervency and agony: whereupon they bound him to the stake, and
> brought the rest of the prisoners with their arms tied each to the other, so setting
> them round the fire. This being done, they went behind the fire, and thrust it for-

wards upon the man, with much laughter and shouting; and when the fire had burnt some while upon him, even till he was near stifled, they pulled it again from him. They danced about him, and at every turn they did with their knives cut collops of his flesh from his naked limbs, and throw them with his blood into his face. When he was dead, they let his body down upon the glowing coals, and left him tied with his back to the stake; where the English Army soon after found him. He was left for us to put out the fire with our tears! Reader, who should be the father of these Myrmidons? (*Magnalia Christi Americana*, bk. 7, p. 69)

Mather clearly tries to create an atmosphere of terror in this passage. In so doing, the simple truth teller and purveyor of "boil'd Indian corn," who denigrates Homer directly as a writer of "mere" poetry and make believe, cannot resist the Homeric figure of the Myrmidons. Mather loves figures of epic encounters, as his continual use of biblical and classical mythology and fairy tale imagery illustrates. After one horrible defeat in the 1637 Pequot War, the Indians come to see their "Barbikewed" friends: "They howled, they roared, they stamped, they tore their hairs; and though they did not swear (for they knew not how!), yet they cursed, and were the picture of so many Devils in Desperation," Mather writes (bk. 7, p. 43). Rowlandson also evokes the Indians as devils when she describes "the roaring, and singing, and dancing and yelling of those black creatures in the night which made the place a lonely resemblance of hell" (Clark and Vaughan 36).

As it did in witchcraft tales, infanticide pervades the Indian captivity narratives. Mather's stories of James Key, Mehetabel Goodwin, Mary Plaisted, and Mary Ferguson all feature the gory murders of children. Key, a five-year-old, is threatened when he cries for his parents. Continuing to weep, he's stripped, bound to a tree, and beaten. After he is thrown on the ground and taunted about missing his parents, "it was not long before the child had a sore eye . . . whereupon, laying hold on the head of the child with his left hand, with the thumb of his right he forced the ball of his eye quite out. . . . About nine or ten days after . . . the child being tired and faint, sat him down to rest, at which this Horrid fellow being provoked, he buried the blade of his hatchet in the brain of the child, and then chopped the breathless body to pieces before the rest of the company" (Mather, C., *Magnalia Christi Americana*, bk. 7, pp. 69–70).

Rowlandson adds to this highly detailed gore a substantial portion of sentimentality by detailing the death of her six-year-old daughter, Sarah, after nine days of journeying without food through the snowy woods:

Thus nine days I sat upon my knee with my babe in my lap till my flesh was raw again; my child being ever ready to depart this sorrowful world, they bade me carry it out to another wigwam (I suppose because they could not be troubled with such spectacles), wither I went with a heavy heart, and down I sat with the picture of death in my lap. About two hours in the night my sweet babe like a lamb departed this life on Feb. 18, 1675 [76], it being about six years and five months old. It was nine days from the first wounding in this miserable condition without any refreshing of one nature or another except a little cold water. I cannot but take notice how at another time I could not bear to be in the room where any dead person was, but now the case is changed; I must and could lie down by my dead babe side by side all the night after. I have thought since of the wonderful goodness of God to me in preserving me in the use of my reason and senses in that distressed time that I did not use wicked and violent means to end my own miserable life. (Clark and Vaughan 39)

Such tearful relations heighten the drama of these narratives. The melodramatic tension and gothic horror is balanced by Rowlandson's reason, which God has restored through his supernatural means.

Violence as Entertainment and the Rise of the Ambiguous Modern Hero

Melodramatic scenes of gothic horrors in captivity narratives are heightened by dramatic escapes from death. The story of Quentin Stockwell's captivity, first published in 1684 in Increase Mather's *Essay*, contains several of these deliverances. Stockwell describes his capture from Deerfield in 1678, after he has returned to rebuild his farm burnt down in an earlier raid. On several occasions during the journey to Canada, an Indian approaches him with an upraised hatchet but doesn't use it. In one instance, unable to move because he has reinjured a war wound while crossing a river, Stockwell's pain dissipates seconds before he would have received the deathly knock on the head. Such last-minute deliverances repeat themselves several times during his captivity.

Humor cuts the drama of these scenes somewhat, and complicates the hard-edged representation of good and evil one would expect from a more traditional religious narrative. Instead of killing Stockwell, the Indians argue over who owns him and who should kill him. They argue over whether or not he should be killed at all. They argue over the style of the shirts he sews for them. These images of Indian dissension and doubt produce a more complex and human story. Stockwell's lack of heroism has similar effects. Instead of carrying out actions like Hannah Dustan's forceful revenge, Stockwell, contemplating killing his sleeping captors, "removed out of the way all the guns and hatchets, but [his] heart failing [him], [he] put all things where they were again" (Clark and Vaughan 83). Asked to make three different styles of shirts for three different Indians, he says he'll make them as his chief master asked, "whereupon," he says, "one Indian struck [me] on the face with his fist. I suddenly rose up in anger ready to strike again." He finally backs down, "and the matter was put up." Stockwell accepts his fate with a mixture of resignation, cowardice, and resistance. His weaknesses further obscure the boundary between savage and civilized behavior, between the damned and the elect.

Mather claims Stockwell's story is true because it is a firsthand account given him by a reliable person. The story is set firmly in a providence tale context in the *Essay*, after two "proofs" of remarkable occult prodigies and before a variety of well-documented sea deliverances and recoveries from grotesque physical injuries. But its diverse elements complicate the idea of the narrative as a straightforward, empirical depiction of God's providential designs. Stockwell has his virtues, and he can be loyal and compassionate. Left alone with a sick Indian who is unable to carry his gun and hatchet, Stockwell does not try to escape to avoid endangering other captives by making his captors angry. His friend Benoni Stebbins does escape, and the Indians threaten to retaliate by killing Stockwell and the other remaining captives. But they find deliverance from a captain among the Indians, one who was "always," he says, "our great friend." This Indian captain convinces the others that the remaining captives should not be punished for Stebbins's escape. Thus we see a virtuous side of Indian behavior, reported by an Englishman, and contrasted with cowardly and traitorous behavior by Stebbins. Stockwell's Indians show kindness in other ways. While the prisoner sits frozen and prepares to die on the ice on Lake Champlain, an Indian comes along, cuts out his pockets and wraps them about his face. The veteran gets "a bit of Biscake as big as a walnut," is helped up and put on a sled, and told he will get a pipe of tobacco.

Stockwell's deceptiveness also undermines his narrative's claims to absolute truthfulness. He tricks the Indians several times. Even though he doesn't report praying at all during his narrative, the Indians, starving and unable to find food, ask him to pray they will kill something on their next hunt. Stockwell "prays," and the next day they kill a bear. Stockwell presents his prayers as a trick played on the Indians, not as a pious, devotional act. During the raid on Deerfield, he holds up his "uncharged" gun to Indians about to split his head with a hatchet. The Indians flee. Stockwell seems delighted by these tricks, especially since he finds the Indians sadistic and cunning in other situations. He tells how an Indian advises him, when he is frozen and nearly starved, to save a piece of raccoon meat under his coat. When the other Indians discover it, they force him to drink raccoon grease, and laugh when it makes him sick.

Stockwell and his enemies switch moral roles throughout the story. Surely the Indians and the French felt they could get a good price for him, but they still treat him in ways that demonstrate their own humanity. Stockwell's description of his deliverance from ice-bound Lake Champlain has a dreamlike quality in which Stockwell becomes a child with two fathers, one Indian, the other French. After trying to catch up with the Indians, he sits, waiting to die, beside a tree lying on the ice. He writes that

> Whilst I was thinking of death, an Indian hallooed, and I answered; he came to me and called me bad names and told me if I could not go he must knock me on the head. I told him then he must then do so; he saw how I had wallowed in that snow but could not rise. Then he took his coat and wrapped me in it and went back and sent two Indians with a sled. One said he must knock me on the head, the other said no, they would carry me away and burn me. Then they bid me stir my instep to see if that were frozen. I did so; when they saw that, they said that was wurregen (wun-negen, a good thing). There was a surgeon at the French that could cure me. (Clark and Vaughan 86)

The Indians make him some otter broth, which he drinks eagerly, and give him warm clothes. Eventually the French buy him from the Indians. He almost dies of frostbite, but manages to survive. His tale tells almost as much of English low cunning and Indian kindness as it does of the reverse.

These mixed elements in Stockwell's narrative, of melodrama, humor, and realism, embody theories of narration advocated by Cotton Mather in *Magnalia Christi Americana*. At the beginning of book 6, Mather writes of hoping to excite his readers while they sit comfortably in their armchairs: "I will carry my Reader abroad upon the huge Atlantic, and without so much as the Danger of being made Sea-sick he shall see Wonders of the Deep" (bk. 6, ch. 1, p. 3). Mather believes that to keep his readers amused, narratives should include chiaroscuro and rhythm. In the middle of a long, gloomy section recounting defeats suffered by the English in King Philip's War, he suddenly stops the narrative to say, "But reader, be content that this paragraph relate a few more of the pernicious things done by the barbarians, about this time, in several parts of the country, and for thy comfort we will give in the next a relation of an unexpected alteration and revolution" (bk. 7, p. 51). The unexpected characterizations and plot twists in the Stockwell narrative illustrate Mather's program for satisfying readers. Mild satire, complex personalities, and alternating rhythmic elements, in a genre designed to make serious and stern religious points, cut against a black and white depiction of Indians and Puritans. To vary the tone of his own Indian war history, Mather describes actions taken by converted or praying Indians helpful to the Puritan cause. Just as providence tales and captivity narratives synthesize diverse elements such as rationalism and sensationalism, so they exhibit variations in mood, genre, and in their considerations of their characters' moral characteristics. These different configurations of elements humanize the narratives, distinguishing them from more narrowly delineated theological or purely scientific genres. Such narratives include diverse relationships between Indians and Puritans, between good and evil.

Mary Rowlandson depicts herself in sensational and ambiguous terms. Contrary to the image of a truthful innocent, she commits a variety of the deadliest sins. Though her confessions do function as atonements, her sins also bring her closer to the savage level of an Indian. In the preface by "Per Amicum," Rowlandson is too modest and self-effacing to want to publish her book, but when her Indian mistress's papoose dies, she comments, "There was one benefit in it, that there was more room" (Clark and Vaughan 55). On seeing her son, who tells her "he was as much grieved for his father as for himself," she says, "I wondered at his speech, for I thought I had enough upon my spirit in reference to myself, to make me mindless of my Husband and everyone else; they being safe among the French" (54). Meanness and selfishness characterize her in these incidents. She has a "wolfish" appetite, and is so eager to eat she burns her mouth with hot food (57). She takes a chunk of horse leg away from an English child, who, because it is so tough, "lay sucking, gnawing, chewing and slobbering it in the Mouth and Hand" (60). The very language she uses here makes her sound more worldly than innocent. She seems quite cunning when, to explain why she won't ask her husband to redeem her, she says, "For there was little more trust to them [the Indians] than to the masters they served" (62). She writes a worldly account of an old, drunken Indian's inability to catch a young squaw. Instead, he settles for an older woman, and Rowlandson relates how "he ran to her; and so through the lord's mercy, we were no more troubled with him that night" (67).

Eventually enjoying much of the "savage" food she has to eat, Rowlandson casts this food as a prodigy of God's mercy, but her enjoyment of it identifies her with the Indians. These predilections become more than just a matter of similar tastes, especially when she marvels at the Indians' ability to survive despite eating food "that a Hog or Dog would hardly touch" (69). She considers this ability a remarkable providence, in that God must have been keeping them alive in order to afflict the English, but the fact is she herself survives by eating such "Indian" food.

Not only does Rowlandson give herself Indian attributes; the Indians themselves appear quite civilized. Despite being away from any "Christian soul" and being surrounded by Indians she had "no knowledge of," she admits that "not one of them offered the least imaginable miscarriage to me." She attributes their politeness to God's mercy, but nevertheless their manners do show the Indians in a positive light. Wandering cold and without a fire to warm herself by, Rowlandson receives an invitation into the wigwam of some Indians she doesn't know. She goes in, and they tell her they would buy her if they could. The following example of some positive Indian traits highlights their dual nature for Rowlandson: "In the morning they took the blood of the deer and put it into the paunch and so boiled it; I could eat nothing of that, though they ate it sweetly, and yet they were so nice in other things that when I had fetched water and had put the dish I dipped the water with into the kettle of water which I brought, they would say they would knock me down. They said it was a sluttish trick" (57).

Rowlandson also depicts the Indians as deceitful liars. She asks to see her son and the Indians tell her they have eaten him. She says, "I considered their horrible addictedness to lying and that there is not one of them that makes the least conscience of speaking the truth" (52). Similarly, she says the Indians tried to make her believe her husband had forgotten her, had remarried, and even thought she was dead. "So like were these barbarous creatures," she says, "to him who was a liar from the beginning" (53).

The Indians are two-faced. But Rowlandson can scheme too. She refuses to send for her husband, she says, because she fears the Indians will hurt him. The line between Puritan truth and Indian error blurs in her narrative. On her return, she makes a surprising analogy between the control her Indian captors had over her and the stifling attentions she receives from her fellow Puritans: "I was not before so much hemmed in with the merciless and cruel heathen but now as much with pitiful, tenderhearted, compassionate Christians" (71). She finds herself then, in the end, in quite a modern place, a no-man's-land, the very realm of modern fiction.

The Battle To Be Believed

In a world of lies and insecurity, characters in providence tales either seek something to believe in or try to create belief in others. John Williams's captivity narrative dramatizes the battle between Papist and Puritan ministers in order to convince congregants of their separate versions of the truth. Williams exposes French lies in his attempt to win the minds of the English, whom he describes as sheep surrounded by wolves. Early in his sermon, he says of his fellow captives, "God has upheld many poor souls . . . and kept them from falling though crafty adversaries were under all advantages, and painful endeavours used to seduce them" (Clark and Vaughan 161).

Throughout seventeenth-century New England literature, the Puritans describe themselves as innocents threatened by deceptive adversaries. In Bradford's *Of Plimouth Plantation*, a substantial part of the narrative concerns the suspicious practices of business agents such as Thomas Weston and Isaac Allerton. Chapter 5 of book 7 of *Magnalia Christi Americana*, "Wolves in Sheeps Clothing," relates the stories of several notorious false ministers who afflicted New England during this period, including John Lyford and Samuel May. *Decennium Luctuosum* and histories by Increase and Cotton Mather, William Hubbard, John Winthrop, and others detail instances in which, during peace negotiations with Indians, the "savages" victimized the Puritans with their treachery. Con artists lurk everywhere in these texts, poised to subvert the Puritan's historical destiny. They represent distorted images of New England heroes who also strive to create belief in their followers. Williams shows the wolves' lies are indeed a serious threat, that the French and the Indians can be convincing liars. At Fort St. François he finds "several poor children who had been taken from the Eastward the summer before, a sight very affecting, they being in habit very much like Indians and in manner very much symbolizing with them" (Clark and Vaughan 183). Later, an English maid taken in the last war appears "dressed up in Indian apparel, [who] could not speak one word of English, who said she could neither tell her own name or the name of the place from whence she was taken" (185). His own daughter Eunice, who married a converted Indian, is compelled to pray in Latin. The few times she does see her family again, she can no longer speak English.

Conversion then entails a loss of one's language along with a loss of one's faith. The battle over souls and beliefs becomes a battle over language, too. Those who convert, who accept another version of truth, can no longer tell their story to their original people, and thus cannot declare the works of the lord. They cannot, that is, tell a convincing providence tale. The battle over belief is a literary battle, and the person with the most convincing words becomes the most effective storyteller who, in turn, can inspire other stories to be told. When people convert, as Eunice does, the loss of their language hurts their families as much as their physical absence does. Losing one's native tongue becomes a symbol of spiritual infidelity. Regaining one's own language equals renewing one's faith. Therefore, writing and reading providential captivity narratives become literary forms of a Mass.

The words in books and letters, the tools of knowledge and reason, are among the primary weapons used in Williams's battles with his French and Indian adversaries. He presents his strongest arguments in his two letters to Samuel. Williams reports that according to the French a letter from Queen Anne to the governor of Port Royal has started the present war. The French claimed to have found the letter on a captured English ship. The queen allegedly wrote, Williams says, "how she approved his [the governor's] design to ensnare and deceitfully to seize on the Indians. . . . [So] they began the present war. I told them the letter was a lie forged by the French" (Clark and Vaughan 184). Another epistolary scene occurs in Samuel's letter to his father, concerning the two women who had supposedly converted on their deathbeds. Samuel writes that they had died in possession of letters calling on other Englishmen and women to convert. But when Williams looks over Samuel's letter, he "presently knew it to be of Mr. Merial's composing" (208). He also concludes that Merial has probably had Samuel rewrite or translate many letters into English in order to persuade others to convert. Creating belief is a matter of writing convincingly.

Williams's narrative seeks to persuade people to believe him rather than the Jesuits. In one scene the struggle becomes a battle of the books, and books become literal weapons. Of his own debates with Jesuits holding him in isolation fifteen miles from his fellow captives, he relates, "When I used their own authors to confute some of their positions, my books, borrowed of them, were taken away from me, for they said, I made an ill use of them. They having, many of them, boasted of their unity in doctrine and profession, were loath I should show them, from their own best approved authors, as many different opinions as they charge against me" (Clark and Vaughan 195–96). Williams emphasizes the power of words. Books are weapons for him. The French work to force captives to pray at Mass, which of course they perform in Latin, a tongue foreign to youths such as Eunice Williams. Williams calls on the Lord to reveal their false words, to "turn the counsels of these Ahitophels [who also caused a separation between a father and a son] into foolishness, and make the counsels of the heathen of none effect" (191).

The Papists use more than letters and books in their stratagems to "allure souls" (Clark and Vaughan 197). They offer to bribe Williams with "a great and honorable pension from the king" (195), if he will "stay among them and be of their religion." They tell his son that his father has agreed to defect for two hundred pounds per year. They tell all the children that their parents have converted and forgotten them. They threaten their prisoners, and offer consolations such as marriages, too: "Some made it their work to allure poor souls by flatteries and great promises. Some offered abusive carriages to such as refused to go to church and be present at Mass; for some they industriously contrived to get them married among them" (196–97).

The French also use providence tales to scare their captives. They circulate apparition stories in which Indians who haven't converted are recognized in hell (201). But just as Williams matches their cunning in using their own authors' arguments to refute the consistency of their beliefs, so he also uses providence tales as weapons and describes similarly sensational events to prove the truthfulness of his own beliefs.

Williams's tales use gothic elements just as More, Baxter, Glanvill, and Sinclair did in England. After a dispute with a mendicant friar sent to Quebec to convert the English there, Williams is sent back to Chateauriche, where he has been held apart from the other prisoners. Rather than concocting his own argument against the friar, Williams lets God show who is right in more compelling and dramatic ways. The story he tells is a providence tale, a remarkable account of some preternatural effects of lightning and thunder. The story provides spectacular and empirical evidence of God's presence: "The day after my being sent away, by the Priest's means, from Quebec, at first, there was a thunder storm, and the lightning struck the seminary in the very place where the fire [which then burned it down, and had been caused by a joiner letting a fiery coal drop into a pile of shavings] now began" (Clark and Vaughan 200).

Another popular providence tale form concerned the remarkable effects of prayer. Williams uses it when he tries to certify Puritan prayer as more effective than Jesuitical methods of seeking God's aid. He proves the power of prayers he offers against some mocking, anti-English Jesuit verses by noting that "upon an observation of the time of these verses being composed, I find that near the same time the bishop of Canada, with twenty ecclesiasticks, were taken by the English, as they were coming from France, and carried into England as prisoners of war" (Clark and Vaughan 193).

When some Jesuit priests brag that it rained the previous day after their morning prayers for rain, and after they held a procession carrying "an holy relick, one of the bones of St. Paul" (193), Williams claims he saw signs of rain that morning in "a great moisture on the stone of the hearth and chimney jamb" (193), and that moreover the rain had begun around dinner time (midday), before the procession began. After these empirical refutations of Jesuit superstition, he adds, "we had been answered when praying for rain, when no such signs of rain, and the beginnings of rain, preceded, as now with them, before they appointed or began their procession" (193).

Williams himself is a master of convincing people to believe. He uses many of the same methods to persuade as those employed by his archenemy, Merial. When he is offered a steady income and the right to see his children regularly if he will convert, we see him poised on the line between truth and deception, although, in fact, he has been on this border continually. He rejects the offer, instead composing a poem "in the plain style," in which he laments that "crafty designs are us'd by Papists all / In ignorance of truth, these [the captives] to inthrall" (198). Williams's business is the mirror image of the work of the lying priests and French con artists he confronts. Williams differs from them as much in the technical superiority of his stories as in any claim to higher morals he may have. His persuasive literary repertoire not only includes theology and homespun verse; he also employs a subtle form of satire. He tells, for example, of a "barefoot and barelegged" soldier on a pilgrimage to get his captain, the governor's brother-in-law, out of purgatory. This soldier has been sent to the home where he is staying to "gain [Williams's] credit of their devised purgatory," but Williams "would not be reclaimed from a denial of purgatory by such a miraculous providence." Here and in the following passage, Williams portrays his adversaries as an inept, comical bunch, similar to Stockwell's haggling Indians: "[Eventually] the soldier's conversation was such, that several among the French themselves judged it to be a forgery. And though the captain spoken of was the governour's lady's brother, I never more heard any concernment or care to get him out of purgatory" (200–201).

Williams can be seen as the foremost among this group of persuasive theologians. The most reasonable of captives, he also brings God on stage in the most spectacular manner. He describes at length his aching feet and his inability to walk across some rough ice because of them. He prays, and his prayers are answered by a soft covering of fluffy snow that cushions his feet and enables him to continue walking (181). He and his captors then cannot canoe across a lake because of a fierce wind. Williams describes how his prayers lead to an abatement of God's anger and of the contrary breeze (187). Williams's varied use of melodrama, theology, common sense, and satire illustrates his persuasive powers. His technical skills parallel those of his French adversaries. This connection to his enemies ironically diminishes his claims to spiritual superiority, while it furthers his political and literary potency as well as the secular characteristics of providence tales.

The "Unauthorized" Texts: Into the Wigwam

The most extreme examples of English assimilation to French and Native American cultures appear in stories of captives who either stayed with the Indians for extended periods or did not return at all. Such characters became, as the next century progressed, a more popular variant of the Indian captivity narrative. The beginnings of this assimilation can be seen in Mary Rowlandson's tale, as well as in earlier relations such as Cabeza de Vaca's. Rowlandson confesses that her reunion with her husband is marred, partly, by despair over their children, one of whom died and two of whom are unaccounted for; this, she writes, "abated . . . our comfort each in the other." When she also states "I was not before so much hem'd in with the merciless and cruel Heathens, but now as much with pitiful, tender hearted compassionate Christians," she seems reluctant to return.

Other characters were even more reluctant to return, and expressed greater admiration for the Indians than Rowlandson did. Perhaps for these reasons their stories were not published for years, sometimes for centuries. A full account of the captivity of John Williams's son Stephen was not published until 1889. A story of the Deerfield raid by Stephen's friend Remembrance Sheldon only appeared in 1920. Their stories reflect greater ambiguity and secularization than those texts that were published at the time the events occurred. As a group, these later "unauthorized" texts reflect many of the most significant cultural characteristics the earlier narratives were developing.

I have already mentioned Eunice Williams, seven at the time of her capture in 1704 during the same raid in which her father, mother, and several siblings were also carried away. Eunice married a Caghnawaga Indian in 1714 and resisted all attempts to redeem her, but (except for brief references in her father's narrative) her story did not begin to be widely told until the publication of works such as John Fessenden's 1837 sermon about her, "Sermon preached . . . in Deerfield in the hearing of several Indians of both sexes supposed to be descendants of Eunice Williams," Elizabeth Williams Champney's *Great Grandmother's Girls in New France: The History of Little Eunice Williams* (1887), C. Alice Baker's *True Stories of New England Captives Carried to Canada During the Old French and Indian War* (1897), and C. Johnson's *An Unredeemed Captive* (1897).

In *Decennium Luctuosum*, Cotton Mather writes brief accounts of captives whose stories were more highly developed much later. Margaret Otis was captured from Dover, New Hampshire, then called Cocheco, in 1686, along with Sarah Gerish. Indians captured Mary Plaisted in York, Maine, in 1696. Mather employs Plaisted and Gerish in brief, sentimental accounts of savage violence. Information about these captives in C. Alice Baker's 1897 work complicates the simple and grim picture of maligned innocence Mather presents. Two daughters of Plaisted captured with her converted to Catholicism and never returned to the English settlements. Mary Plaisted herself does return, but Mather fails to add that "In October 1696, a year after Mary Plaisted's redemption, she was presented at the court of Wells for not attending Ye Publick worship of God upon ye Lord's Day." Baker also writes of Gerish's next-door neighbor in Dover, Margaret Otis, captured in the same raid as Gerish, though Mather says nothing about her. Otis, four then, was baptized Christine in Canada, married a Frenchman, and finally ran off with one of the men who helped redeem her, the well-known Indian fighter Thomas Baker. C. Alice Baker writes that in 1727 Thomas Baker was tried at Springfield, Massachusetts, on a charge of blasphemy: "There being a discourse of God's having in his providence put in Joseph Jennings, Esquire of Brookfield, a Justice of the Peace, Captain Baker said, 'If I had been with the Almighty, I would have taught him better.'"

Ex-captives (Thomas Baker had been held captive by the French) with such satirical views of providence, or who, like Plaisted, seemed so ungrateful or un-repentant despite their deliverances, were not the stuff of Matherian captivity narratives. The Mathers also repress or omit information in their detailed ac-count of the captive Nathaniel Belding's horrible wound and miraculous recov-ery. More details of Belding's captivity, which he underwent with his father, sis-ter, and a friend, did not appear until the complete publication of Stephen Williams's 1704 captivity journal in 1889. Williams describes a less than excruci-ating ordeal: "The Indians kept Mr. Belding himself, and his daughter with them, and gave John Gillet and N.B. to the French. John Gillet worked as a ser-vant to the nuns at their farm, and N.B. worked for the Holy Sisters. . . . Mr. Belding was sold to the French and lived as a servant with the Jesuits at the sem-inary. His business was to wait upon them, and cut wood, make fires, &c., and tend the garden, and accepted himself favourably dealt by, &c" (116).

John Williams's son Stephen, eleven at the time of his capture during the Deerfield raid of 1704, kept a journal that includes an account of his captivity experience. The entire journal remained unpublished until a third edition of John Williams's narrative appeared in 1758, but a substantial part of Stephen's story did not see print until 1837, and only in 1889 was the entire manuscript published. Ambiguity dominates this text. He depicts himself as a typically in-sensitive and self-centered eleven-year-old, totally out of line with the ideal children of the primers, exemplums, and providence tales such as those in Jane-way's *Tokens for Children*. Rather than emphasize the gothic and tragic horror of his predicament, Stephen Williams consistently introduces subjects of more vital immediate self-concern: "After they had broken into our house and took us prisoners . . . they barbarously murdered a brother and sister of mine, as they did several of our neighbors. . . . Before they departed from the place they barbarously murdered a child of about two years old. There my master took away my English shoes, and gave me Indian ones in the room of them, which I think were better to travel in" (Stephen W. Williams, 1837, 103).

This abrupt shift from death to more everyday, practical matters occurs again, when, three short sentences after mentioning the death of his "ever hon-ored mother," he writes, "Here they searched me and took away my silver but-tons and buckle which I had on my shirt" (103). He cannot write of things beyond his immediate self-interest for more than one sentence: "Here they killed near a dozen women and children, for their manner was, if any loitered, to kill them. My feet were very sore so that I was afraid they would kill me also"

(103). He notices that Jacob Hix "was nothing but skin and bones . . . [and] died at the first carrying place of the French River (now Onion River). This was an exceedingly tedious march to me, we being so loaded" (106).

His adventures with the Indians have a more idyllic flavor than Hannah Swarton's accounts of survival and comradeship with Indian women. Stephen goes hunting for two or three months with his master's brother. The Indians are kind to him and take care of his frozen toe. They give him deer skin to lie on and a bearskin covering. He eats well, although he complains, like his father, of a lack of bread and salt. He also objects that he is forced to carry wood and a heavy pack for long distances, and that he has no society but with "inhuman pagans." But these inconveniences don't stop him from deeply admiring the Indian boys. They "do kill the geese with their bows and arrows, they are so bold. Fish are taken easily with hooks. One day as we sailed in the lake, two young Indians shot a fish with a bullet and took it into the canoe. It was as large as I am" (106).

At times, Stephen Williams does act the part of a minister's son. Once, as he's crying out because he is lost in the snow, an angry Indian "lifted up the breach of his gun in order to kill me, but God kept back his hand, for which I desire [he says] his name might be praised." Another time Williams does refer to God's role in his deliverance: "And I desire that the name of the Lord may be praised and adored for his wonderful goodness to me in sparing my life when I was as it were, on the brink of eternity, and that he stayed the hands of those that took up their weapons to slay me with them" (110). But apart from these two instances, God plays little role in his deliverance. More typically, he is saved by Indians themselves, as when a ten-year-old Indian girl relieves his hunger with moose meat and leads him out of the woods after he loses his way.

Williams does follow some providence tale conventions in more traditional ways. He records his adventures in lively detail, even when the anecdotes reflect his laziness. He fails to cut wood because the weather is bad, even though his Indian master has ordered him to. He forgets to stir the maple sap as it "c[a]me to sugar." He also writes descriptively of the wounds he suffers trying to cross a river with a load of firewood. In that scene, he sounds like his father, complaining of his feet: "This was an exceedingly tedious march to me, we being so loaded. The other Indians left us. I suffered much in this journey for when we came to the French River it was as much as our canoes would carry our lumber, the water was so shallow, so that I was forced to travel a foot, on that bank, which cut out my shows, my feet were much galled, and one or two of my toes almost cut off with the stones" (106).

These injuries to his toes appear again in a second captivity story from this period which was not published for 202 years. This narrative of the Deerfield raid, the *Story of Remembrance Sheldon*, was transcribed from the original manuscript by Matilda S.(Stang) Hyde and published in 1920. Where Stephen Williams's account is often obscure and jagged, Sheldon's is a smooth, well-executed work. It exhibits many important providence tale tropes, while it also, more than any other narrative, indicates the direction these narratives were moving toward. That the hero of this piece also happens to be Stephen Williams makes it even more interesting.

Remembrance Sheldon was eleven at the time of the raid. He waited fourteen years, until 1718, to write about his experiences. Instead of seeking to show God's mercies, he says he wants to memorialize his mother, Hannah, so his bride to be, also named Hannah, might remember her: "And that this Hannah may better know and love the other whose memory we both so reverently do cherish, I, Hannah Sheldon's youngest boy, Remembrance, but meanly versed in writing, do now for the first time set on paper the events that follow" (Hyde 3).

Sheldon writes to reveal the wonders of Hannah, not the wonders of God. Like any other providence tale writer, he is humble ("I . . . but meanly versed in writing"). He also relates that his father had been away at the time of the raid, "nor has he to this day forgiven himself for being absent on that wretched night." His father feels so guilty that he never returns to live in Deerfield, despite having atoned by helping to bring some of the captives back, and despite the fact that some of his children still live there. The figure of the missing father figures prominently in this tale, but here he is never restored. Instead, this narrative, through a wealth of vivid details, offers one example after another of the assimilation of the English to the surrounding Indian culture, and vice versa.

Remembrance says he is happy that he no longer lives in Deerfield, where he would have to see his older brother and sister "dispense hospitality at Deerfield tavern to scores of Mohawk Indians whom they (Mary and Ebenezar) durst not turn away, giving them free bed and board because, forsooth, of having lived captive in their lodge" (3). Sheldon describes the life of the young Deerfield boys in the weeks prior to the 1704 raid. He shows their frustration at not being able to go outside the thick, wooden palisades being erected, and describes their yearning for the outdoors: "Much to our disgust . . . we were not let out even to help with the harvests in the field." In the midst of this captivity, in a winter of deep snows, he presents an admiring description of an Indian sent from Albany to warn them of the impending raid: "We were much startled to see the Indian, tall, and with an almost noble cast of countenance, glide into our midst" (4).

Cooped up, the boys play their favorite game, "Puritans and Indians." In this game they reenact the capture of the two Nims boys, who were caught while searching the meadows for their cattle: "It was one of our favorite sports (I blush even now to think of) to enact this scene in one barn or another, each of us clamoring for his turn to play the Indian" (7). Sheldon also describes the boys' interest in cock fights, which they watch secretly, on the lookout for the parson and schoolmaster. Whenever either of those two appear, the boys pretend to be busy, "a spinning of tops." Only one boy has no interest in the cock fights: Stephen Williams, whose nose, Sheldon says, is always in a book.[13] He first appears then as the one boy in town without savage inclinations.

Sheldon relates the story of the unknown person, who in escaping the village leaves open a back door which allows the Indians to enter. He describes his own skill at mumble-de-peg, which serves him well during the raid when he's surprised by an Indian, as "his hand instinctively went to his dirk and he killed the Injun." He also gives several reasons for Eunice's not wanting to return: her anger over hearing her father has remarried; the French telling her she will be damned if she returns, and the brave she married being the finest Indian Sheldon had ever met. Sheldon also says young English captives refuse or appear to be unable to speak English when they are allowed to see English people again because they are taunted by the Indians if they do speak English. Stephen Williams offers the same explanation in his journal.

But what most attracts my attention to Sheldon's narrative is the image he presents of Stephen Williams on his return from captivity:

> Before he left Deerfield he was one person; in the years since his captivity he has been another, very different. Small and puny and over much given to books, how he stood the march to Canada is to this day to me a mystery.
>
> But never have I known man or boy who could endure as he can today, nor who is so versed in the lore of the woods. On snowshoes he is tireless, and he can outswim us all. Every trick in trapping game, large and small, he knows by heart, and he has a deadly aim, whether with gun or with bow and arrow. I believe that with two sticks he could kindle a fire in a deluge.
>
> I asked him once if all these things were not worth a year alone among the savages. He looked at me very steadily for a moment. Then, to my surprise, he leaned over and bared one of his feet. There were ugly scars at the base of the toes. As I gazed I marveled that the toes had ever grown to the foot again.
>
> "You see those scars?" he said. "Those wounds have healed, but I tell you, Remembrance"—here his dark eyes flashed and he laid a hand to his heart—"I tell you that here is a hurt that will never heal." (13–14)

Remembrance's admiration for Stephen's skills illustrates the attraction Indian life held for New England youths. Stephen's transformation, along with remarks of praise for the Indian boys' skills in his journal, prove that many aspects of Indian life impressed him. His last remarks in the above passage, in their intimation of unspeakable horrors and their evocation of his own and the rest of his family's suffering, show his simultaneous hatred of the Indians. Caught in this anger, he expresses no repentance or acceptance of God's judgments. His suffering speaks through his flashing dark eyes, and seems as savage as the Indian torture inflicted on him. All his emotions regarding Indians have a wild quality. This Stephen Williams contains the seeds of future American Indian haters as depicted by Judge Hall in *Legends of the West,* by Robert Bird in *Nick of the Woods,* or by Herman Melville in *The Confidence Man.* In learning Indian ways so well, he foreshadows American pioneer figures such as Daniel Boone and Natty Bumpo. Through Remembrance Sheldon's eyes, Stephen appears as the untameable American boy, forever lighting out for the territories.

Stephen Williams is not just a savage young man. He is also a student of Indian culture and an explorer. This Enlightenment side of Williams contrasts with the more religious figure described in John Demos's book about Eunice Williams, *The Unredeemed Captive.* Here Williams appears primarily as a devout Puritan minister, with "intense, often agonized spirituality" (172). Demos follows his lifelong efforts to bring his sister Eunice out and back: out of the hands of the Catholic church and her Indian/Catholic husband, and back to New England, the Puritan church, and her family. Stephen Williams was also active, Demos informs us, in efforts to educate, Christianize, and otherwise civilize young Indians.

Stephen Williams's captivity experience has split him at least in half. Demos senses this tension when he wonders, "Did [Williams] recognize his work with these boarder/pupils for the turnabout it transparently was? Did he remark anew his own boyhood experience with Indians, who taught him to hunt and fish 'after their own manner,' who cut his hair 'like an Indian, one side long and the other short'? . . . Perhaps at some level, his interest in this 'civilizing' project touched long-buried feelings about his own captivity" (182). Perhaps Stephen Williams's lifelong preoccupation with bringing Eunice back and with converting Indian youths was one way of resolving his Indian, explorer side with his deeply Puritanical side. Like Robert Montgomery Bird's Nathan Slaughter, and like Ahab, Melville's great navigator of the wild ocean, Stephen has developed "deadly aim," and suffers from "a hurt that will never heal."[14]

Demos's Eunice Williams is a mysterious figure throughout *The Unredeemed Captive.* She no longer speaks English. Indeed, for many years she refuses to speak in any tongue to the emissaries the Williamses send. The few words she does utter in her Indian language are oracular in their terseness and ambiguity. When she finally does come to Massachusetts, she arrives in full Indian regalia, and pointedly refuses the offer of new clothing. She remains thoroughly disguised or concealed, the subject of endless interpretation and reinterpretation. After years of effort, Stephen does get her to hint she might come home, but only with her converted Indian husband and her mixed-breed children. But return she never does. Her hints of doing so, Demos suggests, are calculated to regain her inheritance. Although she never receives the entire estate, Stephen gives her gifts, and gets his government to give her more money to induce her to come home. Once again, questions of credibility, belief, and identity dominate a tale of Indian captivity.

Confidence schemes hover around Eunice throughout Demos's account of her story. In 1729 John Williams died, and in his estate "Eunice the Second Daughter" was bequeathed "two hundred and twenty pounds and Eight pence" (177). In February of 1734, a woman appeared in Newport, Rhode Island, who said her name was Williams, and whose history, according to her story, matched Eunice's. After much hesitation, hope, doubt, and correspondence, Stephen went to see for himself. He discovered "her to be a meer cheat, a vile wick'd woman yt had followd ye army for a great while" (181). Six months later another cheat with similar claims appeared. "Taken together," Demos concludes, "the two episodes showed a growing danger that outright impostors might claim the identity—not to mention the patrimony—of the (still) 'unredeemed captive'" (181).

These women are by no means the only actresses or con artists who take part in captivity-related dramas. One of the two Tarbell boys, captured during Queen Anne's War, is noted a few years after his capture by a Massachusetts merchant visiting Albany, for his "Indian dress and . . . his Indian complexion (for by means of grease and paints but little difference could be discerned)" (186). Finally, in Demos's epilogue, he describes two of Eunice's great-grandchildren, brought to Longmeadow (Stephen's home) in 1800 by their father, to be educated and civilized by Stephen's granddaughter's husband, Deacon Nathaniel Ely. The boys startle Longmeadow by their colorful costumes and their "very grotesque and attractive appearance" (243). They wear "beaded wampum . . . about the loins" and their hair is "carelessly stuck with feathers." Demos quotes Ely saying that in church

"the whole congregation, on Sunday, instead of looking at the minister . . . could . . . think of little but the Indians." Their teachers were obliged "to humour . . . the wildness of their nature and habits . . . [and] to endure the disorder which their manners at first created." From time to time they would "jump up and cry 'Umph' or some other characteristic and guttural exclamation, and then perhaps spring across the room." Occasionally they would "dart out" of the schoolhouse altogether, "and take to their heels in such direction as their whims might incline them." (243)

The younger boy, John Sunwattis, returned to Kahnawake in Canada (where Eunice had lived with her husband, Arosen) at the age of twelve, after five years in Massachusetts. Eleazar, now sixteen, remained and became a local favorite. He was favored and "introduced into the best society in New England," primarily because he was "descended of the famous Reverend John Williams" (244). But after showing promise of being a fine and reputable Puritan, he was labeled "a fat, lazy, good for nothing Indian" by one detractor (245). Still Eleazar was not finished. Demos writes, "Eleazar was about to make a spectacular, if short lived comeback. Somehow in the late 1840's, he conceived the idea that he was not, biographically speaking, the man he seemed to be. Instead, he was the 'lost Dauphin': Louis XVII, scion of the Bourbon dynasty and rightful heir to the throne of France. In fact, Eleazar was one of at least forty such pretenders (worldwide), but his ingeniously argued claim put him near the front of the pack" (245). Even the distant sequels to captivity narratives concern the slipperiness of truth and focus on mysterious half-breeds like Eleazar Thorakwineken Williams. Indian captivity was like the fall; it divided a soul and stained it with sins handed down to subsequent generations.

CONCLUSION

The use of providence tales as analytical models for witchcraft relations and Indian captivity narratives spotlights a large and neglected group of seventeenth-century British and early American texts. The addition of this discourse to the Colonial American canon enriches a field that has been considered imitative and relatively lifeless. Providence tales' lively sensationalism belies widespread notions of Puritan rigidity and gloom. The tales' empirical methodology makes them valuable records of the period's cultural history.

These characteristics of sensationalism and empiricism produced increasingly more dramatic and believable prose narratives. Writers could now represent the theories, subjects, and accounts of seventeenth-century theological debates, scientific research, and voyages of discovery in entertaining prose relations. In these tales, the new science's testimony renewed the supernatural world, while scientific research seemed a livelier and more dramatic occupation. The end products of this unique literary collision were germinal forms of early fiction, imaginary worlds depicted in accordance with the rules of empirical analysis. The unique aesthetic structure of providence tales grounded the supernatural world in the material world and made possible the perseverance of Reformation spirituality in an enlightened era. This aesthetic structure also allowed prose narratives to become a form which could carry a divine theme; this new ability furthered the growth of fiction at the expense of poetry.

The providence tale model of witchcraft relations and of the captivity narrative demonstrates the deep dependency of early American literature on British forebears. But it also clarifies creative American transformations of those precursors. Distinctions between the supernatural and the material worlds, between good and evil, and between concepts of savagery and civilization became increasingly ambiguous in Salem trial discourse and in captivity narratives. The tenuousness and instability of the Salem judges' political positions, the Native American characters, and the wilderness setting led the tales in the direction of the morally relative world so familiar in modern fiction. These captivity narratives' aesthetic vision subsequently permeated the main line of American discourse, not just its lower levels of political propaganda and mass market thrillers. It seems hard to miss the emotional terror of Poe's super-rationalistic gothic tales in these witchcraft and captivity relations. Traces of Melville's Ishmael and Ahab, innocent and truth seeker facing the gothic whale in a gothic ocean on board a gothic ship, appear in these early captivities. The images of cultural assimilation and transformation presented by Stephen Williams and the seven-year-old Eunice Williams show us a much earlier source for R.W.B. Lewis's "American Adam" than is usually acknowledged. The innocent figure Lewis describes as facing the darkness of time and history or rejecting the past dominates these early Indian captivity narratives. Struck by some nightmarish wound, captives spend the rest of their lives reenacting that moment of injury.

The view of the captivities as providence tales supports Annette Kolodny's idea that America's frontier literature deserves a far more prominent place in American literary studies. The captivity narratives fit precisely into her definition of frontier literature as "a locus of first cultural contact, circumscribed by a particular physical terrain in the process of change" (Kolodny, "Letting Go," 9). Certainly apparition tales recognize "the relation between human beings and the non-human world" (4), another important characteristic of frontier literature for Kolodny. Indeed, Joseph Glanvill anticipated Kolodny when he called the psychic world a new frontier and a "kinde of America." The continued study of frontier literature, Kolodny says, "promises liberation from the stultifying habit of regarding that literature [early American] merely as a precursor to an authentic literature yet to follow or as transition pieces between British forebears and American identities" (3). New England's providence tales, with their shipwrecks, captivities, Indian conversions, phony ministers, maddened Quakers, criminal confessions, ghost tales, and assorted magnalia dei, constitute one current frontier in American literature which needs further exploration.

Notes

PREFACE

1. From the 1980s until now, some of these authors and their works include: Nancy Armstrong and Leonard Tennenhouse, *The Imaginary Puritan: Literature, Intellectual Labor, and the Origins of Personal Life*; Rosalie Baum and others, in Frank Shuffelton's *A Mixed Race: Ethnicity in Early America*; Mitchell Robert Breitwieser, *American Puritanism and the Defense of Mourning: Religion, Grief, and Ethnology in Mary White Rowlandson's Captivity Narrative*; Christopher Castiglia, *Bound and Determined: Captivity, Culture Crossing, and White Womanhood from Mary Rowlandson to Patty Hearst*; John Demos, *The Unredeemed Captive: A Family Story from Early America*; Kathryn Derounian-Stodola and James Levernier, *The Indian Captivity Narrative, 1550–1990*; Evan Haefeli and Kevin Sweeny, "Revisiting the Redeemed Captive"; Susan Howe, *The Birth Mark: Unsettling the Wilderness in American Literary History*; Annette Kolodny, "Letting Go Our Grand Obsessions: Notes Toward a New Literary History of the American Frontier" and *The Land before Her*; and June Namias, *White Captives: Gender and Ethnicity on the American Frontier*.

2. Williams's book is *Pillars of Salt: An Anthology of Early American Criminal Narratives*; Cohen's is *Pillars of Salt, Monuments of Grace: New England Crime Literature and the Origins of American Popular Culture, 1676–1860*.

3. See Demos, *The Unredeemed Captive*; Dorson, ed., *America Begins: Early American Writing*; Levernier's introduction to Increase Mather's *Essay for the Recording of Illustrious Providences*; and Parson's introductions to both George Sinclair's *Satan's Invisible World Discovered* and Joseph Glanvill's *Saducismus Triumphatus*.

4. However, recent books such as Ian Steele's *The English Atlantic, 1675–1740* suggest that this view was somewhat more grounded in religious myth than in fact.

1. Such as Boccaccio's *The Fate of Illustrious Men* (1358).

2. For the view of the captivities as a rapidly declining genre, see chapter 1, note 1.

3. See Richard Hakluyt, *The Principall Navigations, Voiages, and Discoveries of the English Nation* (London, 1589).

4. From Clarke's *A Mirrour or Looking Glass Both for Saints and Sinners*, 4th ed. (London, 1671), 1:512. See chapter 4 below for more details on this story.

Chapter 1. Remapping Colonial Discourse from Providence Tale to Indian Captivity Narrative

1. Philip Carleton, Roy Harvey Pearce, Richard Slotkin, James Levernier, Alden Vaughan, Daniel Richter, Edward Clark, Hennig Cohen, Richard VanDerBeets, Kathryn Zabelle Derounian, Joseph Norman Heard, and Frances Roe Kestler are among these critics.

2. Kolodny includes as frontier narratives: "Eskimo legends of the Tunnit; Christopher Columbus's 'Letter to Lord Sanchez . . . on His First Voyage'; Amerigo Vespucci's *Mundus Novus*; Gaspar Perez de Vallagra's *Historia de la Nueva Mexico*; William Bradford's *History of Plimmouth Plantation*; Mary Rowlandson's captivity narrative; and Daniel Boone's putative autobiography" (Kolodny, "Letting Go Our Grand Obsessions," 5). She feels her approach "promises liberation from the stultifying habit of regarding that literature [early American] merely as a precursor to an authentic literature yet to follow or as a transition piece between British forbears and American identities" (3).

3. See Kolodny's article in *American Literature* 64, no.1(1992) for more writers reconfiguring early American history.

4. The following picture of the demographics of Indian captivity in seventeenth-century New England come largely from five works. Alden Vaughan and Daniel Richter, in their "Crossing the Cultural Divide: Indians and New Englanders, 1605–1763," and Richard Slotkin, in *Regeneration through Violence*, both acknowledge drawing much of their primary information from works by two other authors I have consulted: Charlotte Alice Baker's 1897 *True Stories of New England Captives Carried to Canada during the Old French and Indian Wars* and Emma Lewis Coleman's 1925 *New England Captives Carried to Canada between 1677 and 1760 during the French and Indian Wars*. Another valuable book for demographic material is David Cressy's 1987 *Coming Over: Migration and Communication between England and New England in the Seventeenth Century*.

5. This and other figures regarding literary taste in seventeenth-century New England were culled from the following works: *Literary Culture in Early New England*, by Thomas Goddard Wright; "The Publication, Promotion, and Distribution of Mary Rowlandson's Indian Captivity Narrative in the Seventeenth Century," by Kathryn Zabelle Derounian; *Golden Multitudes: The Story of the Best Seller in the United States*, by Frank Mott; and *The Popular Book: A History of America's Literary Taste* by James Hart.

6. The other best sellers on Mott's list between 1660 and 1720 which reached the

same sales levels mentioned above for Rowlandson, Dickinson, and Williams are: *The Day of Doom*, Michael Wigglesworth, 1662; *A Call to the Unconverted*, Richard Baxter, 1664; *The Practice of Piety*, Lewis Bayly, 1665; *A Guide to Heaven*, Samuel Hardy, 1679; *The Pilgrim's Progress*, John Bunyan, 1681; *Essays*, Francis Bacon, 1688; *Seven Sermons*, Robert Russell, 1701; *Husbandry Spiritualized*, John Flavel, 1709; *Mother Goose's Melodies for Children*, 1719; and *Divine and Moral Songs for the Use of Children*, Isaac Watts, 1719. Mott also lists better sellers for the period which had total sales equal to at least "one per cent of the population of . . . the English Colonies in the years before the Revolution." These are: *Meat Out of the Eater*, Michael Wigglesworth, 1670; *The Fountains Opened*, Samuel Willard, 1700; *A Token for Children*, James Janeway, 1700; *Treatise on the Lord's Supper*, Thomas Doolittle, 1700; and *The Day of Grace*, Nathaniel Vincent, 1722.

7. Paul Kocher, in *Science and Religion in Elizabethan England*, notes where these writings can be found: Augustine, *The City of God* (1909 edition), bk. 5, ch. 8, 153 ff.; Boethius, *The Consolation of Philosophy*, bk. 5; Aquinas, *Summa Theologica*, pt. 1, q. 22 ff. (Kocher, 94).

8. For more information on providence tales, see James Levernier's introduction to Increase Mather's 1684 providence tale collection, *An Essay for the Recording of Illustrious Providences*, chapter 5 of Keith Thomas's *Religion and the Decline of Magic*, Coleman Parson's introductions to Joseph Glanvill's *Saducismus Triumphatus* and to George Sinclair's *Satan's Invisible World Discovered*, Paul Kocher's *Science and Religion in Elizabethan England*, as well as chapters 2 and 3 herein.

9. For more information on the Cambridge Platonists, see chapter 2 herein, and the following authors, listed in the bibliography: Cassirer, Cragg, Patrides, Powicke, Wiley, and Willey.

10. James Levernier, in his 1977 introduction to Increase Mather's *Essay*, notes this scientific bent of providence tale writers; he says, "In many respects, Mather's *Essay* is as much a scientific treatise as it is a theological one. All the selections in the *Essay* were collected by means of what were, at least for the time, sound scientific methodology" (xiii).

11. Perry Miller, in *The New England Mind: The Seventeenth Century*, quotes William Perkins expressing this idea: "Sometimes he governs according to the usual course and order of nature . . . yet so, as he can and doth most freely order all things by means either above nature or against nature" (Miller 228).

12. Perry Miller, in *The New England Mind: The Seventeenth Century*, wrote of special providences that they "differed from miracle[s] in that God wrought [them] through or with means, by natural instruments, by arranging the causes or influencing the agents, rather than by forcible interposition and direct compulsion." In the words of John Preston, whom Miller quotes, special providences are where "nature is turned off its course" (228).

These special providences were similar to preternatural phenomena described by Lorraine Daston, Keith Thomas, and Increase Mather in his introduction to the *Essay*. Generally, preternatural and supernatural phenomena both confounded natural law, but the supernatural usually indicated the direct hand of God, while in the former, God acted more indirectly, through angels, demons, witches, or some rearrangement of the natural order.

13. The Antinomian Crisis, King Philip's War, and Andros's and Randolph's post-Restoration moves against Massachusetts's sovereignty had been just the most obvious factors in the central church's declining influence and control.

14. As Levernier says, Mather does indeed cite a meeting of September 9, 1646, of the commissioners. In Ebenezer Hazard's *Historical Collections*, however, this meeting is headed September 24, 1646. In any case, this sermon, "A Discourse Concerning the Danger of Apostasy," was printed in 1679 as part of *A Call to Heaven*. Mather writes in this sermon: "I pray you in the name of the Lord, that a Speedy and Effective course may be taken, that the great things that God did for our Fathers, in planting these Heavens, and laying the Foundations of the Earth, be faithfully recorded and transmitted to Posterity. . . . One-half of the Old Testament is a chronicle of things done by the Lord for his people." And Mather calls for a "record of the great works of God towards them, for the benefit of the Generation that shall follow" (70–71).

15. The "prodigious" was a category closely related to the preternatural and to Miller's idea of special providences. Interest in it paralleled Bacon's turn to the unusual and abnormal. Increase Mather's "Magnalia Dei," defined in his preface, also fit here. Mather calls them "things wherein the glorious finger of God is eminently to be seen, but not always immediately to be understood (qtd. in Levernier's introduction, x).

16. Boyle was an eminent scientist and member of the Royal Society, and wrote, for example, *On the Usefulness of Experimental Natural Philosophy*; yet he was also governor of the Company for the Propagacion of the Gospell in New England and the Parts Adjacent in America, the fund-raising arm in England of American efforts to convert Indians during the reign of Charles II.

17. See Kathryn Derounian's article "The Publication, Promotion, and Distribution of Mary Rowlandson's Indian captivity Narrative in the Seventeenth Century." Also see Amy Schraeger Lang's introduction to Rowlandson in William Andrews's *Journeys in New Worlds: Early American Women's Narratives*, where she says, "At least one scholar has proposed the minister Gershom Bulkeley as its author" (Andrews 31n).

18. More's "Advertisements" to Glanvill's apparition tales were added to the 1681 edition of *Saducismus Triumphatus*. They follow each tale and add philosophical commentary and attestations of witnesses' veracity, and confront various skeptical adversaries of these stories. Increase Mather's "Cases of Conscience" ponder such questions as "Whether it be lawful to try witches by casting them into the water" (248), as well as other theoretical questions pertaining to the occult.

19. According to "Per Amicum," Rowlandson published her narrative only because her friends were affected by it and what it said about God's power and mercy. "This Gentlewoman's modesty," he writes, "would [never have] thrust it into the press" (x).

20. Many Cambridge Platonists, such as More, Cudworth, and Whichcote, as well as Boyle, Kenelm Digby, and other scientists, added their testimony to Greatrakes's own defense of his "preternatural" healing powers, his 1666 *A Briefe Account of M. Valentine Greatrak's, and Divers of the Strange Cures by Him Lately Performed*. An eminent, noble

lady and Neoplatonist philosopher, the Lady Anne Conway held court at her estate at Ragley to a group of eminent intellectuals, including the above men, who shared a belief in the presence of occult, supernatural forces in human affairs.

21. Gary Lindberg, in his 1982 *The Confidence Man in American Literature*, argues that the shifting nature of the new world, its lack of firm social identities, created a free rein for confidence men or anyone who could create belief (3–12).

22. Williams's 1707 narrative is a chronological exception for Pearce.

23. The film "Dances with Wolves" shows how persistent this trait is.

24. Miller says of providence tales:

> The New England literature is part of a wider movement, inspired no doubt, as among the Cambridge Platonists and in the works of Joseph Glanvill, by apprehensions lest the all-conquering science result in a theory of blind mechanism or endorse the blasphemies of Thomas Hobbes. Therefore the renewed insistence upon special providences in late seventeenth-century New England is the most noticeable response of its theologians to the new science, almost the only respect in which they were compelled to reorient their thinking or overhaul their doctrines in order to adjust themselves to the new era. . . . Yet this redistribution of emphasis meant no innovation in their theory. . . . The treatments of special providences written in the later decades of the century, whatever the occasion for their composition, added nothing new to the content of Puritan theory. . . . Cotton Mather, who ever followed with unequal steps the mighty strides of his father, wrote much that posterity will never read upon every kind of providence. *The New England Mind* 228–31)

25. Leslie Fiedler, in his *Return of the Vanishing American*, also takes a psychoanalytical view of the captivities, calling them imaginative enactments of "that basic white male desire at once to relish and deplore, vicariously share and publicly condemn, the rape of white female innocence" (93).

26. Armstrong and Tennenhouse see the captivity narrative as a mutation, a precursor itself of a subsequent English form, the sentimental, epistolary novel, rather than as the result of a previous English form, the providence tale, being transformed by the culture of the New World.

27. I am thinking in particular of Melville's extended descriptions and explanations of the whaling industry when I mention *Moby Dick*'s scientific realism.

CHAPTER 2.   THE PROVIDENCE TALE IN ENGLAND, 1597–1697

1. "Josephus states that the doctrine of free will was maintained by the Pharisees both against the Sadducees, who attributed everything to chance, and the Essenes, who ascribed all the actions of man to predestination and Divine Providence" (Hertz 882n).

2. Glanvill did not attend Cambridge, but he wished he had. He did have an intimate literary association with Henry More, and shared many of More's theological and

philosophical ideas. He was close enough to the Cambridge Platonists to be considered one.

3. Neile, 1562–1640, was Archbishop of York. Laud was his protégé. He sat on the High Commission and in the Star Chamber, and was always in favor of the divine right of the Episcopacy. As early as 1614 he declared himself against the House of Commons and for the royal prerogative.

4. Arminians in this context were English followers of Laud and Charles I who opposed a church independent of the state. They also tended to oppose many Calvinist (either Presbyterian, Congregational, or Independent) forms and practices. Although Puritans considered them popish, they actually stood somewhere between Rome and Geneva.

5. Bancroft, 1544–1610, was Archbishop of Canterbury from 1604 to 1610. A favorite of Whitgift's, he compelled the clergy to subscribe in 1604 to all the articles in a new book of canons he himself had compiled. As a result of this subscription, three hundred Puritan preachers were ejected from their livings, including some who eventually went to Plymouth.

6. This oath was passed in 1640. According to Orme, a contemporary of Baxter's, it was "an oath binding fallible men never to change themselves, or give their consent to alterations, however necessary, and including an 'et caetera' nobody knows what" (Lee 1:1352).

7. This was a petition of fifteen thousand London citizens made to Commons to destroy episcopacy "root and branch." It was passed in May of 1641, and dropped in August of that year. It proposed commissioners one-half lay and one-half clerical to "exercise ecclesiastical jurisdiction" over bishops.

8. Twelve Puritan ministers and twelve bishops discussed Puritan/church relations and the liturgy at this conference. A failure to come to an agreement led to the Act of Uniformity and the exclusion of over two thousand Puritans.

9. This 1662 Act was the fourth act so named. It insisted on the use of a revised *Book of Common Prayer*. It declared that bearing arms against the king was illegal and denied the binding force of the Solemn League and the Covenant. Schoolmasters henceforth needed a license from a bishop and episcopal ordination to hold a benefice. Heads of colleges and lecturers had to subscribe to the 39 Articles. Over two thousand ministers resigned their preferments as a result of its passage.

10. The Covenant was an old Scottish custom, a bond to the death for a common cause. In 1557 the Scotch barons and Protestant reformers joined together in this fashion against popery. King James I signed one in 1581. In 1638 Charles I, trying to force the English liturgy on Scotland, caused a new covenant to be forged there against the bishops. By then the Covenant had become the war cry of the Presbyterian party. In 1643 the English Parliament sought Scotish aid and the Scots in turn demanded mutual engagement by sworn pact, which was also called the Solemn League and Covenant. This was adopted by the Westminster Assembly but never effectively imposed on the nation. Charles II signed the Covenant in 1650, "at the invitation of the Estates," but he had it burned after the Restoration. By then the term *Covenanters* came to mean insurgents, and they some-

times joined with the outed ministers in conventicles. Such insurgents eventually had to be put down by an army of fifteen thousand under the Duke of Monmouth in 1679.

11. This act of 1673 excluded Charles II's Catholic councilors from the government. The king was hereby forced to stop his efforts to dispense with the penal laws against Dissenters. Anyone in state office had to take the oath of allegiance and supremacy, and subscribe to the declaration against transubstantiation.

12. This act, designed for the relief of Protestant dissenters, was advocated after the Test Act was enacted, but was finally dropped, as another like it had been in 1663. It would have freed ministers of the established church and members of universities from subscribing to the 39 Articles if only they would support "the doctrine, worship, and government of the Church of England." It would have left "scrupled ceremonies to discretion" and also would have allowed Presbyterian ministers to practice provided they "submitted to imposition by a bishop." This formal bill of 1681 was mutilated in the upper house, after which the king was to call the houses of convocation for ecclesiastical matters. Nonconformists also disliked the subscriptions required of them by the bill.

13. This act, 1665, stated the Nonconformist ministers had to stay out of places they'd ministered in. They could not teach without taking the oath of nonresistance. The act was a part of the regressive Clarendon Code.

14. See the entry on Hartlib in Sidney Lee, *The Dictionary of National Biography*.

15. This neglect has probably been fostered by the same pragmatic rationalism that prevailed over the Nonconformists and Neoplatonists by the eighteenth century, and which has remained dominant as a cultural outlook. This outlook, in turn, has denied religion its true place in the history of the imagination's development, which place, in some small measure, this study seeks to promote.

16. See the *Dictionary of National Biography* entry on Janeway for more on his life.

17. A conventicle was any meeting of five or more people (not including family members) in a private home "under color of religion" (Abrams 243).

18. See the entry on Baxter in *The Dictionary of National Biography*.

19. Book 3 of *Antidote* begins with a section entitled "That, good men not always faring best in this world, the great examples of Divine vengeance upon wicked and blasphemous Persons are not so convincing to the obstinate Atheist." More then illustrates this section with "The irreligious Jeers and Sacrileges of Dionysius of Syracuse." By chapter 2 he is telling stories, mostly from older anthologies of witchcraft tales written by Wierus and Bodin. He titles some of these sections "The Moving of a Sieve by a Charm" and "A Story of a Sudden Wind that had like to have Thrown down the Gallows at the hanging of two Witches." In chapter 3 he tells his most famous tale, "The Devil of Mascon," while chapter 7 is a long account of a contemporary witchcraft trial from 1653, the story of Anne Bodenham. By chapter 9 he returns to theory ("Of Fairy Circles, Questions propounded concerning Witches Leaving Their bodies, as also Their Transformations into bestial shapes"), but the new narrative form has already been established.

1. The appendix to Rowlandson's 1682 narrative was the last sermon preached by her husband Joseph before his death, titled "A Sermon of the Possibility of God's Forsaking a People that Have Been Near and Dear to Him." The sermon explores the problem of the suffering of the righteous. Rowlandson's text itself also refers to this theme frequently.

2. Another justification, witnesses' credibility, has been mentioned, and will be discussed in detail in the next section of this chapter.

3. Increase Mather's scientific side and relationship to Bacon can be seen in his preface to Rowlandson, when the preface is viewed next to this passage from Bacon; Mather writes, "and forasmuch as not the general but the particular knowledge of things makes deepest impression upon the affections, this narrative particularizing the several passages of this providence, will not a little conduce thereunto."

4. See Winship, "Prodigies, Puritans, and the Perils of Natural Philosophy: The Example of Cotton Mather."

5. Francis Hutchinson's eminent *Essay on Witchcraft*, written in 1718 and considered by many to have been the knock-out blow to the belief, estimated that out of the thousands of executions for witchcraft in Europe from 1484 until 1718, only 140 or so of them occurred in England, most of these happening during Cromwell's Protectorate (Lecky, 120n).

6. Henry Cornelius Agrippa wrote *Of the Vanities and Uncertainties of Artes and Sciences* (1569). Kocher considers his work a part of the "skeptical thought coming into England in the last decades of the sixteenth century. Wallace Notestein (*History of Witchcraft in England from 1558 to 1718*) says Agrippa "attacked the tyranny and superstition upon the Continent" (62). Montague Sumners, still pursuing witches in his early-twentieth-century *Geography of Witchcraft*, cites Agrippa's *De Occulta Philosophia*, and says, "More than once he was openly proclaimed as 'heretic and magician,' and I suspect the charge went little, if at all, beyond the truth" (489).

7. This motif is especially interesting in view of Tennenhouse and Armstrong's idea about Rowlandson asserting female independence and subjectivity; I would say the Indian captivity narratives instead create a new feminist perspective while simultaneously trying to push that perspective away. Providence tales, as I've been saying, increasingly set up and explore such dualities, the most prominent of which is the science/sensation tension.

8. These changes were discussed in chapter 2.

9. Hariot and Cotton Mather, to certain degrees, also imposed orthodox economic and religious ideas on the facts they collected, just as Aristotle imposed classical conceptions of the universe on his own and others' observations of nature. Such "editing," of course, cut against Bacon's proposed methods.

10. One example of this decline in religious fervor is told by C. F. Adams in his *Three Episodes in Massachusetts History*. Adams notes in his section on the Antinomian Crisis

that after the Restoration, Puritan religious severity and concern with theological wrangling became subjects of scorn and ridicule in works such as Samuel Butler's *Hudibras*. Old religious certainties were dissolving, and with such uncertainty came much doubt. England had ancient traditions, customs, and laws and a social hierarchy to ease the prevailing religious anxiety, but in New England, where so much remained wide open, this anxiety struck harder.

11. Brown's Carwin in *Wieland* is one character I have in mind here. Cooper often has disguised characters, or figures whose identities remain a mystery until the end, or outright hypocrites in his stories, as we see in *The Spy* (Harvey Birch), *The Water Witch*, *The Pioneers* (Richard Jones and Oliver Edwards/Effingham), and *Satanstoe* (Jason Newcome). Melville's *Confidence Man* has numerous con artists, while Hawthorne deals in such figures constantly: note Judge Jaffrey Pyncheon and Holgrave, so "thirsty for novelty" in the words of Gary Lindberg, in *House of the Seven Gables*, or Hollingsworth the reformer gone bad in *Blithedale Romance*. Poe wrote "Diddling Considered as One of the Exact Sciences." Lindberg sees him as "willing not only to burlesque his own serious themes but to capitalize on the suspicion that he is a trickster" (62). Poe's possible hoax in "solving" the 1842 murder of Mary Rogers in his "Mystery of Marie Roget" has been discussed widely too. Lindberg adds that he "explores the creation of belief [and] . . . shows the machinery of illusion while creating it out of often 'absurd' occasions" (73).

12. Descartes would have said that if these events were truly caused by God, they would be absolutely inexplicable, and therefore not worth studying.

CHAPTER 5.   THE BIRTH OF THE INDIAN CAPTIVITY NARRATIVE

1. Nancy Armstrong and Leonard Tennenhouse, to take one contemporary example, argue in *The Imaginary Puritan* that Mary Rowlandson's narrative was responsible for the creation of the sentimental, epistolary novel.

2. Kathryn Derounian ("The Publication, Promotion, and Distribution of Mary Rowlandson's Indian Captivity Narrative in the Seventeenth Century") and David Minter ("By Dens of Lions") explain this connection in detail.

3. In her focus on physical appearance and dress, as well as on the Indians' unique and even bizarre habits, Rowlandson, though less scientific, follows patterns set down earlier by explorers, scientists, and artists such as Thomas Hariot, Robert Boyle, and John White. Hariot's and White's observations can be seen in the Theodor DeBry's 1590 edition of their notes and drawings about Virginia, *A Briefe and True Report of the New Found Land of Virginia* (though DeBry Europeanizes White's Indians). For the originals see the *Virginia Magazine of History and Biography* 35 (1927): 419–30, and 36 (1928): 17–26, 124–34. In DeBry's work, engravings with notes of subjects such as "Of the Chieff Ladyes of Secota," "A Young Gentill Woeman Doughter of Secota," and "Their Danses Which They Use att Their Hyghe Feastes" are denser, more scientific renditions of the women and dances Rowlandson explores in the ensuing quoted passages. Similarly, Boyle and other members of the Royal Society, in that institution's *Philosophical Transactions*, reported on a wide variety of prodigies, such as a monstrous calf and colt Boyle

described "whose hinder leggs had no Joynts, and whose tongue was, Cerberus-like, triple." Lorraine Daston and Katharine Parks, in the article by Daston listed in my bibliography, describe more of these *Philosophical Transactions*.

4. This influence can be seen in an entry from Mather's diary from November 1706, upon Williams's return. Clark and Vaughan cite this entry to support their admission that Mather "may" have somewhat helped Williams. They don't, however, include the full quotation, which makes their hesitation questionable: "I now satt with him [Mather writes of Williams], and studied and contrived and united counsels with him, how the Lord might have revenues of glory from his Experiences. And I particularly employ'd him, to preach my Lecture, unto a great Auditory (the general Assembly then also sitting) and, directed him, to show how great things God had done unto him" (575).

Williams's sermon about his captivity experiences was delivered on December 5, 1706, and was published with the narrative in 1707. It is called "Reports of Divine Kindness; or, Remarkable Mercies Should Be Faithfully Published for the Praise of God the Giver."

5. Book 6, *Remarkables of the Divine Providence among the People of New England*, begins, as does Increase Mather's *Essay* after the introduction, with a chapter of sea deliverances, which is then followed, also like his father's work, with a chapter on a wider selection of deliverances. Cotton's second chapter is called "Hosea: Relating Remarkable Salvations Experienced by others beside the Sea Faring," and it, like Increase's second chapter, contains his first captivity narrative.

6. In his own preface to his *Essay*, Increase wrote, "It is not easie to give an Account of Things, and yet no circumstantial mistakes attend what shall be related. Nor dare I averr, that there are none such in what follows. Only I have been careful to prevent them; and as to the substance of each passage, I am well assured it is according to truth" (A7, A8, a1).

7. The *OED* defines this as "the battle of the frogs and mice, a mock heroic poem, possibly of the Homeric Age."

8. Devils could be saved too. Rowlandson notes how God enabled the Indians to survive on the "trash" they ate, so they would be healthy enough to afflict the English.

9. Ferguson was captured in a raid on Salmon Falls, Maine, in 1690.

10. Baker's 1897 *New England Captives Carried to Canada* presents extensive data mined from colonial archives about New Englanders captured by Indians. She adds considerably to earlier accounts.

11. The threats of flagellation, conversion, and damnation unfolded in this epistolary manner seem similar to threats later innocents depicted in works such as Richardson's *Pamela*; where Tennenhouse and Armstrong see only Rowlandson influencing Richardson, a providence tale model for the captivity narratives, in which Williams's narrative figures so prominently, suggests a broader source for later eighteenth-century prose narrative developments.

12. I keep equating God's power and reason because Puritans thought that not believing in God was equivalent to an utter lack of reason. Puritan theology held that nature's complex order had to have been created purposefully, and not by chance, because

her design so far exceeded the order and complexity of the works of mankind, which in themselves were awesome and had been purposefully made.

13. The second story in Increase Mather's *Essay* tells of a drunken student who, after communion, while the other students "repaired to their closets . . . went immediately to a Drunken meeting, and then to a cockfight, where he fell to his accustomed madness, and pouring out a volley of Oaths and Curses; while these were between his lips, God smote him dead in the twinkle of an eye." Thus we can clearly see the evil connotation to cockfights.

14. According to David Proper, librarian of the PVMA library in Deerfield, Massachusetts, Hyde's Sheldon tale was made up. Even if this were the case (and I suspect she was working from some less-than-fictional materials such as family legends, perhaps), the striking persistence of so many providence tale tropes in the story demonstrates the continued power of the form.

Works Consulted

PRIMARY SOURCES

Acosta, Jose de. *The Natural and Moral History of the Indies*. Trans. Edward Grimston, 1604. Ed. Clements Markham. London, 1880.

Agrippa, Henry Cornelius. *Three Books of Occult Philosophy on Magic*. 1533. Trans. Henry Morley, 1651. Inwood, N.Y.: E. Loomis, 1897.

Bacon, Francis. *Essays*. Ed. Michael Kiernan. Cambridge, Mass.: Harvard University Press, 1985.

———. *The New Organon and Other Related Writings*. Ed. Fulton Anderson. New York: Liberal Arts Press, 1960.

———. *The Works of Francis Bacon*. Ed. Robert Leslie Ellis, Douglas Dean Heath, and James Spedding. 15 vols. Boston, 1860–64.

Baxter, Richard. *A Call to the Unconverted; Containing Directions and Persuasions to a Sound Conversion; or, A Seasonable Antidote Against Religious Delusion. Designed as an Appendix to the Saints Everlasting Rest*. Manchester, 1799.

———. *The Certainty of the World of Spirits. And Consequently, of the Immortality of Souls. Of the Malice and Misery of the Devils and the Damned. And of the Blessedness of the Justified. Fully Evinced by the Unquestionable Histories of Apparitions [and] . . . Witchcrafts. . . . Written as an Addition to Many of the Treatises, for the conviction of Sadducees and Infidels*. London, 1691.

———. *Reliquae Baxterianae*. Ed. M. Sylvester. London, 1696.

———. *The Saint's Everlasting Rest*. London, 1650.

Beard, Thomas. *The Theatre of God's Judgements. Wherein is Represented the Admirable Justice of God . . . Collected out of Sacred, Ecclesiastical, and Prophane Histories: now Secondly Printed, and Augmented with at least Two Centuries of Examples*. London, 1612.

Belknap, Jeremy. *The History of New Hampshire*. Philadelphia, 1784–92.

Bernard, Richard. *Guide to Jurymen*. London, 1627.

Blome, Richard. *The Present State of Her Majestie's Isles and Territories in America*. London, 1687.

Boccaccio, Giovanni. *The Fate of Illustrious Men*. Trans. Louis B. Hall. New York: Ungar, 1965

Bodin, J. *De la Demonomanie des Sorciers*. Paris, 1580.

Boyer, Paul, and Stephen Nissenbaum. *Salem Witchcraft Papers: Verbatim Transcripts of the Legal Documents of the Salem Witchcraft Outbreak of 1692*. New York: Da Capo, 1977.

Boyle, Robert. *General Heads for the Natural History of a Country*. London, 1692.

———. "Reflections upon a Theological Distinction. According to Which, 'Tis Said, That Some Articles of Faith are Above Reason but not Against Reason . . . " In *The Christian Virtues*. London, 1690.

———. *Robert Boyle on Natural Philosophy: An Essay with Selections from his Writings by Marie Boas Hall*. Westport, Conn.: Greenwood Press, 1980.

———. *Select Philosophical Papers*. Ed. M. A. Stewart. Totowa, N.J.: Barnes and Noble, 1979.

———. *Some Considerations Touching the Usefulness of Experimental Natural Philosophy*. Oxford, 1663.

———. *Tracts . . . Containing New Experiments, Touching the Relation Betwixt Flame and Air. And About Explosions. An Hydrostatical Discourse Occasion'd by Some Objection of Dr. Henry More Against Some Explications of New Experiments Made by the Author of these Tracts*. London, 1673.

Bradford, William. *Of Plymouth Plantation, 1606–1646*. 1856. Ed. Samuel Eliot Morison. New York: Knopf, 1963.

Burr, George Lincoln, ed. *Narratives of the Witchcraft Cases*. New York: Scribners, 1914.

Burrage, Champlin, ed. *Early English Dissenters in the Light of Recent Research, 1550–1641*. 2 Vols. New York: Russell and Russell, 1967.

Caesarius of Heisterbach. *The Dialogue on Miracles*. Trans. C. C. Swinton Bland and H. Von E. Scott. London: Routledge, 1929.

Calder, Isabel M., ed. *Colonial Captivities, Marches, and Journeys*. New York: Macmillan, 1935.

Calef, Robert. *More Wonders of the Invisible World*. London, 1700.

Calvin, Jean. *Institutes of the Christian Religion*. Trans. Henry Beveridge. 2 vols. Edinburgh, 1869. Grand Rapids, Mich.: Erdmans, 1966.

Campagnac, E. T. *The Cambridge Platonists*. Oxford: Oxford University Press, 1901.

Carleton, George. *A Thankfull Remembrance of Gods Mercie. In an Historicall Collection of the Great and Mercifull Deliverances of the Church and State of England, Since the Gospell Beganne Here to Flourish, from the Beginning of Queen Elizabeth. Collected by Geo. Carleton*. 3rd ed. London, 1627.

Casaubon, Meric. *A Treatise Concerning Enthusiasme, as it is an Effect of Nature: but is Mistaken by Many for Either Divine Inspiration or Diabolical Possession*. 1655. Gainesville, Fla.: Scholar's Facsimiles and Reprints, 1970.

Catlin, George. *Letters and Notes on the Manners, Customs, and Conditions of the North American Indians.* 1844. New York: Dover, 1973.

Chillingsworth, William. *The Religion of Protestantism a Safe Way to Salvation. Or, An Answer to a Booke Entitled "Mercy and Truth, or Charity Maintained by Catholiques," which Pretends to Prove the Contrary.* Oxford, 1638.

Churchill, Awnsham and John. *A Collection of Voyages and Travels.* London, 1704.

Cicero. *Of the Nature of the Gods and Divinations.* Trans. and ed. C. D. Younge. London, 1907.

Clark, Edward, and Alden Vaughan, eds. *Puritans among Indians: Accounts of Captivity and Redemption, 1676–1724.* Cambridge, Mass.: Belknap Press of Harvard University Press, 1981.

Clarke, Samuel. *A Mirrour or Looking Glass Both for Saints and Sinners, Held Forth in Some Thousands of Examples; Wherein is Presented, as God's Wonderful Mercies to the One, so His Severe Judgements Against the Other.* London, 1671.

Cohen, Hennig, and James Levernier, eds. *The Indians and Their Captives.* Westport, Conn.: Greenwood Press, 1977.

Cooper, James Fenimore. *Wept of the Wish Ton-Ton.* Philadelphia, 1829.

Cotton, John. *The Bloody Tenant, Washed and Made White in the Blood of the Lamb.* 1647. New York: Arno, 1972.

———. *Congregational Church in Massachusetts. Cambridge Synod of 1648. A Platform of Church Discipline Gathered Out of the Word of God.* 1649. (In R. Mather's hand but of John Cotton's composition mostly.)

———. *God's Promise to His Plantations . . . As it was Delivered in a Sermon.* London, 1634.

———. *The New Covenant, or, A Treatise, Unfolding the Order and Manner of Giving and Receiving the Covenant of Grace.* London, 1654.

———. *The Way of Congregational Churches Cleared, in Two Treatises.* London, 1648.

Cragg, Gerald, ed. *The Cambridge Platonists.* New York: Oxford University Press, 1968.

Cudworth, Ralph. *The True Intellectual System of the Universe.* 1678. Stuttgart-Bad Cannstatt: F. Frommann Verlag, 1964.

Darrell, John. *A True Narration of the Strange and Grevous Vexation by the Devil of Seven Persons in Lancashire and Wm. Somers of Nottingham. Wherein the Doctrine of Possession and Dispossession of Demoniakes out of the Word of God is Particularly Applied unto Somers. In Collections of Scarce and Valuable Tracts.* Ed. Walter Scott, Esq. Vol. 3. London, 1810.

Defoe, Daniel. *Robinson Crusoe.* New York: New American Library, 1961.

Delbanco, Andrew, and Alan Heimert, eds. *The Puritans in America: A Narrative Anthology.* Cambridge, Mass.: Harvard University Press, 1985.

Descartes, Rene. "Descartes and Henry More on the Beast Machine. A Translation of their Correspondence Pertaining to Animal Automation." *Annals of Science* 1:48–61.

———. *Philosophical Essays: Discourse on Method: Meditations. Rules for the Direction of the Mind.* Indianapolis: Bobbs Merrill, 1964.

————. *The Philosophical Works of Rene Descartes*. Cambridge: Cambridge University Press, 1973.

Dickinson, Jonathan. *God's Protecting Providence, Man's Surest Help and Defense, in Times of the Greatest Difficulty and Most Imminent Danger. Evidenced in the Remarkable Deliverance of Divers Persons, from the Devouring Waves of the Sea; Amongst Which They Suffered Shipwrack; and also, from the More Cruelly Devouring Jaws of the Inhumane Canibals of Florida. Faithfully Related By One of the Persons Concerned Therein, Jonathan Dickinson*. Philadelphia, 1699.

Diebold, Robert Kent. "A Critical Edition of Mrs. Mary Rowlandson's Captivity Narrative." Ph.D. dissertation, Yale University, 1972.

Dorson, Richard M., ed. Introduction. *America Begins: Early American Writing*. New York: Pantheon, 1950

Drake, Samuel Gardner. *Indian Captivities: Being Remarkable Narratives of Persons Taken Captive by the North American Indians . . . To Which are Added Notes, Historical Background, and . . . .* Boston, 1839.

————. *Tragedies of the Wilderness; or, True and Authentic Narratives of Captives, Who Have Been Carried Away by the Indians from Various Frontier Settlements of the United States, from the Earliest to the Present Time. Illustrating the Manners and Customs, Barbarous Rites and Ceremonies, of the North American Indians, and their Various Methods of Torture Practised Upon Such as Have, from Time to Time, Fallen into Their Hands*. Boston, 1841.

————. *The Witchcraft Delusion in New England*. 1866. New York: Burt Franklin, 1970.

Felt, Joseph. *Annals of Salem*. Salem: Ives, 1845–49.

Fitzgerald, F. Scott. *The Great Gatsby*. 1925. New York: Scribners, 1953.

Folsom, James, and Richard Slotkin,, eds. *So Dreadful A Judgement: A Puritan Response to King Philip's War. 1676–1677*. Middletown, Conn.: Wesleyan University Press, 1978.

Fowler, S. P. *Salem Witchcraft*. Boston, 1865.

Foxe, John. *The Actes and Monuments*. 1563. New York: AMS Press, 1965.

Gaule, John. *Select Cases of Conscience Touching Witches and Witchcrafts*. London, 1646.

Glanvill, Joseph. *Saducismus Triumphatus or, Full and Plain Evidence Concerning Witches and Apparitions*. 1689. Ed. Coleman Parsons. Gainesville, Fla.: Scholar's Facsimiles and Reprints, 1966.

————. *The Vanity of Dogmatizing*. London, 1661.

Gookin, Daniel. *Historical Account of the Doings and Sufferings of the Christian Indians in New England, in the Years 1675, 1676, 1677*. New York: Arno Press, 1972.

Greatrakes, Valentine. *A Brief Account of Mr. Valentine Greatrak's, and Divers of the Strange Cures by Him Lately Performed*. 1666. Dublin, 1688.

Guazzo, Brother Maria Francesco. *Compendium Maleficarum*. Milan, 1608.

Gyles, John. "Memoirs of Odd Adventures, Strange Deliverances, Etc. 1736. In Edward Clark and Alden Vaughan, eds., *Puritans among Indians*. Cambridge: Harvard University Press, 1981.

Hakewell, George. *An Apologie or Declaration of the Power and Providence of God in the*

Government of the World, Consisting in an Examination and Censure of the Common Error Touching Nature's Perpetuall and Universal Decay. Oxford, 1627.

Hakluyt, Richard. *The Principall Navigations, Voiages and Discoveries of the English Nation.* 1589. Cambridgeshire: For the Hakluyt Society and Peabody Museum of Salem at the University Press, 1965.

————. *Virginia Richly Valued.* Ann Arbor, Mich.: University Microfilms, 1966.

Hale, Matthew. *The Works, Moral and Religious.* 2 vols. London, 1805.

Hall, David. *Witch Hunting in Seventeenth-Century New England: A Documentary History, 1638–1692.* Boston: Northeastern University Press, 1991

Haller, William, ed. *Tracts on Liberty in the Puritan Revolution, 1638–1647.* 1934. New York: Octagon Books, 1965.

Hariot, Thomas. *A Briefe and True Report of the New Found Land of Virginia.* Ed. Theodore Debry. 1590. New York: Dover, 1972.

Harsnett, Samuel. *A Declaration of Egregious Popish Impostures, to With-draw the Harts of Her Majesties Subjects from Their Allegeance, and from the Truth of Christian Religion Proferred in England, Under the Pretense of Casting out Devils. Practiced by Edmunds, Alias Weston a Jesuit, and Divers Romish Priests His Wicked Associates. Where-unto are Annexed the Copies of the Confessions and Examinations of the Parties Themselves, which were Pretended to be Possessed and Dispossessed, Taken Upon Oath Before Her Majesties Commissioners, for Causes Ecclesiastical.* London, 1603.

————. *A Discourse of the Fraudulent Practices of John Darrell . . . Detecting in some Sort the Deceitful Trade in These Latter Dayes of Casting Out Devils.* London, 1599.

Hazard, Ebenezer. *Historical Collections: Consisting of State Papers, and other Authentic Documents: Intended as Materials for a History of the United States of America.* 1792–94.

Heard, Norman J. *White into Red: A Study of the Assimilation of White Persons Captured by Indians.* Metuchen, N.J., Scarecrow Press, 1973.

Heckewelder, John Gottlieb. *History, Manners and Customs of the Indian Nations Who Once Inhabited Pennsylvania and the Neighboring States.* 1876. New York: Arno, 1971.

Hertz, J. H., ed. *The Pentateuch and Haftorahs.* London: Soncino Press, 1958.

Higginson, Francis. *New England's Plantation.* 1630. New York: Da Capo Press, 1970.

Hobbes, Thomas. *Leviathan.* 1651. Harmondsworth: Penguin, 1968.

Hodge, Frederick W., ed. *Spanish Explorers in the Southern United States, 1528–1543.* New York: Scribners, 1907.

Hooker, Thomas. *A Survey of the Summe of Church Discipline.* 1648. New York: Arno, 1972.

Hrotswitha. "Gallicanus." In *Plays of Hrotswitha of Gandersheim.* Trans. Larissa Bonfante. New York: New York University Press, 1979.

Hubbard, William. *A General History of New England.* 1815. New York: Arno, 1972.

————. *A Narrative of the Troubles with the Indians in New England: From the First Planting Thereof in the Year 1607, to the Present Year 1677.* Boston, 1677.

Hutchinson, Francis. *An Essay on Witchcraft*. London, 1748.

Hyde, Matilda (Strang). *The Story of Remembrance Sheldon, Transcribed from the Original Manuscript by Matilda Hyde*. Olde Deerfield, Mass.: Olde Deerfield Doll House, 1920.

Irving, Washington. *The Sketch Book*. 1819–1820. New York: New American Library, 1961.

Janeway, James. *Invisibles, Realities, Demonstrated in the Holy Life and Triumphant Death of Mr. John Janeway*. 3rd ed. Boston, 1703.

―――. *Mr. Janeway's Legacy to His Friends, Containing Twenty Seven Famous Instances of God's Providence in and about Sea Dangers and Deliverances, with the Names of Several That Were Eyewitnesses to Many of Them*. London, 1674.

―――. *A Token for Children*. Boston, 1771.

―――. *A Token for Mariners*. London, 1708.

Johnson, C. *An Unredeemed Captive. Being the Story of Eunice Williams, Who at the Age of Nine Years, Was Carried Away from Deerfield by the Indians in the Year 1704*. Holyoke, Mass., 1897.

Johnson, Edward. *The Wonder Working Providence of Sion's Saviour in New England*. 1654. Delmar, N.Y.: Scholar's Facsimiles and Reprints, 1974.

Johnson, Thomas, and Perry Miller, eds. *The Puritans*. New York: American Book Co., 1938.

Josselyn, John. *New England's Rarities Discovered in Birds, Beasts. Fishes, Serpents, and Plants of the Country*. 1672. Boston, 1865.

Kestler, Francis Roe, ed. *The Indian Captivity Narrative: A Woman's View*. New York: Garland Publishing Co., 1990.

King James I. *Daemonologie*. 1597. New York: Barnes and Noble, 1965.

Kramer, Heinrich, and James Sprenger. *Malleus Maleficarum*. Trans. Montague Summers. New York: Dover, 1971.

Laud, William. *A Relation of the Conference Betweene William Laud . . . Now Arch-Bishop of Canterbury; and Mr. Fisher the Jesuite, by the Command of King James . . . .* London, 1639.

―――. *A Speech Concerning Innovations in the Church*. 1637. New York: Da Capo, 1971.

Lincoln, Charles H., ed. *Narratives of the Indian Wars, 1675–1699*. New York: Scribners, 1913.

Linschofen, Jan Huygen von. *His Discours of Voyages into the Easte and Weste Indies*. Trans. W. P. London. 1598.

Lithgow, William. *History of Nineteen Years of Travel*. London, 1682.

Lloyd, David. *Wonders no Miracles, or Mr. Valentine Greatrates Gift of Healing Examined*. London, 1666.

Loudon, Archibald. *A Selection, of Some of the Most Interesting Narratives, of Outrages, Committed by the Indians, in Their Wars, With the White People. Also, an Account of Their Manners, Customs, Traditions, Religious Sentiments, Mode of Warfare, Military tactics, Discipline and Encampments, Treatment of Prisoners, Etc. Which Are Better Explained and More Minutely Related, Than Has Been Heretofore Done, by Any Other Author on That Subject. Many of the Articles Have Never Before Ap-*

peared in Print. The Whole Compiled From the Best Authorities. 2 vols. Carlisle, Pa.: Loudon, 1808–11.

Lydgate, John. *Fall of Princes.* Ed. Henry Berger. 4 vols. Washington, D.C.: Carnegie Institute of Washington, 1923–27.

———. *Mirror for Magistrates.* 1559. New York: Barnes and Noble, 1960.

Mandelslo, Johann Albrecht von. *The Voyage and Travels of J. Albrecht de Mandelslo (a gentleman belonging to the embassy, sent by the Duke of Holstein, to the great Duke of Muscovy, and the King of Persia) into the East Indies.* In A. Olearius, *The Voyages and Travels of the Ambassadors Sent by Frederick, Duke of Holstein.* 2nd ed. London, 1669.

Mather, Cotton. *A Brand Pluck't Out of the Burning.* In George Lincoln Burr, ed., *Narratives of the Witchcraft Cases.* New York: Scribners, 1914.

———. *Decennium Luctuosum. A History of Remarkable Occurrences in the Long War, Which New England hath had with the Indian Salvages, From the Year 1688. To the Year 1698. Faithfully Composed and Improved.* Boston, 1699.

———. *Diary of Cotton Mather.* 2 Vols. 1681–1709 and 1709–1729. New York: Ungar, 1957.

———. *Good Fetch'd Out of Evil: A Collection of Memorables Relating to our Captives.* Boston, 1706.

———. *Humiliations Follow'd With Deliverances. A Brief Discourse on the Matter and Method, of That Humiliation Which Would Be an Hopeful Symptom of Our Deliverance From Calamity. Accompanied and Accommodated With a Narrative, of a Notable Deliverance Lately Received by Some English Captives, From the Hands of Cruel Indians. And Some Improvement of the Narrative. Whereto Is Added a Narrative of Hannah Swarton, Relating to Her Captivity and Deliverance.* 1697. In *Days of Humiliation, Times of Affliction and Disaster; Nine Sermons for Restoring Favor With an Angry God* (1697–1727) by Cotton Mather. Ed. George Harrison Orians. Gainesville, Fla.: Scholars' Facsimiles and Reprints, 1970.

———. *Late Memorable Providences Relating to Witchcrafts and Possessions.* London, 1691.

———. *Magnalia Christi Americana: or, the Ecclesiastical History of New England, From Its First Planting in the Year 1620 Unto the Year of Our Lord 1698.* 1702. New York: Arno Press, 1970.

———. *Memorable Providences Relating to Witchcrafts and Possessions.* Boston, 1689.

———. *Manuductio ad Ministerium: Directions for a Candidate of the Ministry.* New York: Published for the Facsimile Text Society, Columbia University Press, 1938.

———. *Pillars of Salt. An History of Some Criminals Executed in this Land, For Capital Crimes.* Boston, 1699.

———. *Wonders of the Invisible World. Being an Account of the Tryals of Several Witches Lately Executed in New England. To Which is Added, A Further Account of the Tryals of the New England Witches, by Increase Mather.* Boston, 1693.

Mather, Increase. *Angelographia: A Discourse Concerning the Nature and power of the Holy Angels.* Boston, 1696.

———. *A Brief History of the War with the Indians in New England.* Boston, 1676.

———. *Burnings Bewailed.* Boston, 1711.

———. *A Call From Heaven to the Present and Succeeding Generation.* Boston, 1679.

———. *Cases of Conscience Concerning Evil Spirits Personating Men, Witchcrafts, Infallible Proofs of Guilt in Such as are Accused with that Crime.* Boston, 1693.

———. *A Discourse Concerning Comets* (Kometographia). Boston, 1683.

———. *A Discourse Concerning the Uncertainty of the Times of Men and the Necessity of Being Prepared for Sudden Change and Death. Delivered in a Sermon Preached at Cambridge in New England, Dec. 6, 1696, On Occasion of the Sudden Death of Two Scholars Belonging to Harvard College.* Boston, 1697.

———. *An Essay for the Recording of Illustrious Providences.* 1684. Ed. James Levernier. Delmar, N.Y.: Scholars and Facsimiles and Reprints, 1977.

———. *Heavens Alarm to the World.* Boston, 1682.

———. *A Relation of the Troubles Which Have Hapned in New England by Reason of the Indians There, from the Year 1614 to the year 1675.* 1677. New York: Arno Press, 1972.

———. *Times of Men; or, A Sermon Occasioned by That Awfull Providence Which Hapned in Boston in New England the Fourth Day of the Third Month 1675 (When Part of a Vessel was Blown Up in the Harbor, and Nine Men Hurt, and Three Mortally Wounded) Wherein is Shewed How We Should Sanctifie the Dreadfull Name of God Under Such Awful Dispensation.* Boston, 1675.

———. *The Times of Men are in the Hands of God.* Boston, 1675.

———. *Wo To Drunkards.* 2nd ed. Boston, 1712.

Mather, Richard. *Church Covenant: Two Tracts.* 1643. New York: Arno, 1972.

Miller, Arthur. *The Crucible.* New York: Viking, 1953.

Miller, Perry, ed. *The American Puritans, Their Prose and Poetry.* New York: Columbia University Press, 1982.

Montaigne, Michel de. *The Essays.* Trans. M. A. Screech. New York: Penguin, 1991.

More, Henry. *An Antidote Against Atheism.* In *A Collection of Several Philosophical Writings of Henry More.* 2nd ed. London, 1666.

———. *Enchiridion Metaphysicum.* London, 1671.

———. *The Immortality of the Soul.* Hingham, Mass.: Kluwer Academic Pub., 1987.

———. *A Modest Enquiry into the Mystery of Iniquity.* 2 vols. 1664. New York: Garland, 1978.

———. *Philosophical Writings of Henry More.* Ed. Flora Isabel MacKinnon. 1925. New York: AMS Pub., 1969.

Morse, John Howard. *Morse Genealogy, Comprising the Descendants of Samuel, Anthony, William and Joseph Morse, and John Moss: being a revision of the Memorial of the Morses, published by Rev. Abner Morse in 1850 / compiled by J. Howard Morse and Emily Leavett under the auspices of the Morse Society.* Cloverdale, N.Y.: Springfield Printing and Binding, 1903.

Morton, Nathaniel. *New England's Memorial; or, A Brief Relation of the Most Memorable and Remarkable Passages of the Providence of God Manifested to the Planters of New England, in America; with Special Reference to the First Colony Thereof called New Plymouth.* 1669. A. Danforth, 1826.

Newes from Scotland. 1591. In *Elizabethan and Jacobean Quartos*. Ed. G. B. Harrison. New York: Barnes and Noble, 1966.

Nider, Johanne. *Formicarius*. Cologne, 1475.

Oakes, Urian. *The Sovereign Efficacy of Divine Providence*. Los Angeles: William Andrew Clark Memorial Library, University of California, 1955.

Patrides, C. A., ed. *The Cambridge Platonists*. Cambridge: Harvard University Press, 1970.

Perkins, William. *A Discourse on the Damnable Art of Witchcraft*. London, 1608.

———. *A Golden Chaine, or, The Description of Theologies, Containing the Order of the Causes of Salvation and Damnation, According to God's Word*. London, 1591.

———. *Works*. 1603. In *Early English Books, 1475–1640*, reel 1425. Ann Arbor: Michigan University Microfilms, 1976.

———. *The Works of William Perkins*. Abingdon (Berks.): Sutton Courtenay Press, 1970.

———. *William Perkins, 1558–1602, English Puritanist; His Pioneer Works on Casuistry: "A Discourse of Conscience," and "The Whole Treatise of Cases of Conscience*. Ed. and with an introduction by T. F. Merrill. Nieuwkoop: B. De Grief, 1966.

Philosophical Transactions of the Royal Society. Vols. 1–70. London, 1665–1780.

Pike, James. *The New Puritan: New England Two Hundred Years Ago. Some Account of the Life of Robert Pike, the Puritan Who Defended the Quakers. Resisted Clerical Domination, Opposed the Witchcraft Persecution*. New York, 1879.

Pliny the Elder. *The Natural History of C. Plainest Secundum*. Trans. Philemon Holland. London, 1601.

Plumstead, A. W., ed. *The Wall and the Garden: Selected Massachusetts Election Sermons, 1670–1775*. Minneapolis: University of Minnesota Press, 1968.

Potts, Thomas. *The Wonderfull Discoverie of Witches in the Countie of Lancaster*. London, 1613.

Psellus, Michael. *La Demonologie de M. Psellos*. Trans. Karl Svoboda. Brno: Filosoficka Fakulta, 1927.

Ramus, Petrus. *Arguments in Rhetoric Against Quintilian*. Trans. Carole Newlands. De-Kalb, Ill.: Northern Illinois University Press, 1986.

Remy, Nicoles. *Demonolatry*. 1595. Secaucus, N.J.: University Books, 1974.

Rowlandson, Mary. *A True History of the Captivity and Restoration of Mrs. Mary Rowlandson, a Minister's Wife in New England. Wherein is Set Forth the Cruel and Inhumane Usage She Underwent Amongst the Heathens, for Eleven Weeks Time: and Her Deliverance From Them. Written by Her Own Hand, for Her Private Use: and Now Made Publick at the Earnest Desire of Some Friends, for the Benefit of the Afflicted. Whereunto is Annexed, a Sermon of the Possibility of God's Forsaking a People That Have Been Near and Dear to Him. Preached by Mr. Joseph Rowlandson, Husband to the Said Mrs. Rowlandson: It Being His Last Sermon*. London, 1682.

Schoolcraft, Henry Rowe. *The American Indians: Their History, Conditions, and Prospects*. Buffalo, 1851.

———. *On'eota: or, Characteristics of The Red Race of America*. New York, 1845

———. *Western Scenes and Reminiscences: Together with the Thrilling Legends and Tra-*

ditions of the Red Men of the Forest. To Which is Added Several Narratives of Adventures Among Indians. Auburn, 1853.

Scot, Reginald. *The Discoverie of Witchcraft.* 1584. London: Arundel Centaur Press, 1964.

Scott, Walter. *Peveril of the Peak.* Edinburgh, 1847.

Shea, John Dawson Gilmary. *Perils of the Oceans and Wilderness; or, Narratives of Shipwreck and Indian Captivities.* Boston, 1857.

Sheldon, George. *What Befell Stephen Williams in His Captivity.* Deerfield, Mass., 1889.

Shepard, Thomas. *The Autobiography.* Boston, 1832.

———. *The Clear Sunshine of the Gospel Breaking Forth Upon the Indians in New England.* London, 1648.

———. *The Day Breaking, if not the Sun Rising, of the Gospel with the Indians in New England.* London, 1647.

———. "Eye Salve, or, A Watchword from our Lord Jesus Christ Unto His Churches." Preached on day of election, Boston, Mass., May 15, 1672. Cambridge, Mass., 1673.

———. *New England's Lamentation for Old England's Present Errors.* London, 1645.

———. *The Sincere Convert.* London, 1640.

Sinclair, George. *Satan's Invisible World Discovered.* 1685. Gainesville, Fla.: Scholar's Facsimiles and Reports, 1969.

Smith, John. *Travels and Works of Capt. John Smith.* Ed. Edward Arber. 2 vols. New York: B. Franklin, 1967.

Sprat, Thomas. *History of the Royal Society.* 1667. Ed. Jackson Cope and Harold Whitmore Jones. 1958. St. Louis: Washington University Press, 1966.

Stoughton, William. *New England's True Interest, Not to Lie. Delivered in a Sermon Preached in Boston . . . April 19 1668.* Cambridge, 1670.

Stubbes, Phillip. *The Anatomie of Abuse.* 1583. New York: Garland, 1973.

Turner, William. *A Compleat History of the Most Remarkable Providences.* 1697.

Underhill, John. *Newes from America.* 1638. Amsterdam, N.Y.: Da Capo, 1971.

Upham, Charles W. *Salem Witchcraft.* 1867 New York: F. Ungar, 1959.

VanDerBeets, Richard, ed. *Held Captive by Indians: Selected Narratives, 1642–1836.* Knoxville: University of Tennessee Press, 1973.

Vincent of Beauvais. *Speculum Historiale.* In Richard Hakluyt, ed., *The Texts and Versions of John de Plano Carpini and William de Rubruquis.* 1598. London, 1903.

Vincent, Thomas. *God's Terrible Voice in the City. The History of the . . . Plague and Fire in London.* 1667. Bridgeport, Conn., 1811.

Voragine, Jacobus de. *The Golden Legend.* Trans. Caxton, 1483. Ed. Frederick Ellis. 3 vols. Hammersmith, 1892.

———. *Golden Legend.* Trans. Helmut Ripperger and Granger Ryan. London: Longman, Green, 1941.

Ward, Nathaniel. *The Simple Cobbler of Aggawam in America.* 1647. Lincoln: University of Nebraska Press, 1969.

Webster, John. *Book of Witchcraft.* Ed. Frances Shirley. 1623.

Wier, Johannes. *Pseudomarchia Daemonum.* Trans. T. R. Basil, 1563.

Wigglesworth, Michael. *The Day of Doom.* New York: Russell and Russell, 1966.

Williams, Daniel. *Pillars of Salt: An Anthology of Early American Narratives*. Madison, Wis.: Madison House, 1993.

Williams, John. *The Redeemed Captive Returning to Zion. A Faithful History of Remarkable Occurrences, in the Captivity and Deliverance of Mr. John Williams, Minister of the Gospel in Deerfield, Who, in the Desolation Which Befell That Plantation, By an Incursion of the French and Indians, Was by Them Carried Away, With His Family, and His Neighborhood, unto Canada. Whereto There is Annexed a Sermon Preached by Him, Upon His Return, at the Lecture in Boston, Dec. 5, 1706. On Those Words, Luk.8, 35., Return to Thine Own House and Shew How Great Things God Hath Done Unto Thee.* 2nd ed. Boston, 1720.

Williams, Roger. *The Bloody Tenant Yet More Bloody*. London, 1652.

———. *Complete Writings*. 7 vols. New York: Russell and Russell, 1963.

Williams, Stephen. *A Biographical Memoir of Rev. John Williams . . . with an Appendix Containing the Journal of Stephen Williams . . . During His Captivity*. Greenfield, Mass., 1837.

Winstanley, Gerrard. *The Work of Gerrard Winstanley*. New York: Russell and Russell, 1965.

Winthrop, John. *The History of New England 1630 to 1649*. Ed. James Savage. New York: Arno, 1972.

Wood, William. *New England's Prospect*. London, 1634.

Woodward, W. E. *Records of Salem Witchcraft*. 1866. New York: Burt Franklin, 1972.

Young, Alexander, ed. *Chronicles of the First Planters of the Colony of Massachusetts, 1623–1636*. 1846. New York: Da Capo, 1970.

———. *Chronicles of the Pilgrim Fathers of the Colony of Plymouth*. 1844. New York: Da Capo, 1971.

Secondary Sources

Abrams, Robert Martin. *The Land and Literature of England: A Historical Account*. New York: Norton, 1983.

Adams, Charles Francis. *Three Episodes in Massachusetts History*. 1892. New York: Russell and Russell, 1965.

Andrews, William. *Journeys in New Worlds: Early American Women's Narratives*. Madison: University of Wisconsin Press, 1990.

Armstrong, Nancy, and Leonard Tennenhouse. *The Imaginary Puritan: Literature, Intellectual Labor, and the Origins of Personal Life*. Berkeley: University of California Press, 1992.

Axtell, James, ed. *Essays in the Ethnohistory of Colonial North America*. New York: Oxford University Press, 1981.

Axtell, James. *The Invasion Within: The Contest of Cultures in Colonial America*. New York: Oxford University Press, 1985.

Baker, Charlotte Alice. *True Stories of New England Captives Carried to Canada during the Old French and Indian Wars*. Cambridge, 1897.

Barbeau, Marius. "Indian Captivities." *Proceedings of the American Philosophical Society* 94 (1950): 522–48.

Barnett, Louise. *The Ignoble Savage: American Literary Racism, 1790–1890*. Westport, Conn.: Greenwood Press, 1975.

Baum, Rosalie Murphy. "John Williams' Captivity Narrative: A Consideration of Normative Ethnicity." In Frank Shuffelton, ed., *A Mixed Race: Ethnicity in Early America*. New York: Oxford University Press, 1993.

Behan, Dorothy Forbis. "The Captivity Story in American Literature, 1577–1826: An Examination of Authentic and Fictitious Narratives of the Experiences of the White Men Captured by the Indians North of Mexico." Ph. D. dissertation, University of Chicago, 1952.

Benton, Richard P. "The Problem of Literary Gothicism." *ESQ: A Journal of the American Renaissance* 18 (1972): 5–9

Bercovitch, Sacvan. *The American Jeremiad*. Madison: University of Wisconsin Press, 1978.

———. *The American Puritan Imagination: Essays in Revaluation*. London: Cambridge University Press, 1974.

———. *The Puritan Origins of the American Self*. New Haven: Yale University Press, 1975.

———. *Typology and Early American Literature*. Amherst: University of Massachusetts Press, 1972.

Berkhofer, Robert. *The White Man's Indian: The History of an Idea from Columbus to the Present*. New York: Knopf, 1978.

Billington, Ray Allen. *Westward Expansion: A History of the American Frontier*. New York: Macmillan, 1947.

Bourne, Russell. *Red Kings Rebellion: Racial Politics in New England, 1675–1678*. New York: Athenaeum, 1990.

Boyer, Paul, and Stephen Nissenbaum. *Salem Possessed: The Social Origins of Witchcraft*. Cambridge, Mass.: Harvard University Press, 1974.

Breitwieser, Mitchell Robert. *American Puritanism and the Defense of Mourning: Religion, Grief, and Ethnology in Mary White Rowlandson's Captivity Narrative*. Madison: University of Wisconsin Press, 1990.

Buckley, George. *Atheism in the English Renaissance*. New York: Russell and Russell, 1965.

Carleton, Phillip. "The Indian Captivity Narrative." *American Literature* 15 (1943): 169–80.

Cassirer, Ernest. *The Platonic Renaissance in England*. 1953. New York: Gordion, 1970.

Castiglia, Christopher. *Bound and Determined: Captivity, Culture Crossing, and White Womanhood from Mary Rowlandson to Patty Hearst*. Chicago: University of Chicago Press, 1996.

Chase, Richard. *The American Novel and Its Tradition*. Garden City, N.Y.: Doubleday, 1957.

Cohen, Daniel. *Pillars of Salt, Monuments of Grace: New England Crime Literature and the Origins of American Popular Culture, 1676–1860*. New York: Oxford University Press, 1993.

Coleman, Emma Lewis. *New England Captives Carried to Canada During the French and Indian War*. 2 vols. Portland, Maine: Southworth Press, 1925.

Cowie, Alexander. *The Rise of the American Novel*. New York: American Book Co., 1948.

Cragg, Gerald. *From Puritanism to the Age of Reason*. Cambridge: Cambridge University Press, 1950.

Cressy, David. *Coming Over: Migration and Communication between England and New England in the Seventeenth Century*. Cambridgeshire: Cambridge University Press, 1987.

Cronon, William. *Changes in the Land: Indians, Colonists, and the Ecology of New England*. New York: Hill and Wang, 1983.

Daston, Lorraine. "Marvelous Facts and Miraculous Evidence in Early Modern Europe." *Critical Inquiry* 1.1 (Autumn 1991).

Debo, Angie. *A History of the Indians of the United States*. Norman: University of Oklahoma Press, 1970.

Delbanco, Andrew. *The Puritan Ordeal*. Cambridge, Mass.: Harvard University Press, 1989.

Demos, John. *Entertaining Satan: Witchcraft and the Culture of Early New England*. New York: Oxford University Press, 1982.

———. *The Unredeemed Captive: A Family Story from Early America*. New York: Knopf, 1994.

Derounian, Kathryn Zabelle. "A Note on Mary (White) Rowlandson's English Origins." *Early American Literature* 24.1 (1990): 70–72. (Added to and Corrected *EAL* 25.5)

———. "The Publication, Promotion, and Distribution of Mary Rowlandson's Indian Captivity Narrative in the Seventeenth Century." *Early American Literature* 23.3 (1988): 239–61.

———. "Puritan Orthodoxy and the 'Survivors Syndrome' in Mary Rowlandson's Indian Captivity Narrative." *Early American Literature* 22 (Spring 1987): 82–93.

Derounian-Stodola, Kathryn Zabelle, and James Levernier. *The Indian Captivity Narrative, 1550–1990*. New York: Twayne, 1993.

Dondore, Dorothy. "White Captives among the Indians." *New York History* 13 (1932): 292–300.

Dorson, Richard M. *American Folklore*. Chicago: University of Chicago Press, 1959.

Downing, David. "Streams of Scripture Comfort: Mary Rowlandson's Typological Use of the Bible." *Early American Literature* 15 (1981): 252–59.

Drinnon, Richard. *Facing West: The Metaphysics of Indian Hating and Empire Building*. Minneapolis: University of Minnesota Press, 1980.

Dudley, Edward, and Maximillian Novak, eds. *The Wild Man Within: An Image in Western Thought from the Renaissance to Romanticism*. Pittsburgh, Pa.: University of Pittsburgh Press, 1973.

Fiedler, Leslie. *The Return of the Vanishing American*. New York: Stein and Day, 1969.

Frank, Frederick Stilson. "Perverse Pilgrimage: The Role of the Gothic in the Works of Charles Brockden Brown, Edgar Allan Poe, and Nathaniel Hawthorne." Ph. D. dissertation, Rutgers University, 1967.

Godbeer, Richard. *The Devil's Dominion: Magic and Religion in Early New England.* Cambridgeshire: Cambridge University Press, 1992.

Greene, David. "New Light on Mary Rowlandson." *Early American Literature* 20 (1985): 24–38.

Haefeli, Evan, and Kevin Sweeney. "Revisiting the Redeemed Captive." William and Mary Quarterly 52:1 (January 1995): 3–46.

Hall, David. *Worlds of Wonder, Days of Judgement: Popular Religious Belief in Early New England.* New York: Knopf, 1989.

Haller, William. *The Rise of Puritanism.* 1938. Philadelphia: University of Pennsylvania Press, 1972.

Hallowell, A. Irving. "American Indians, White and Black: The Phenomenon of Transculturation." *Current Anthropology* 4 (1963): 519–31.

Hart, James. *The Popular Book: A History of America's Literary Taste.* Berkeley and Los Angeles: University of California Press, 1961.

Hill, Christopher. *Society and Puritanism in Pre-Revolutionary England.* New York: Schocken, 1964.

Howe, Susan. *The Birthmark: Unsettling the Wilderness in American Literary History.* Hanover, N.H.: University Press of New England for Wesleyan University Press, 1993.

Hume, Robert E. "Gothic Versus Romantic: A Revaluation of the Gothic Novel." *PMLA* 84 (1967): 282–90.

Jennings, Francis. *The Invasion of America: Indians, Colonialism, and the Cant of Conquest.* New York: W. W. Norton, 1975.

Jennison, Keith, and John Tebbel. *The American Indian Wars.* New York: Harper and Bros., 1960.

Jones, Howard Mumford. *O Strange New World!* 1952. New York: Viking Press, 1967.

Karlsen, Carol. *The Devil in the Shape of a Woman: Witchcraft in Colonial New England.* New York: Norton, 1987.

Keiser, Albert. *The Indian in American Literature.* New York: Octagon Books, 1970.

Kibby, Ann. "Mutations of the Supernatural: Witchcraft, Remarkable Providences, and the Power of Puritan Men." *American Quarterly* 34:2 (1982): 125–48.

Kittredge, George Lyman. *Witchcraft in Old and New England.* 1929. New York: Russell and Russell, 1956.

Knowles, Nathaniel. "The Torture of the Captive by the Indians of Eastern North America." *Proceedings of the American Philosophical Society* 82 (1940): 151–225.

Kocher, Paul Harold. *Science and Religion in Elizabethan England.* New York: Octagon, 1969.

Kolodny, Annette. "Among the Indians." *New York Times Book Review* 98 (January 31, 1993): 1, 26–28.

———. "The Integrity of Memory." *American Literature* 57 (May 1985): 291–307.

———. *The Land before Her: Fantasy and Experience of the American Frontiers, 1630–1860.* Chapel Hill: University of North Carolina Press, 1984.

————. *The Lay of the Land: Metaphor as Experience and History in American Life and Letters.* Chicago: University of Chicago Press, 1975.

————. "Letting Go Our Grand Obsessions: Notes Toward a New Literary History of the American Frontier." *American Literature* 64 (March 1992): 1–18.

————. Review of *Narratives of North American Indian Captivities,* ed. Wilcomb Washburn. *Early American Literature* 14 (1979): 228–35.

Kopper, Philip, et al., eds. *The Smithsonian Book of North American Indians before the Coming of the Europeans.* Washington, D.C.: Smithsonian Books, 1986.

Kupperman, Karen Ordahl. *Settling in with the Indians: The Meeting of English and Indian Cultures in America, 1580–1640.* 1920. Totowa, N.J.: Rowman and Littlefield, 1980.

Leach, Douglas Edward. "The 'Whens' of Mary Rowlandson's Captivity." *New England Quarterly* 34 (1961): 353–63.

————. *Flintlock and Tomahawk: New England in King Philip's War.* New York: Macmillan, 1958.

Lecky, W. E. H. *History of the Rise and Influence of the Spirit of Rationalism in Europe.* 2 vols. New York: Appleton, 1867.

Lee, Sidney, and Leslie Stephens, eds. *The Dictionary of National Biography.* 1917. Oxford University Press, 1963–64.

Levernier, James. "Indian Captivity Narratives: Their Function and Forms." Ph. D. dissertation, University of Pennsylvania, 1975.

Levine, Paul. "The American Novel Begins." *American Scholar* 35 (1966): 134–48.

Lewis, R. W. B. *The American Adam.* Chicago: University of Chicago Press, 1965.

Lindberg, Gary. *The Confidence Man in American Literature.* New York: Oxford University Press, 1982

Low, Sidney, and F. S. Pulling et al., eds. *The Dictionary of English History.* 1928. London: Cassell, 1884.

McKeon, Michael. *The Origins of the English Novel, 1660–1740.* Baltimore: Johns Hopkins University Press, 1987.

McQuade, Donald M. *The Harper American Literature.* 2nd ed. Vol.1. New York: Harper and Row, 1994.

Maddox, Lucy. *Removals: Nineteenth-Century American Literature and the Politics of Indian Affairs.* New York: Oxford University Press, 1991.

Martin, Calvin. *Keepers of the Trade: Indian Animal Relationships and the Fur Trade.* Berkeley: University of California Press, 1978.

Martin, Calvin, ed. *The American Indian and the Problem of History.* New York: Oxford University Press, 1987.

Meade, James. "The 'Westerns' of the East: Narratives of Indian Captivity from Jeremiad to Gothic Novel." Ph. D. dissertation, Northwestern University, 1971.

Merchant, Carolyn. *Ecological Revolutions: Nature, Gender, and Science in New England.* Chapel Hill: University of North Carolina Press, 1989.

Miller, Perry. *Errand into the Wilderness.* 1956. New York: Harper Torchbooks, 1964.

————. *The New England Mind: From Colony to Province*. 1939. Boston: Beacon Press, 1961.

————. *The New England Mind: The Seventeenth Century*. 1939. Boston: Beacon Press, 1961.

Minter, David. "By Dens of Lions: Notes on Stylization in Early Puritan Captivity Narratives." *American Literature* 45 (1973): 335–47.

————. "The Puritan Jeremiad as Literary Form." In *The American Puritan Imagination: Essays in Revaluation*, ed. Sacvan Bercovitch. London: Cambridge University Press, 1974.

Mott, Frank Luther. *Golden Multitudes: The Story of Best Sellers in the United States*. New York: Macmillan, 1947.

Murdock, Kenneth B. *Literature and Theology in Colonial New England*. New York: Harper Torchbooks, 1962.

Murray, Marjorie. *The Witch Cult in Western Europe*. Oxford: Clarendon Press, 1962.

Namias, June. *White Captives: Gender and Ethnicity on the American Frontier*. Chapel Hill: University of North Carolina Press, 1993.

Nelson, Lowry, Jr. "Night Thoughts on the Gothic Novel." *Yale Review* 52 (1962): 231–57.

Nicolson, Marjorie, ed. *The Conway Letters: Correspondence of Anne, Viscountess Conway, Henry More, and Their Friends, 1642–1684*. New Haven: Yale University Press, 1930.

————. *Mountain Gloom and Mountain Glory: The Development of the Aesthetics of the Infinite*. 1959. New York: Norton, 1963.

Notestein, Wallace. *A History of Witchcraft in England from 1558 to 1718*. New York: Russell and Russell, 1965.

O'Brien, Edward. *The Advance of the American Short Story*. New York: Dodd, Mead and Co., 1923.

Pattee, Fred Lewis. *The Development of the American Short Story*. New York: Harper and Brothers, 1923.

Pearce, Roy Harvey. *The Savages of America: A Study of the Indian and the Idea of Civilization*. Baltimore: Johns Hopkins University Press, 1953.

————. "The Significance of the Indian Captivity Narrative." *American Literature* 15 (1947): 1–20.

Peder, William. *The American Short Story: Front Line in the National Defense of Literature*. Boston: Houghton Mifflin, 1964.

Petter, Henri. *The Early American Novel*. Columbus: Ohio State University Press, 1971.

Powicke, Frederick J. *The Cambridge Platonists: A Study*. Hamden, Conn.: Archion Books, 1971.

Richter, Daniel, and Alden Vaughan. "Crossing the Cultural Divide: Indians and New Englanders 1605–1763." *American Antiquarian Society Proceedings* 90.1 (April 16, 1980): 23–99.

————. "Whose Indian History?" *William and Mary Quarterly*. 3rd series, 50:2 (April 1993): 379–93.

Russell, Jason A. "The Narratives of Indian Captivity." *Education* 51 (1930): 84–88.

Sargent, Marc. "The Witches of Salem, the Angel of Hadley, and the Friends of Philadelphia." *American Studies* 34:1 (1993): 105–20.

Schwab, Gabrielle. "Seduced by Witches: Nathaniel Hawthorne's *Scarlet Letter* in the Context of New England Witchcraft Fiction." In *Seduction and Theory*, ed. Dianne Hunter. Chicago: University of Illinois Press, 1989.

Seelye, John. *Prophetic Waters: The River in Early American Life and Literature.* New York: Oxford University Press, 1977.

Shea, Daniel. *Spiritual Autobiography in Early America.* Princeton, N.J.: Princeton University Press, 1968.

Shuffelton, Frank, ed. *A Mixed Race: Ethnicity in Early America.* New York: Oxford University Press, 1993.

Simpson, Alan. *Puritanism in Old and New England.* 1955. Chicago: University of Chicago Press, 1970.

Slotkin, Richard. *Regeneration through Violence: The Mythology of the American Frontier, 1600–1860.* Middletown, Conn.: Wesleyan University Press, 1973.

Steele, Ian. *The English Atlantic, 1675–1740: An Exploration of Communication and Community.* New York: Oxford University Press, 1986.

Stephen, Sir Leslie. *History of England in the Eighteenth Century.* New York: Harcourt, Brace and World, 1963.

Summers, Montague. *The Geography of Witchcraft.* 1927. Evanston, Ill.: University Books, 1958.

Thomas, Keith. *Religion and the Decline of Magic.* New York: Scribners, 1971

Ulrich, Laurel. *Image and Reality in the Lives of Women in Northern New England, 1650–1750.* New York: Knopf, 1982.

Utley, Robert Marshall, and Wilcomb Washburn. *The American Heritage History of the Indian Wars.* New York: American Heritage Pub. Co., 1977.

Vail, R. W. G. *The Voice of the Old Frontier.* Philadelphia: University of Pennsylvania Press, 1949.

VanDerBeets, Richard. "The Indian Captivity Narrative: An American Genre." Ph. D. dissertation, University of the Pacific, 1973.

———. "The Indian Captivity Narrative as Ritual." *Early American Literature* 43 (1972): 548–62.

———. "A Surfeit of Style: The Indian Captivity Narrative as Penny Dreadful." *Research Studies* 40 (1972): 297–306.

———. "A Thirst for Empire: The Indian Captivity Narrative as Propaganda." *Research Studies* 40 (1972): 207–15.

Vaughan, Alden. *Narratives of North American Captivity: A Selective Bibliography.* New York: Garland Publishing Co., 1983.

———. "Pequots and Puritans: The Cause of the War of 1637." *William and Mary Quarterly* 21 (April 1964): 256–69.

Voss, Arthur. *The American Short Story: A Critical Survey.* Norman: University of Oklahoma Press, 1973.

Waring, Edward G. *Deism and Natural Religion: A Source Book.* New York: Ungar, 1967.

Washburn, Wilcombe. *The Indian in America.* New York: Harper and Row, 1975.

————. *The Indians and the White Men.* Garden City, N.Y.: Doubleday, 1964.

————. *Red Man's Land, White Man's Law: A Study of the Past and Present Status of the American Indian.* New York: Scribners, 1971.

Webb, Stephen Saunders. *1676, The End of American Independence.* New York: Knopf, 1984.

Whitford, Kathryn. "Hannah Dustan: The Judgment of History." *Essex Institute Historical Collection* 108 (1972): 304–25.

Wiley, Margaret. *The Subtle Knot: Creative Skepticism in Seventeenth Century England.* London: Allen and Unwin, 1952.

Willey, Basil. *The Seventeenth-Century Background: Studies in the Thought of the Age in Relation to Poetry and Religion.* 1934. New York: Columbia University Press, 1957.

Wimsatt, William, and Cleanth Brooks. *Literary Criticism: A Short History.* New York: Knopf, 1957.

Winship, Michael. "Prodigies, Puritans, and the Perils of Natural Philosophy: The Example of Cotton Mather." *William and Mary Quarterly,* 3rd series, 51.1 (1994): 92–105.

Winter, Yvor. *Maule's Curse.* Norfolk, Conn.: New Directions, 1938.

Wright, Thomas Goddard. *Literary Culture in Early New England, 1620–1730.* New York: Russell and Russell, 1966.

Index

commentary with narrative in,
67–68; rationale for storytelling in,
68–70; scientific aspects of, 66

Mandelsloe, Johann, 89

Martin, Susanna, 125

Martine, Andrew, 94

materialists, 41

Mather, Cotton, x, 10, 20, 25, 27, 30–31, 54,
72, 131, 169n.24, 172n.9, 174n.4; *A
Brand Pluck't out of the Burning*,
118–23; Indian captivity narratives
of, 20, 144–45, 148–49, 151, 155; *Magnalia Christi Americana*, x, 23–24, 28,
34–35, 37, 49, 91, 98, 107, 119, 132–34,
148–49, 151; *Memorable Providences,
Relating to Witchcrafts and Possession*, 104, 107, 109–18; *Wonders of the
Invisible World*, 48, 107, 118

Mather, Increase, x, 3, 9–10, 25, 27, 28,
54–55, 72, 89, 151, 168nn.14, 15, 18,
172n.3; *An Essay for the Recording of
Illustrious Providences*, 21–22, 24, 32,
34, 37–38, 52–53, 89, 103, 106–9, 117,
131–32, 146–48, 167n.10, 174n.6,
175n.13

Mathie, Jennet, 94

Maxwell, Sir George, 94, 95, 144

Maxwell, John, 94

May, Samuel, 151

McHenry, James, 100

McKeon, Michael, x–xi, 4–10

medieval exempla, 18

Melville, Herman, 11, 49, 91, 160, 163,
169n.27

*Memorable Providences, Relating to
Witchcrafts and Possession* (Mather),
104, 107, 109–15

Miller, Arthur, 100, 101, 102, 105–6

Miller, Perry, 15, 31–32, 100, 167nn.11, 12,
169n.24

Milton, John, 53

Mirror for Magistrates (Lydgate), 18, 40

*Mirrour or Looking Glass for Saints and
Sinners, A* (Clarke), 9, 49–50, 88, 142

Moby Dick (Melville), 10, 38, 49, 169n.27

Mompesson, John, 78, 80–82, 93

More, Henry, 7, 9–10, 19, 25, 26–27, 44, 48,
53–54, 57–63, 67, 78, 79, 82–83, 85–86,
92–93, 107, 143–44, 169–70n.2

More, Thomas, 41

Morse, William, 108, 109

Mott, Frank Luther, 21

Mountain Gloom and Mountain Glory
(Nicolson), 61

Munday, Arthur, 18

Murray, Margaret, 63

Narratives of the Witchcraft Cases (Burr),
x

Nash, Thomas, 43

Natural History (Pliny), 50

Natural History of Oxfordshire (Platt),
118–19

Neff, Mary, 135

Neile, Bishop, 44–45, 170n.3

Neoplatonists, 67. *See also* Cambridge
Platonists

*New England Mind: From Colony to
Province* (Miller), 100

Newes from Scotland, 74–77, 79, 144

Nicolson, Marjorie Hope, 61–62, 89

Nider, Jon, 65, 70

Nissenbaum, Stephen, x, 105–6

Nonconformists, as authors of providence tales, 44–63

Notestein, Wallace, 73

novel: captivity narrative as precursor of,
169n.26, 173n.1; providence tale as
paradigm for, x–xi, 7, 10

Novum Organum (Bacon), 5, 8, 20, 112

Nullibists, 19, 41

Of Plymouth Plantation (Bradford), 151

Old Man and the Sea, The (Hemingway),
12

Origins of the English Novel (McKeon),
x–xi, 4

Otis, Margaret, 155

pamphlets. *See* witchcraft trial pamphlets

Parker, Henry, 18

Parsons, Coleman, x, 11, 37, 90

Patrides, C. A., 53–54, 61

Pearce, Roy Harvey, 30

Pelham, Edward, 9, 88
Pepper, Robert, 143
Perkins, William, 18, 107, 167n.11
Philosophical Transactions (Royal Society), 8, 173n.3
Phips, William, 120
Pilgrim's Profession (Taylor), 45
Pilgrim's Progress (Bunyan), 45
Plaisted, Mary, 145, 155
Plato, 19
Platt, Robert, 118–19
Pliny, 2, 42, 50
Plotinus, 19
Plutarch, 42
Poe, Edgar Allan, 63, 91, 126, 163
Poole, Matthew, 19, 21, 44, 46, 52–55, 96
Potts, Thomas, 26, 95, 131
Preston, John, 167n.12
printing, as cultural force, 4–6
Proper, David, 175n.14
Protestant belief, as cultural force, 6–7
providence tales: affliction as theme of, 28, 96–97, 136–37; Baxter as author of, 47–49; Beard as influence on, 40–41, 44–45; the Bible as, 18; captivity motif in, 27–28; Clarke as author of, 49–52; evolution of, 4–9; Glanville as author of, 57–61; impact of on American prose narrative, xi, 1–14, 162–63; Indian captivity narratives as, ix–x, xi, 15–18, 23, 26, 27, 28–29, 34–38, 51, 54, 163; influences on, 39–40; Janeway as author of, 56; markers of, 13–14, 108; Henry More as author of, 57–63; Nonconformist authors of, 44–63; objectives of, 2; as paradigm for the novel, x–xi; Poole as influence on, 52–55; as response to atheism, 41–44, 47–48; science as concern of, 78–91; in seventeenth-century England, 18–20; in seventeenth-century New England, 21–25; Sinclair as author of, 56–57, 90–91; sources for, 2–3; transatlantic perspectives on, xi, 18–20; truth as concern of, 25–27, 132–34. *See also*

Indian captivity narratives; witchcraft tales
Psellis, Michael, 65
Pseudomarchia Daemonum (Wier), 72
purgatory, 140
Puritan culture: and Indian captivity narratives, 30–32, 33; and providence tales, ix, 2–3
Puritan Mind, The: The Seventeenth Century (Miller), 31–32

reason: as manifested in Indian captivity narratives, 136–37, 141–44, 174n.12; as manifested in providence tales, 134–35. *See also* science
Records of Salem Witchcraft (Woodward), x
Redeemed Captive Returning to Zion, The (Williams), 24
Reformation. *See* Protestant belief
Regeneration through Violence (Slotkin), 32–33
religion: as cultural force, 2–3, 12; as imaginative art form, xii; providence tales as vehicle for, 3–4, 19–20, 41–44, 128–29
Removals (Maddox), 15
Remy, Nicoles, 65
Richter, Daniel, 16
"Rip Van Winkle" (Irving), 12
Robinson Crusoe (Defoe), 11
Robinson, Edmund, 95
Robinson, John, 18
Rogers, Robert, 144
Rowlandson, Joseph, 51, 139, 172n.1
Rowlandson, Mary, 10, 16, 22–23, 25, 26, 28, 29, 30, 33–34, 35–36, 68, 91, 117, 129–32, 135, 136, 137, 142, 143, 145–46, 149–50, 154–55, 172n.1, 173n.1, 173n.3
Rowlandson, Sarah, 136, 145–46
Royal Society of London, as advocate of science, 1, 7, 8, 59, 114, 120, 129
Ryther, John, 9, 89

Sadducees, 41
Saducismus Triumphatus (Glanvill), 19,

Library of Congress Cataloging-in-Publication Data

Hartman, James D.
  Providence tales and the birth of American literature / James D. Hartman.
    p.   cm.
  Includes bibliographical references (p.   ) and index.
  ISBN 0-8018-6027-x (acid-free paper)
  1. American literature—Colonial period, ca. 1600–1775—History and criticism.
2. Providence and government of God in literature. 3. English literature—Early modern, 1500–1700—History and criticism. 4. American literature—English influences.
5. Geographical discoveries in literature. 6. Indian captivities—United States. 7. Supernatural in literature. 8. Shipwrecks in literature. 9. Witchcraft in literature. I. Title.
PS195.P76H37   1999
818′.10809382315—dc21   98-36542
                                                                                    CIP